Drenched in Grace

Drenched in Grace

Essays in Baptismal Ecclesiology Inspired
by the Work and Ministry of Louis Weil

Edited by Lizette Larson-Miller
and Walter Knowles

PICKWICK *Publications* · Eugene, Oregon

DRENCHED IN GRACE
Essays in Baptismal Ecclesiology Inspired by the Work and Ministry of Louis Weil

Biblical quotations, unless otherwise noted, are from the New Revised Standard Version Bible, copyright 1989, Division of Christian Education of the National Council of the Churches of Christ in the United States of America. Used by permission. All rights reserved.

Pickwick Publications
An Imprint of Wipf and Stock Publishers
199 W. 8th Ave., Suite 3
Eugene, OR 97401

www.wipfandstock.com

ISBN 13: 978-1-62032-726-5

Cataloguing-in-Publication data:

Drenched in grace : essays in baptismal ecclesiology inspired by the work and ministry of Louis Weil / edited by Lizette Larson-Miller and Walter Knowles

xiii + 238 pp. ; 23 cm. Includes bibliographical references.

ISBN 13: 978-1-62032-726-5

1. Baptism. 2. Baptism—History of doctrines. 3. Church. I. Larson-Miller, Lizette. II. Knowles, Walter. III. Weil, Louis, 1935–

BV811.3 L37 2013

Manufactured in the U.S.A.

Thus we see now what in these days God calls us to. We are now planted by the waters in which some Christians wade to the ankles (and be we thankful for that), some can but creep, as it were in the way of grace, and some, it may be, can walk on with some strength; some have yet gone deeper, till they be wholly drenched in grace, and this should we all labor after.

JOHN COTTON, *WAY OF LIFE OR GOD'S WAY AND COURSE*
(1641)

Contents

Baptismal Faith Healing Division

Baptismal Life Transforming the World

Contributors

J. Neil Alexander is a bishop of The Episcopal Church. He presently serves as Dean and Professor of Liturgy in the School of Theology of the University of the South, Sewanee, TN.

Michael B. Aune is a pastor in the Evangelical Lutheran Church in America. He is Professor of Liturgical and Historical Studies at Pacific Lutheran Theological Seminary in the Graduate Theological Union, Berkeley, CA.

Paul Avis is a presbyter in the Church of England. He served as General Secretary of the Council for Christian Unity and theological consultant to the Anglican Communion Office. He is editor-in-chief of *Ecclesiology* and honorary professor of theology in the University of Exeter.

John F. Baldovin, SJ, is a presbyter in the Roman Catholic Church and a member of the Society of Jesus. He is Professor of Historical and Liturgical Theology in the School of Theology and Ministry at Boston College in Boston, MA.

Andrea Bieler is a pastor in the Evangelische Kirche. She is Professor of Practical Theology at the Kirchliche Hochschule of Wuppertal/Bethel in Wuppertal, DL.

Paul De Clerck is a presbyter in the Roman Catholic Church. He was Professor of Liturgy at the Institut Catholique de Paris.

Donald Gerardi is Emeritus Professor of History and Religious Studies at Brooklyn College, City University of New York, NY.

Frank T. Griswold was the 25th Presiding Bishop of the Episcopal Church.

Contributors

Jeffrey Gros, FSC, is Catholic Scholar in Residence at Lewis University. He was Distinguished Professor of Ecumenical and Historical Theology at Memphis Theological Seminary, Memphis, TN and Director of Faith and Order of the National Council of Churches USA.

Arthur Holder is a presbyter in the Episcopal Church. He is Dean, Vice President for Academic Affairs, and John Dillenberger Professor of Christian Spirituality at the Graduate Theological Union, Berkeley, CA.

David Holeton is a presbyter in the Anglican Church of Canada. He is Professor of Liturgics in the Hussite Theological Faculty of the Charles University in Prague, CZ.

Walter Knowles is a presbyter in the Episcopal Church. He is an independent scholar and musician in Seattle, WA.

Lizette Larson-Miller is a presbyter in the Episcopal Church. She is Nancy and Michael Kaehr Professor of Liturgical Leadership and Dean of the Chapel at the Church Divinity School of the Pacific in the Graduate Theological Union in Berkeley, CA.

Mary E. McGann, RSCJ, is a Religious of the Sacred Heart. She is Professor of Liturgy and Music at the Franciscan School of Theology in the Graduate Theological Union in Berkeley, CA.

Ralph McMichael is a presbyter in the Episcopal Church. He is Executive Director of the Center for the Eucharist in St. Louis, MO.

Louis Weil is a presbyter in the Episcopal Church. He is the James F. Hodges and Harold and Rita Haynes Professor Emeritus of Liturgics at the Church Divinity School of the Pacific in the Graduate Theological Union in Berkeley, CA.

Introduction

LIZETTE LARSON-MILLER

TO BE DRENCHED IN God's grace is to be immersed in the fullness of God's love and a never-ending action, and it is both of these for individuals and for communities. Starting in Baptism with new identity, new orientation, and new formation has been at the heart of baptismal theology for centuries, particularly as it is applied to individuals. But it is also the reality that every new Baptism and every newly baptized individual changes the whole community. The community is baptized again, drenched in God's grace again. Here baptismal theology becomes ecclesiology—and all of it flowing from the first person of the Trinity, through the Son and in the Holy Spirit, through the church—the body of Christ, and for the sake of the whole world.

In the ecumenical liturgical renewals of the twentieth century, the Rev. Dr. Louis Weil has been a primary voice among Anglicans, particularly Episcopalians in the United States, in articulating the interface between the rites of initiation and the theology of the church. He has exemplified the application of the best of theological reflection to the doing of liturgy at the same time as challenging liturgical practice to ask "why" certain pastoral practices are chosen and what the choices made might mean in theologically-grounded pastoral liturgical practice. Fr. Weil has invited not only Anglicans into this conversation, however, but has drawn from and shared with an ecumenical community of scholars and practitioners, maintaining and strengthening the bonds begun in his own expansive educational background. From music degrees earned at Southern Methodist University and Harvard University, to the S.T.B. achieved at the General Theological Seminary, to Paris for the S.T.D. from Institut Catholique, Dr. Weil has brought together music as theology, liturgical theology, and ecclesiology. From pastoral work as a parish priest in Puerto Rico, Wisconsin, California, and England, Fr. Weil has brought together the experiences of different cultural expressions and expectations within Anglicanism. From his teaching at El Seminario Episcopal del Caribe, Nashotah House and Church Divinity School of the Pacific, he has taught and collaborated with students and colleagues for more than fifty years, engaging with old ideas and new, reshaping and rearticulating his reflections, research, and teaching.

It is by inspiration of this work and with a desire to join in the conversation with the Rev. Dr. Louis Weil that this collection of essays has been written and gathered. Circling around and through the topics of rites of initiation (inclusive of Baptism, confirmation/chrismation, and Eucharist), ecclesiology, ecumenism, Anglicanism, and pastoral liturgy, the fifteen authors both find common ground with earlier work as well as present challenges to some popular assumptions of the past decades. Like the exegetical reader-response approach to both scriptural work and preaching, many of these essays go beyond the story, beyond the narrative of official liturgical texts, to fill in the gaps; in other words, they are not content with the narrative analysis or standard interpretation, but also focus on what is not said. Particularly in the several essays that call for new ways of understanding the phrase "baptismal ecclesiology," the authors raise up questions about interpretations of Baptism and of the church in contemporary conversations. But the wealth of the collection is that these new questions are approached from so many different perspectives. Several of the writers focus on the spirituality of Baptism and its meaning not only for the individual's lifelong journey into God but for the understanding of church. Others take a historical approach, finding in the particularities of our rich tradition a springboard for broader appropriation of wisdom from the past. Reflecting on the decades-old work on ecumenism and the defining of Anglicanism, two of our authors issue a call for revisiting questions of ecumenical agreement and difference with fresh eyes. Another author raises the urgent question of the relationship of ecology to sacramental theology through the very waters of Baptism. Several authors reignite needed theological reflection on the meaning and import of church for sacramental understanding in a changed world view of Christianity. All of the writers engage with questions that have been part of Louis Weil's work and scholarly passion for years.

The title of the collection was chosen by Fr. Weil suggested by a title used at an Inclusive Church Conference in England, November 2007, at which Fr. Weil spoke. The quote is actually drawn from a longer meditation of John Cotton (1585–1652), titled "The Pouring Out of the Spirit."

There is such a measure of grace in which a man may swim as fish in the water, with all readiness and dexterity, gliding as if he had water enough to swim in. Such a Christian does not creep or walk, but he runs the ways of God's Commandments. Whatever he is to do or to suffer, he is ready for all, so every way drenched in grace, as let God turn him any way, he is never drawn dry.

Thus we see now what in these days God calls us to. We are now planted by the waters in which some Christians wade to the ankles (and be we thankful for that); some can but creep as it were in the way of grace, and some it can be walk on with some strength; some have yet gone deeper, till they be wholly drenched in grace, and this should we all labor after.[1]

John Cotton's imaginative description, reminiscent of centuries of images of Christians as fish, at home in the waters of Baptism and yet always striving towards more immersion, more drenching, in order to swim in the ways of God's teaching, is as contemporary as it is old. The church is composed of these; those fully and deeply immersed in Christ, others walking with confidence, some creeping, some to the ankles, others planted on the banks waiting for the water to rise toward them. These waters immerse and surround the church, sometimes refreshing, sometimes challenging in their dangerous call to go deeper regardless of cost according to the world's view. These waters flow through the faithful voices of the theologians contained in this volume also—each caring deeply about the church, the body of Christ in earth and in heaven, and the unity of the communion of saints in all places and in all times.

As the authors in this collection were invited into an ongoing conversation with the Rev. Dr. Louis Weil about the richness of liturgy and church in contemporary Christianity, so we invite you into the conversation. Read, mark, learn, and inwardly digest these writings with us, and join in the conversation for the sake of the mystery exercised, glimpsed and given in the church's celebrations.

1. John Cotton, *Way of Life Or God's Way and Course* (London, UK: Fawne and Geilbrand, 1641), 105–6.

Baptismal History Informing the Present

1

Bodies at Baptism

ANDREA BIELER

THE SACRAMENT OF BAPTISM is the tangible and corporeal event in which divine grace is being poured out onto bodies in the encounter with Christ. Baptism is the sacrament of deliverance and deep transformation. The human person who is entangled in the powers of sin as alienation from God, neighbor, and the planet Earth is rescued. In Baptism, thus, a saved body emerges through ritual acts that are attentive to words that bear divine promise and to material elements such as water and oil that carry the powers of cleansing, forgiveness, and healing. Both words and elements are directed towards the body being baptized.

There is an intimate dimension to Baptism that lifts up the singularity of the individual person before God: Right before Baptism one's name is uttered and placed in *HaShem,* whom Christians confess as the Triune God.[1] At the same time Baptism is the initiation rite through which individuals become part of a communal body, the church as the body of Christ. In the rite of Baptism, people are absorbed into the body of Christ through water, Word, and Spirit—a body so porous and fluid that human beings can be immersed in it. Belonging to Christ through Baptism evokes a loss of self as egocentric autopoeisis. This loss is acted out in ritualized gestures that pertain in particular ways to the body. These gestures hint at an eccentric understanding of belonging: a particular name is voiced in the assembly and becomes immediately immersed in Divine Mystery. Even in the act of dying, an eccentric dynamic emerges: those who are

1. For a spatial understanding of the Trinity that is grounded in the Jewish tradition of substituting the unspeakable name for the Divine with *HaShem,* which means in Hebrew "The Name." See Frettlöh and Marquardt, *Die Welt als Ort Gottes.*

baptized die and rise *with* Christ. In this interrelatedness a new identity emerges that is signified in the wearing of a new garment.

Baptism can thus be perceived as ritual space of Christian identity formation that is intimate, eccentric, communal, and cosmological. The cosmological dimension transpires through the element of water—the connecting tissue between the individual body and the planet; both depend on it as a matter of death or life. Many early depictions of baptismal rites and theologies imply an understanding of the connection between the physical body and the cosmos that is most intriguing for contemporary discussions that seek to emphasize the theological significance of the ecological dimension of this water ritual.[2] Dale Martin spells out the connection between the microcosmic body of the individual and the macrocosmic body: they resemble each other in terms of the basic materiality of that they consist. They also bear similarities in terms of the way they function in the creation of a healthy balance.[3] These speculations about the micro and the macro body can be found in Plato, pre-Socratic philosophers, and Hippocratic medical theory who converge:

> in assuming that the human self (body and soul) was composed of the same elements as the universe: air (pneuma), earth, water, and fire. Thus the dynamics that one saw at work in the external cosmos could be read onto and into the human body, the inner body being buffeted by the same weather as the outer body. . . . As is already apparent, construing the body as really (not just figuratively) a microcosm blurs any boundaries between the inner and the outer body. The workings of the internal body are not just an imitation of the mechanics of the universe; rather, they are part of it, constantly influenced by it.[4]

In acts of renunciation, anointing, and in immersion the permeability of the microcosmic and the macrocosmic body becomes tangible. What is "inside" the body has an intense relationship to the "outside"—the environment that shapes embodied living every moment as we breathe in and out. For Cyril of Jerusalem, for example, the oil used for exorcisms has the power to drive away the enemy's power, and the breath of the saints can drive out devils. Oil and breath have the capacity to enter the porous body through the skin and other body openings and to remove evil spirits that hover inside.[5]

2. See for instance Mary McGann's essay in this volume.

3. Martin, *The Corinthian Body*, 16.

4. Ibid., 16–17.

5. Yarnold, "Fourth-Century Baptismal Homilies: Cyril of Jerusalem," 77.

It thus seems to be of pivotal theological significance to pay attention to what happens to bodies in Baptism. The saved body is ritualized into existence; from there meaning making and corporeal interpretation emerge. Drawing on a deconstructivist understanding of embodiment as practice, we are led to ask how the saved body emerges from this ritual as words are sung and spoken over the body and things are done to the body. Interpellations (*Anrufungen*) that speak particular bodies into existence as well as the gaze of the gathered assembly that rests upon the body to be baptized come into focus.[6]

A phenomenologically oriented approach to embodiment will also take the subjective dimension into account that explores the felt sense of the participants. Attending to the historical documents that are available to us, we need to acknowledge that there are not very many sources in which participants describe their embodied felt sense of Baptism. One treasured exception is the witness that Ephrem the Syrian (306–73) gave about his own Baptism: "For when the waves of oil lift me up, they hand me over to the sayings about Christ, and then the waves of Christ bear me back to the symbols (mysteries) of oil. The waves meet each other, and I am in their midst."[7] His own Baptism evokes in Ephrem a sense of being overwhelmed; he captures this sense in the wave image: He is carried away on the mighty waves of anointing that evoke an interplay between the teachings about Christ and the sensual experience of anointing. In the dramatic synaesthetic interplay of the audible, the tactile and the olfactory, the baptismal event unfolds.

In what follows, I seek to explore the attention that is given to bodies at Baptism and the theological significance this body awareness might imply. I claim that the performative dimension of bodily engagement in Baptism is pivotal for baptismal theology. I proceed by highlighting two historical examples for the sake of further constructive theological work.

Standing Naked Without Shame

I begin with some glimpses into the Mystagogical Catechesis of Cyril of Jerusalem (fourth century) by focusing on the significance of nakedness. Cyril offers homilies for the neophytes that retrospectively interpret the

6. See Bieler and Plüss, "In This Moment of Utter Vulnerability: Tracing Gender in Presiding" for the interrelatedness of a deconstructivist and a phenomenological perspective regarding the body in liturgy.

7. Ephrem the Syrian, *Hymni de Virginitate* 7, 15.

meaning of the Baptism they had received. The body technologies these homilies reflect are couched in thick descriptions of the tangible quality of the rites themselves. Woven into these descriptions we find intense processes of meaning making, in that the body practices described become an intense field of theological explanation. What is written onto the body becomes almost a site of revelatory knowledge, filled with references to Scripture and theological allusions. Cyril speaks of bodily practices as symbolizing something. Cyril often times juxtaposes symbol and reality in a Platonic way indicating that the symbol is less real than the thing it symbolizes. He nevertheless assumes an ontology of participation that means that the body participates in the reality it signifies.

Cyril explains what happened upon entry into the baptistery:

> Upon entering [the baptistery] you took off your clothing, and this symbolised your stripping off of "the old nature with its practices." Stripped naked, in this too you were imitating Christ naked on the cross, who in his darkness, "disarmed the principalities and powers" and on the wood of the cross publicly "triumphed over them." . . . This was a remarkable occasion, for you stood naked in the sight of all and you were not ashamed. You truly mirrored our first-created parent Adam who stood naked in Paradise and was not ashamed.[8]

The interpretation of nakedness these sequences provide is preceded by a reading of Romans 6 that alludes to Baptism into Christ's death; the cited passage is followed by a description of prebaptismal anointing with exorcistic functions. Then the actual baptismal act happens.

What is written onto the bodies of those who stand naked is the departure of the old nature, of Adam after the fall, a body in whose limbs corrupted desire has lurked. What emerges is Adam in paradise, a body that stands naked and is not ashamed. The naked body right before Baptism is thus already placed in the garden of paradise. The naked body before Baptism does not know shame anymore.[9] Also, in the act of standing naked, Christ on the cross is imitated. The place of deepest despair and vulnerability becomes the place of disarming power. Nakedness thus becomes a means for the performance of eccentric identity in relation to Christ and to

8. Yarnold, "Fourth-Century Baptismal Homilies: Cyril of Jerusalem," 76.

9. Theodore of Mopsuestia offers a different perspective. For him nakedness before Baptism still resembles the shame of Adam and Eve after the fall, while after Baptism nakedness is without shame. See Miles, *Carnal Knowing*, 35. See also Rita Nakashima Brook and Rebecca A. Parker (*Saving Paradise*, 115–40) on the understanding of Baptism as portal to paradise.

the garden of creation. It is a technology of the body that initiates transformation with regard to shame and power. The scene as depicted by Cyril can be interpreted as a liminal practice in which the weakening of the body that has been made vulnerable opens up the possibility of deep transformation.

Margaret Miles provides a summary of the major motives that Christian authors attached to the issue of nakedness in fourth-century sources that are considered orthodox: stripping off of the old man with his deeds, imitation of Christ, leaving the world, death and rebirth, new life, the undoing of shame, and quasi martyrdom.[10]

The historical significance of nakedness in Baptism ought to be discussed by situating the issue of nudity within the larger cultural context. Regarding the cultural customs in Roman bath houses, Miles assumes that mixed naked bathing came to be gradually customary in the fourth century. This tendency to accept mixed bathing practices however was rejected by a variety of Christian authors. Cyprian and Jerome warn consecrated virgins in particular not to go to bath houses in which males are present since the virgins would quench the hot desires of youth. [11] A harsh critique was also uttered against the display of naked bodies in the context of gladiatorial games in the coliseum, which were associated with the devil's pomp. Augustine, pointing to the spectators who went into a frenzy watching the games and their cruelty, spoke of this audience as offering incense to the demons with their hearts.[12] Miles concludes:

> Christian naked baptism, then, cannot be understood as a continuation of secular culture made feasible by Christians' familiarity with and acceptance of secular nakedness. Ironically, the appropriate context for Christian baptism must rather be Christian aversion to secular nakedness, an aversion informed by the sense that a human body because of its intimate connection with the soul should not be casually or carelessly exposed.

---

10. Miles, *Carnal Knowing*, 35.

11. Ibid., 29.

12. In *Confessions* 6.8.13 (Augustine, *Confessions*, 101), Augustine describes at length the uncontrolled desire for bloodshed that emerges from watching the display of naked bodies at the gladiator games. Pointing to the example of his friend Alypius he writes:

> He was struck in the soul by a wound graver than the gladiator in his body whose fall had caused the roar. . . . As soon as he saw the blood, he at once drank in savagery and did not turn away. His eyes were riveted. He imbibed madness. Without any awareness about what was happening to him he found delight in the murderous contest and was inebriated by bloodthirsty pleasure.

> For Christians following an incarnated Christ naked bodies
> have religious meaning; bodies are the site and naked bodies the
> symbol of religious subjectivity.[13]

In contrast, historian Laurie Guy takes another stance regarding the depiction of nakedness as it is portrayed in Cyril's homily as well as in other texts; he doubts that the descriptions we find in these texts indeed reflect actual practice. Guy contends that the allusions to nakedness were rather meant to be understood in a metaphorical sense since nudity was so much disputed by Christian writers.[14] Even if we cannot come to a final conclusion with regard to the historicity of the depiction of nakedness in Baptism, it is nevertheless crucially important for theological inquiry into Baptism to engage the somatic imagination of these early writings.[15] The somatic imagination of the texts offer a powerful reframing of nakedness. When the devil's pomp—a notion that hints at the imperial games—is contested in its cruelty during renunciations and the nakedness of Adam is evoked, the baptized body is removed from the coliseum to the garden of paradise.

In more general terms we may say that early and medieval baptismal rites are filled with dramatic actions that pertain to the body; stripping off clothes and standing naked is just one of them. In addition we can see fasting, anointing of the entire body or of particular parts of the body, the ritual closure of body openings by offering the sign of the cross, breathing into the face, covering of the ear with saliva, putting salt onto the tongue, and immersion and sprinkling practices. Following the baptismal rite, the kiss of peace was exchanged and the participation in the Eucharist was practiced. These diverse rites imply a synaesthetic interplay in which sensual experience inspires religious insights: what Baptism effects and evokes is understood not only through the ears of those who listen to homilies, but also through the senses of taste, smell, and touch. When Cyril speaks of the neophytes as the aroma of Christ to God by referring to postbaptismal anointing, he probably is alluding not only to 2 Cor 2:14–16 but also to the sensual experience such anointings did evoke.[16] When Cyril describes the triple submersion of the neophytes as the symbolic dying

13. Miles, *Carnal Knowing*, 29–30.

14. Guy, *Introducing Early Christianity*, 220ff.

15. My use of the term "somatic imagination" is inspired by Carolyn Walker Bynum's deliberations on the depictions of the human body as a site of religious expression, e.g., when it comes to the relationship with Christ and understandings of the incarnation, salvation, and healing. See Bynum, *Fragmentation and Redemption*, 181–91.

16. Yarnold, "Fourth-Century Baptismal Homilies: Cyril of Jerusalem," 83.

and rising with Christ, he offers a very visceral and embodied interpretation of the reading of Romans 6.

Signing the Cross onto the Body

The era of the Reformation has often been associated with a departure from embodied ritual as a move away from the external body environment towards the interior of the believing self. According to this view, faith is not so much expressed and embodied in the exterior gestures of ritual; rather it is located in the interior space of the believer where faith as the habit of the heart resides.

We could be inclined to interpret Luther's second revision of the *Baptismal Booklet* (*Taufbüchlein*) in this vein. The second edition from 1526 shows a diminution of ritual actions and gestures compared to the version of 1523, which is still very close to the Roman rite.[17]

In the epilogue to the 1523 version of the rite, he already utters his reservations when it comes to particular practices:

> Now remember, too, that in baptism the external things are the least important, such as blowing under the eyes, signing with the cross, putting salt into the mouth, putting spittle and clay into the ears and nose, anointing the breast and shoulders with oil, signing the crown of the head with chrism, putting on the christening robe, placing a burning candle in the hand, and whatever else has been added by many to embellish baptism.[18]

In the 1526 edition, regarding the rites situated in front of the church, Luther suggests reducing the exsufflation to just the words and consequently neglecting the breathing under the eyes of the person to be baptized. In addition he recommends omitting entirely the salt rite, which was

17. The first *Baptismal Booklet* published in 1523 was mainly a translation of the Roman rite of the Magdeburg Agenda of 1497. It contained only minor changes.

18. Leupold, *Luther's Works: Liturgy and Hymns*, 53:102. In German (Luther, "Taufbüchlein," 536.l.2–537.l.3):

> So gedenke nu, daß in dem Täufen diese äußerliche Stücke das geringste sind, als da ist: unter Augen blasen, Kreuze anstreichen, Salz in den Mund geben, Speichel und Kot in die Ohren und Nasen tun, mit Öle auf der Brust und Schuldern salben und mit Cresem die Scheitel bestreichen, Westerhembd anziehen und brennend Kerzen in die Händ geben, und was das mehr ist, das von Menschen, die Taufe zu zieren, hinzugetan ist.

supposed to deliver another exorcism as salt is put into the mouth. Luther also considered the *ephphatha* rite to be a superfluous action in which the priest touches the right ear of the person to be baptized with spittle. Inside the sanctuary, the prebaptismal anointing of the chest and the shoulders, as well as the postbaptismal anointing of the head, particularly the parting, ought to be skipped. This pertains also to the sign of peace.

We might say that Luther indeed devalues in his revisions the external body environment that had been the site of particular ritual actions. He characterizes the rites that ought to be abolished as less valuable pieces, which are only a superficial adornment added onto the baptismal rite. These rites relate to the surface of the skin as well as to the openings of the body: mouth, ears, eyes, and nose. The ritual actions that pertain to such openings do have a dual function in the Roman rite: the *ephphatha* rite is supposed to stimulate the sense of hearing and the ability to speak. It refers back to the healing of the person who was deaf-mute in Mark 7:32–37. The salt rite relates to the body opening of the mouth; it serves as an exorcism that is supposed to inspire the sense of taste for the reception of the gift of wisdom.

The rites have to be understood in the context of exorcisms. Satan as well as evil spirits invade the body through its orifices. The treatment of body openings that occur in baptismal rites should be understood as a practice of defense. Consequently, we might say that prebaptismal anointings that are perceived to have exorcistic power have protective functions; they are also able to drive out evil spirits that lurk inside the body. It is thus not only the openings of the body but also the skin that is a permeable organ through that evil spirits can enter.

The omissions Luther proposes seek to repulse Satan as a power that pushes from the external corporeal environment into the internal body space. Since the reformer is willing to let go of such practices, how does he describe the essential significance of Baptism? How can he describe Baptism as our sole consolation, as foundation for the reception of all divine gifts bestowed upon the believer, and as entrance into the holy assembly?

For the sake of a theology of Baptism that seeks to pay attention to the corporeal and performative aspects, we need to return once more to Luther's reform proposals that he laid out in the 1526 edition of the *Taufbüchlein*. On the one hand the speech acts are retained that were related to the exsufflation, the oration with the flood prayer (*Sintflutgebet*), the exorcisms in shortened form. He also preserves the Lord's Prayer, the words spoken at the entrance into the church, the renunciation of the devil, the creed, and the questions that are to affirm the desire to baptize as well as the answers of the godparents. With regards to the ritual actions before entering the church, he holds on to the sign of the cross to be made on the forehead and the chest with the common words ("receive the sign of the cross"). Luther also suggests keeping the laying on of hands during the Lord's Prayer, the actual baptismal rite through immersion and concluding, the dressing of the neophyte with the christening gown (*Westerhemd*).

We can recognize that the concentration on the openings of the body fades into the background. This shifting attention allows for a reorientation and a focus on the sign of the cross placed on the forehead and the chest. The inscription of the sign of the cross onto the body is the preparation for the Holy Spirit to enter. At the same time the speech acts pertaining to the exorcism that are spoken in front of the church door are retained: "Depart you unclean spirit." This speech act is amplified in the renunciation of the devil that the godparents proclaim on behalf of the child.

I suggest that what we see here is not devaluation of the body or outer ritual practices in favor of an inner conviction of faith. Rather, we see a re-framing and shifting of ritual actions so that a theology of the body comes into focus that is not constrained by binary dualisms such as internal or external, work (ritual) or faith, ritual gesture or word. Luther accentuates over and over again the significance of the external social and corporeal space that is inhabited by living bodies:

> Indeed, it has to be an outward thing that we can touch and comprehend, and thereby draw into our heart, since the entire Gospel is an outward oral proclamation. Summing up, the things God wants to do as an effect in us, God seeks to accomplish through outward orders.[19]

Luther unfolds an understanding of the body as a space that can be inhabited either by unclean spirits or by the Holy Spirit. Baptism effects a fundamental change: people are removed from the sphere of Satan into the sphere of the Holy Spirit. This transformation not only pertains to the individual corporeal space but also has social consequences within communities. Through the power of the Spirit, a new social *Gestalt* is given to the assembly. Through Baptism the assembly is continuously transformed into a community of priests who are rescued through exorcistic speech acts, the sign of the cross,

19. Luther, "Von Der Taufe, Großer Katechismus, Teil 4," 697.l.4–10, "Ja, es soll und muß äußerlich sein, daß man's mit Sinnen fassen und begreifen und dadurch ins Herz bringen könne, wie denn das ganze Evangelion ein äußerliche mündliche Predigt ist. Summa, was Gott in uns tuet und wirket, will er durch solch äußerliche Ordnung wirken."

and the act of immersion from the powers of evil spirits and Satan. For Luther, belonging to Christ through Baptism occurs in a change of power spheres in which the body and its social environment are transformed.[20]

The baptismal booklets of the German Enlightenment, however, brought a devaluation of the corporeal experience in Baptism, as it became imperative to abolish all ritual actions that were considered to be magic or against reason. The worship books of the Enlightenment focused on the homily that was supposed to address the family of the child to be baptized; they also offered alternative rephrasing of the creeds, the Lord's Prayer, or the baptismal formula. These rites focused on an individual address of the family of origin; shared ritual practice disappeared more and more. The power of the baptismal rite was situated in the domain of cognitive expression through language; ritual gestures and embodied participation were not trusted as transmitters of meaningful baptismal theology.

Contemporary Protestant baptismal rites in Germany have reintegrated a variety of ritual practices that highlight bodily engagement; the suspicion of the Enlightenment that devalued bodily intuition in ritual seems not to carry much contemporary weight. Empirical studies on the reception of baptismal practices within the assembly emphasize that the key scenes that leave an impression on the participants are not so much located in the cognitive sphere of words remembered but rather in embodied gestures. The emotional density of memories of baptismal celebrations are related to an overall sense of incorporation into community, as well as to ritual actions such as the signing of the cross, the water ritual, the passing on and the holding of the baby to be baptized, and the baptismal blessing. Parents remember less the wordy explanations of what actions are about; they instead point to the significance of ritual actions.[21]

Bodies at Baptism matter. What is done to the body shapes in significant ways baptismal theologies expressed in liturgical texts, baptismal homilies, and personal reflections. Bodies at Baptism matter: salvation occurs when Spirit sinks into flesh through corporeal rites such as standing naked, anointing, signing the cross, and immersion. In Baptism the mystery of the incarnation is celebrated: the Word becomes flesh and the human body becomes a site of salvation.

20. Gutmann, *Symbole Zwischen Macht Und Spiel*, 247.

21. See Sommer, *Kindertaufe*, 294–300.

Bibliography

Augustine. *Confessions.* Translated by Henry Chadwick. Oxford: Oxford University Press, 1998.

Bieler, Andrea, and David Plüss. "In This Moment of Utter Vulnerability: Tracing Gender in Presiding." In *Presiding Like a Woman,* edited by Nicola Slee and Stephen Burns, 112–22. London: SPCK, 2010.

Brock, Rita Nakashima, and Rebecca Ann Parker. *Saving Paradise: How Christianity Traded Love of This World for Crucifixion and Empire.* Boston: Beacon, 2008.

Bynum, Caroline Walker. *Fragmentation and Redemption: Essays on Gender and the Human Body in Medieval Religion.* New York: Zone, 1992.

Frettlöh, Magdalene L., and Friedrich-Wilhelm Marquardt, editors. *Die Welt als Ort Gottes—Gott als Ort der Welt: Friedrich-Wilhelm Marquardts theologische Utopie im Gespräch.* Gütersloh: Gütersloher Verlagshaus, 2001.

Gutmann, Hans-Martin. *Symbole Zwischen Macht Und Spiel: Religionspädagogische Und Liturgische Untersuchungen Zum »Opfer.«* Göttingen: Vandenhoeck and Ruprecht, 1996.

Guy, Laurie. *Introducing Early Christianity: A Topical Survey of Its Life, Beliefs, and Practices.* Downers Grove, IL: InterVarsity, 2004.

Leupold, Ulrich S., editor. *Luther's Works: Liturgy and Hymns.* Vol. 53. St. Louis, MO: Concordia, 1965.

Luther, Martin. "Das Taufbüchlein Verdeutschet Und Aufs Neu Zugericht." In *Die Bekenntnisschriften Der Evangelisch-lutherischen Kirche.* 2. Rev ed. Göttingen: Vandenhoeck and Ruprecht, 1952.

———. "Von Der Taufe, Großer Katechismus, Teil 4." In *Die Bekenntnisschriften Der Evangelisch-lutherischen Kirche.* 2. Rev. ed. Göttingen: Vandenhoeck and Ruprecht, 1952.

Martin, Dale B. *The Corinthian Body.* New Haven: Yale University Press, 1995.

Miles, Margaret R. *Carnal Knowing: Female Nakedness and Religious Meaning in the Christian West.* Boston: Beacon, 1989.

Sommer, Regina. *Kindertaufe: Elternverständnis und Theologische Deutung.* Stuttgart: Kohlhammer, 2009.

Yarnold, Edward. "Fourth-Century Baptismal Homilies: Cyril of Jerusalem." In *The Awe-Inspiring Rites of Initiation: Baptismal Homilies of the Fourth Century,* 2nd ed., 67–97. Collegeville, MN: Liturgical, 1994.

2

Incorporate into the Society of the Spirit

Baptismal Practice and Ecclesiology in Augustine's North Africa

Walter Knowles

Introduction

AUGUSTINE, IN HIS DEBATES with both the Donatists and the Pelagians, started, as the well-trained rhetorician he was, with that on which he and his opponents agreed—the practice of Baptism in the community of the Western church—and worked out the implications of that practice. However, his theology of Baptism and its relationship to the church is not always obvious in these controversial writings, for in them, Baptism, and infant Baptism in particular, does not function as a ground of the church, but only as a *malleus haereticorum*, a hammer against those who would divide the church into the "holy athletes" and all the rest of us. The practice in late fourth-century Africa is not the individualistic practice that dominates Baptism from the Middle Ages onward, nor is it the cure for a sinfulness which resides primarily in the person. Paul Kolbet wrote:

> For the mature Augustine, sin derives its power less from individual weakness than from the manner in which our souls are embedded in the deeply flawed communities to which we owe our physical existence. It is thereby an unavoidable feature of our social lives and formation.[1]

1. Kolbet, *Augustine and the Cure of Souls*, 131–32.

The paschal power of Baptism in Augustine's church is found in communal salvation from this communal sinfulness. It is the repeated communal constellation of sacraments which embeds us in the new and redeemed community of the Spirit of God. Augustine's own theology and the practice of the church in North Africa have significant implications for baptismal life in the church of our own time. His theologies of baptismal redemption came from the awareness of the church as the redeemed body of Christ and the realization that Baptism is the entrance into the full life of that body, in the power of the Holy Spirit.

Augustine's Early Baptismal Ecclesiology

In *Augustine's Early Theology of the Church*, David Alexander stated that Augustine's early ecclesiology was latent rather than obvious, as it became in his battles with the Donatists.[2] His earliest visions of the church were of the people of God singing[3] and Ambrose preaching,[4] both presumably at morning and evening prayers. His earliest writing was also the work of a educated lay person rather than that of an ecclesial functionary. These pre-controversial writings are important as a source of Augustine's baptismal ecclesiology, for Carol Harrison cautioned that his theology must be considered as a whole, rather than the output of a split personality dominated by its opponents.[5] Augustine's baptismal ecclesiology was grounded in his biographical reflection, and there is no better place to begin an exploration of that theology than in his *anamnesis* of his own journey through the catechumenate into adult baptismal faith that he called *Confessions*.

Confessions was not the biography of a "pagan who found Jesus," but rather an exploration of what it means to be a Christian. Augustine lived in a cultus, as did virtually all educated late-fourth-century persons:

> Augustine probably never "missed church" a week in his life. He was a Catholic catechumen until 18, followed the Manichees enthusiastically for years after, and still participated, at least outwardly, in their cult while living with them in Rome. On going

---

2. Alexander, *Augustine's Early Theology of the Church*.

3. He records the closing lines of Ambrose's *Deus creator optima* at *De beata vita* 4.35, and *De musica*, book VI, is an analysis of that hymn.

4. *Soliloquies* 2.14.26.

5. For example, in Harrison, *Rethinking Augustine's Early Theology*, and her *Beauty and Revelation*.

to Milan he takes up orthodox Christianity again. It is typical of late antique men that they are rarely (if ever) cultless.[6]

This continuing experience of church in relative fullness gave Augustine the basis for his expanding ecclesiology.

Enrollment as a Catechumen

Augustine was the child of Patricius, possibly a catechumen, and Monnica, a baptized Christian. "The atmosphere at their home was Christian, yet he was not baptized."[7] Instead, he was enrolled as a catechumen soon after his birth. In *Confessions,* he wrote:

> Already in my boyhood I was taught about the eternal life promised us through the Lord's lowliness reaching down to our haughtiness—I was signed already with his cross, seasoned with his salt, when I left the womb of my mother, who turned fervently to you.[8]

Augustine did not censure Monnica's failure to have him baptized; indeed, Augustine wrote that "the name of Christ was bestowed on [him] from his infancy."[9] The pattern of "Christian-making" in which Monnica participated is reflected in the early sacramentaries; the Gallican and Gothic sacramentaries titled the prayers for the initiation of the catechumenate in the fourth- and fifth-century tradition: *"ad christianum faciendum."*[10] It is only as the infant catechumenate waned that the Gelasian sacramentary called it *"ad catechumenum ex pagano faciendum."*[11] The sign of the cross in enrollment is "sanctification;" in *De peccatorum meritis et remissione,* Augustine wrote:

---

6. O'Donnell, *Augustine: Confessions: Commentary,* 2:238.

7. Rist, *Augustine,* 2.

8. *Confessions* 1.11.17, translation in *Confessions,* 12. Wright, "Infant Dedication in the Early Church," 354, makes the point that the imperfect tenses of *signabar* and *condiebar* suggest strongly that Augustine is describing a repeated (and probably domestic) ritual.

9. *Confessions* 6.4.5, translation in *Confessions,* 114.

> "I was in a state of confusion, I was changing," but I rejoiced, my God, that the sole church, in which the name of Christ had marked me as a child, was not prey to childish nonsense . . .

10. Mohlberg, *Missale Gallicanum Vetus,* 16, and Mohlberg, *Missale Gothicum,* 65.

11. Wilson, *The Gelasian Sacramentary,* 113.

There is not just one kind of sanctification. For catechumens are sanctified in their way through the sign of Christ and the laying on of hands in prayer. What they receive is not the Body of Christ . . . [12]

and the seal of Christ on the forehead is a fundamental exorcism, for it drives away Satan from the believer.[13]

Augustine was a Christian from that seasoning with salt, but though he trusted in Jesus, he was not a full member of the body of Christ. As a bishop he later encouraged the catechumens to take the step into the fullness of relationship:

Hence, I urged and still urge our brothers and sisters the catechumens. For, if you question them, they have already believed in Jesus; but because they do not yet receive his body and blood, Jesus has not yet trusted himself to them. What must they do for Jesus to trust himself to them? Let them be reborn of water and the Spirit; let the church make known those to whom she has given birth. They have been conceived, let them be brought forth into the light.[14]

Clinical Baptism

There is a note of disapproval almost immediately in Augustine's narrative, for when he fell gravely ill, he was prepared for Baptism, and then, upon recovery, not baptized:

You saw, Lord, how I, while still a boy, almost died from a sudden attack of chest fever. . . . [My mother] made quick arrangements for the rites of my ablution in the saving mysteries, with my testimony to you, Lord Jesus, for forgiveness of my sins. Only, instantly, I recovered—so my cleansing was put off.[15]

In *Confessions*, there is no mention of what came to be known as infant Baptism—the Baptism of presumably healthy young children in Christian

---

12. *De peccatorum meritis et remissione et de baptismo parvulorum* 2.26.42. What they receive is presumably salt.

13. *In Johannis evangelium tractatus* 50.2: "Christ's seal on us drives away the Destroyer, if we receive Christ into our hearts."

14. In *Johannis evangelium tractatus* 12.3, translation in *Homilies on the Gospel of John*, 229–30.

15. *Confessions* 1.11.17 , translation in Augustine, *Confessions*, 13–14.

families, prior to their being able to answer the baptismal scrutinies on their own. Baptism is converting Baptism, and the only example of a Baptism where the candidate cannot answer personally is that of a young friend whom Augustine had lead into Manicheism. The friend, lying insensible in a lethal sweat and given up for lost, was baptized without knowing it.[16] Baptism *in extremis* appears to be the only significant deviation from adult intentional initiation in the fourth and fifth centuries.[17] This is certainly the case in Augustine's discussion of Baptism of infants in *De Genesi ad litteram*, book 10. Here the context is perimortem Baptism, and he reminded the reader that the church teaches that "parents should hasten with their babies while they are still alive and help them while still alive."[18] William Harmless states:

> Infant baptism was often emergency baptism. We should not presume that the *practice* of infant baptism was the pastoral norm, as it is today, just because Augustine and the Pelagians debated the *meaning* of infant baptism so frequently and so vigorously.[19]

The Retreat at Cassiciacum

The salting Augustine received as an infant "took," and it led him through much of the intellectual culture of the late antique western empire. He turned to the Manichees because he understood them to be better interpreters of Paul than the Catholics of North Africa. He turned away from Manicheism to Academic philosophy because Manichean exegesis did not grasp the whole of the Scriptures, nor did its cosmology provide an adequate scientific explanation of the world. Finally, he did not convert to a belief in Christ; he "therefore continued [to be] in the status of

---

16. *Confessions* 4.4.8.

17. Clinical Baptism of infants was frequent throughout this period, though it seems that it was never normative. See Wright, "At What Ages?" Everett Ferguson surveys Ernst Diehl's *Inscriptiones Latinae Christianae Veteres* for funereal inscriptions of infant Christians in "Inscriptions and the Origin of Infant Baptism," 37–46, and finds no instances of epitaphs of infants and children where their Baptisms are not immediately proximate to their deaths. Harmless, "Christ the Pediatrician," 7–34, finds a strong correlation of narratives of infant Baptism and "running to church" with sickly babies and children.

18. *De Genesi ad litteram* 10.11.19. Translation in *On Genesis*, 408. At cum videamus hoc universaliter Ecclesiam retinere, ut cum viventibus curratur, et viventibus succurratur.

19. Harmless, "Christ the Pediatrician," 24.

"catechumen" (in which my parents over time commended me), until the reliable illumination of Baptism would shine on the path I was to follow."[20] He thus answered, "Is it enough to plod along in the path where my parents put me as child, until truth turns up?"[21] with: "I had decided to [keep on being] a catechumen in the church, the way given to me by my parents, until I either found what I was looking for, or until I was persuaded that I wouldn't find it there."[22]

In both of these passages, Augustine used the *present* tense of "to be"; He chose to be what he was—a Christian—not to become something he was not.[23]

Continuing to keep on being a catechumen was at least one of the significant causes for his retreating with some of his friends to an estate at Cassiciacum, where he explored the interface of faith and philosophy. Throughout the Cassiciacum dialogs[24] we have the reflection of someone who had probably seen the public rites of initiation: enrollment into the catechumenate, enrollment into the *competentes*, and the scrutinies. *Mysteria* and its cognates occur relatively frequently, but with a changing meaning. Early on, *mysteria* is knowledge, but later in the Dialogs it refers to the process of acquiring knowledge; *sacramentum* and its cognates do not occur. Baptism is thus a gateway into the community of the enlightened. Monnica, as the only member of the Dialogs community with significant experience as a baptized Christian, shines as a wisdom figure at the end of *De beata vita* (4.28 and 4.36) and in *De ordine* (2.1.1). All the members of the Cassiciacum circle were at least catechumens (Augustine was not yet even one of the *competentes*) and, as we have seen above, all were "Christians," and thus participated in a life of prayer, praise, reflection on Scripture, and theological exploration. It is impossible to see Augustine's prayer in *Soliloquies* as that of anyone other than a committed Christian:

20. *Confessions* 5.14.25: "Statui ergo tandiu esse catechumenus in catholica Ecclesia mihi a parentibus commendata, donec aliquid certi eluceret, quo cursum dirigerem." *Tandiu (tamdiu)* . . . *eluceret* is an interesting pairing. Normally one might translate this as Gary Wills (*Confessions*, 105) does ("provisionally . . . a certain light") as reflecting a lack of commitment on Augustine's part. However, as this passage is close to the rhetorical hinge of *Confessions*, it seems more accurate to understand that Augustine is making reference to his baptismal status.

21. *Confessions* 6.11.18, translation in *Confessions*, 116.

22. *De utilitate credendi* 8.20.

23. See, for example, Ferrari, "Young Augustine: Both Catholic and Manichee."

24. *De beata vita, De ordine, Contra academicos,* and *Soliloquia* were all composed (or discussed) from November, 386, to March, 387, when Augustine and his company returned to Milan for the final preparation for Baptism.

> I come to you for the very things whereby an approach can be
> made to you, so that I might beseech you again. For the one
> whom you abandon is lost forever. But you do not abandon
> anyone, for you are the perfect good, which no one has rightly
> searched for and not found. All those who rightly search for
> you, you have caused to search rightly for you. Make me, father,
> search for you, protect me from evil, and as I search, let there be
> nothing else for me other than you, I beg you father. If there is
> in me a desire for anything that would weigh me down, rid me
> of it yourself and make me fit to see you.[25]

But that April, the philosopher who simply desired to be purified of his
past so that he could continue, with more intensity and authority, his life
of theological and philosophical *otium*, was baptized. With that Baptism,
his theology and philosophy opened out to the church and world around
him. As James O'Donnell writes:

> There is no reason to think that these ideas [developed in the
> Cassiciacum Dialogs] about the liberal disciplines were in any
> essential way incompatible with the practice and belief of Chris-
> tianity in Augustine's time. Though he himself moved beyond
> them, that is at least in part because he believed that those ideas
> about the *disciplinae* were assimilated into and made less ur-
> gently necessary by the *disciplinae ecclesiae*.[26]

Baptizing Augustine

At the culmination of this part of his journey in faith, Augustine turned in
his name for Baptism to Ambrose and was baptized with his son Adeoda-
tus and his friend, Alypius. His account of their final stage as *competentes*
is terse, and may even reflect Ambrose's own caution that the *infantes* not
be underwhelmed by their experience:[27]

---

25. *Soliloquies* 1.1.6, translation in *Soliloquies*, 24.

26. O'Donnell, *Augustine: Confessions: Commentary*, 2:271.

27. See Ambrose, *De mysteriis*, 2.6 (translation in Ambrose, "The Mysteries," 6)
"There you saw the Levite, you saw the priest, you saw the highest priest. Do not consider the bodily forms, but the grace of their ministrations," and 3.15 (translation, p.
10) "Therefore, you should not trust only in the eyes of your body. Rather is that seen
which is not seen, for the one is temporal, the other eternal. Rather is that seen which
is not comprehended by the eyes, but is discerned by the spirit and the mind."

> And when it was time for me to turn in my name [i.e., to enroll
> as one of the *competentes*], we left the country and returned to
> Milan. Alypius chose to be born again in you along with me. . . .
> We took with us my son, Adeodataus.[28]

Typical of Augustine, he was much more moved by the music of hymns and canticles than by the "awe-inspiring rites of initiation," even after we take account of his respect for the *disciplina arcana*. Then, without a further word, he was off to continue his journey south through Rome to Thagaste.

The Standard Pattern: Infant Dedication with Adult Baptism

This early dedication of an infant with the intention of adult Baptism bears all the evidence of normativity, not just in less than fully-committed households such as Augustine's, but also in the best of observant homes. We have Augustine's unique reflection on his inner journey, but he was by no means unusual among the great leaders of Christianity, or even the simple believers, in the fourth and fifth centuries.[29] It seems that a pattern of early catechumenate and adult Baptism was almost a biographical requirement for substantial leadership in the early post-Constantinian church,[30] and its normativity was underscored by Prudentius as he writes in his paean to the martyrs:

> We see patrician families,
> Noble on both male and female side,
> Vowing their pledged offering,
> The child of most distinguished parents.[31]

The families pledged to raise their children "in the knowledge and fear of the Lord" so that they will come to their Baptisms with an adult commitment to Christ.

For Augustine, there was no simple *ordo* of the bath, but rather a complex of ritual and intellectual activity which reached only one of its climaxes in the initiatory washing we call Baptism. There are hundreds of references

28. *Confessions*, 9.6.14.

29. Wright, "At What Ages?," 393.

30. I have to reflect on the importance of being able to remember one's own Baptism as an important component of continuing conversion. It seems that much of the semi-Pelagian nonsense in the Episcopal Church about our ability to keep our baptismal promises and follow the baptismal covenant has come from authors who cannot remember making those promises.

31. Prudentius, *Peristephanon* 2.521–24.

to "Baptism" in his writing, ranging from the water-washing rite proper, to the entire process of conversion, but there is no reference to the complex of rites which the church came to know as "infant Baptism." Baptism, as a sacramental process, clearly brings us into a full relationship with God in God's church, but the water bath, by itself, does not. The entire spectrum of initiatory rites transformed Augustine from one who stood away from God to a person whose restless heart found its rest in God.

What Makes a Christian?

To make sense of the place of water Baptism in its complex of sacraments we need to parse what it means to become a Christian. In the chapter before he mentioned his Baptism, Augustine described the enrollment and Baptism of Victorinus. For Victorinus, being a Christian was to believe and study (a position that Augustine shared at Cassiciacum); for Simplician, it was life in the church, initiated by the catechumenate:

> [Victorinus] said to Simplician, in the confidence of friendship, making no public statement: You can count me a Christian now. Simplician answered: I put no trust in that nor rank you among Christians, till the day I see you in Christ's church. And he taunted back: Are Christians made by walls? . . . But then he said out of the blue, when Simplician was least expecting it: Go we to the church, I would be a Christian. . . . There Victorinus was steeped in the basic mysteries of the faith, and shortly after entered his name for the rebirth of baptism.[32]

Walls—or at least pillars of the salt of the catechumenate—*do* make one a Christian.

Similarly, early in his episcopate, Augustine addressed a mixed congregation of faithful, catechumens, and baptized who have fallen into sin, and called them all Christians:

> Obviously, the person whom I tell, "Believe in the gospel," is not yet a Christian. There is no one, I take it, listening to me in this congregation, who does not yet believe in the gospel. There are many listening to me who have not yet taken their place among the faithful by baptism, and are still catechumens; not yet born, but already conceived. But when or how would they have been

---

32. *Confessions* 8.2.4, translation in *Confessions*, 164.

conceived in the womb of mother Church, if they had not been signed with some sacrament of faith?[33]

What we have in Baptism then is a journey through many sacraments, beginning with the sacrament of salt (enrollment), through sacraments of scrutiny and enlightenment, and at the apex of an arc which continues with the Eucharist and instruction, the water rite. Thus Augustine continued to understand catechumens in general to be Christians—bearers of the name of Christ—though not yet faithful. In his instructional letter on the practice of the catechumenate to the catechist Deogratias, he repeatedly referred to the stages of the catechumenate, from enrollment through Baptism as *sacramenta, sacramentae,* and *primae sacramentae.*[34]

This process corresponds to his view of the church as a mixed body, tares and wheat, redeemed and sinful, a fundamental concept in his debates with both the Donatists and Pelagians. For example, in his debate with Julian, a Pelagian, he made reference to a rite which seems to have occurred many times in the normal process of the formation of *competentes,* but in the case of clinical Baptism of young children was still considered to be required: "Little ones contract original sin and thus they must undergo the rite of exsufflation in exorcisms so that they are rescued from the power of darkness and transferred to the kingdom of their savior and lord."[35]

The set of sacraments that made up Baptism as a whole varied with the local church. For example, foot-washing was part of the baptismal rites, whereas in Hippo, it seemed to be part of the penitential sequence. In his letter to Januarius, Augustine tried to clear up the confusion that two washings for the forgiveness of sins caused:

> But many have refused to accept this as a custom for fear that it should seem to belong to the sacrament of baptism. Some have also not hesitated to remove it as a custom. But in order to practice this at a less public time and to distinguish it from the sacrament of baptism, some have chosen to do this action either on the third day of the octave, . . . or on the eighth day itself.[36]

A careful reading of the beginning of *De fide et operibus,* a middle anti-Pelagian work, shows that the distinction between the water rite and the

---

33. *Sermo* 352/A.3, translation in *Sermons: Newly Discovered Sermons,* 88 (Hill lists Dolbeau 14 as Sermon 94A).

34. See particularly *De catechizandis rudibus* 13.19 and 26.50.

35. Contra *Juliani opus imperfectum* 1.117, translation in *Answer to the Pelagians* III, 133.

36. *Epistula* 55.18.33, translation in *Letters 1–99,* 233.

process of Baptism was maintained late in Augustine's episcopate. The treatise begins with:

> There are some people who understand that anyone should be admitted to the bath of regeneration, which is in Christ Jesus our Lord, even though they will not change an immoral and even evil life, obvious by bad deeds and scandal, and even openly assert that they will continue to live that way.[37]

and continues in the next section:

> People who argue this way seem particularly concerned with those who have not been admitted to Baptism because they divorced their wives and married other women or divorced their husbands and married other men. Our Lord Christ testifies, without any doubt, that these are not marriages but adultery.[38]

The distinction between *lavacrum regenerationis* and *baptismum* is critical here. Public adultery was one of the reasons for denying a person admission to the catechumenate, while failure to live up to the moral standards of the Christian community would have been discovered during the scrutinies, and thus the person would then be barred from the water rite.

The water-bath at Easter may have been the high point of the baptismal journey, but it was not the conclusion for the church at Hippo. In a sermon for the Sunday after the Paschal festival, Augustine told his congregation—and especially the *infantes*:

> Then we return, as it were, to the starting point. You see, just as when these seven days have been spent, the eighth is the same as the first; in the same way, after the ages of the fleeting course of time have run and come to their end, we shall return to that immortality and blessedness from which man fell. And that's why this octave rounds off the sacraments of the *infantes*.[39]

Baptism and the Church

In Augustine's theology of Baptism, the church has two deeply intertwined roles. In the first place, it is the body which does the baptizing, but also it is the body into which one is baptized. Baptism converts the catechumen

---

37. *De fide et operibus* 1.1.

38. Ibid., 1.2.

39. *Sermo* 259.2, translation in *Sermons (230–272B)*, 176.

into faithfulness and it commissions the new faithful to an evangelical mission of "proclaiming by word and example the Good News of God in Christ."[40] These images of the baptizing church are profoundly trinitarian (the mother, the body of Christ, the dove) and unitive (the community).

In *De moribus ecclesiae catholicae*, Augustine wrote of "the catholic church, most true mother of all Christians."[41] While God is the father to Christians, the church is mother to the new *infantes*, and the church's womb is the baptistery.

> God is Father, the Church, mother. You will be born of the parents very, very differently from the way you were born of [your natural parents]. The birth of offspring here will not be accompanied by labor, by woe, by weeping, by death; but by easiness, by happiness, by joy, and by life. Being born of those is something to be mourned, being born of these is something to be desired. Those parents, in giving us birth, bear us to eternal death, because of the ancient fault; these in giving us new birth, cause both fault and punishment to disappear.[42]

This image of church as mother was intertwined with Augustine's, or more properly, Monnica's, biography and with Baptism as a process, not an instantaneous sacramental moment. The theme returns in Augustine's own lectures to the *compententes* on John 3:

> So therefore there are two births, but [Nicodemus] knew only the first. One is of earth, the other of heaven; one is of flesh, the other of the Spirit; one is of mortality, the other of eternity; one is of male and female, the other of God and the Church.[43]

In his discussion of Psalm 57, Augustine enlarges the maternal metaphor. The mother's womb is a place of gestation, of growth in faith. His use of birth metaphors localizes this place of birth within the baptistery ("you have been sacramentally born within the bowels of your mother").[44] The

---

40. The first and third baptismal promises in the Episcopal Church's Book of Common Prayer (1979), 305, most directly reflect Augustine's theology.

41. *De moribus eccleseae catholicae* 30.62.

42. *Sermo* 216.8. translated in *Sermons (184–229Z)*, 172. *Sermo* 22.10 is another classic example of the two sets of parents, also in the context of Baptism. There he ties together the parental image with that of the *totus christus*. The church, by itself as mother, is a fundamental image in *De baptismo*, e.g., in 1.16.25 and 3.14.19.

43. In *Johannis evangelium tractatus* 11.6.

44. *Ennaratio in Psalmos* 57.5. "sacramento quodam natus es in visceribus matris."

metaphor of church as mother is further developed, hinting at the other great sacramental complex of the Eucharist in *De quantitate animae*:

> Then we will perceive how perfect has been our nourishment within [our] mother church. . . . To accept such nourishment when fed by one's mother is most proper; when already grown, shameful; to refuse it when needed would be bad; to find fault with it at any time or to disdain it would be wicked and impious; but to discuss it and communicate it with kindness is the mark of an overflow of goodness and charity.[45]

Augustine's place in the life of his mother, the church, seemed to be one of those who would discuss and communicate that nourishment. Indeed, for him the church and its constituent community was a place of instruction and learning, and a primary vocation of the baptized Christian is to take part in that communal conversation.

The church as the body of Christ emerged as a theme during Augustine's time at Thagaste, particularly in *De Genesi adversus Manicheos*, but soon after his ordination to the presbyterate, he found a phrase that permeated his ecclesiology: *totus Christus*. The union of Christ and his church, through Baptism, becomes a hermeneutical center for Augustine's interpretation of the Psalms.[46] In his commentary on Psalm 30[31] (probably from the time of his presbyterate and part of his baptismal teaching) he preached:

> Without him, we are nothing, but in him, we too are Christ. Why? Because the whole Christ consists of Head and body. The Head is he who is the savior of his body, he who has already ascended into heaven; but the body is the Church, toiling on earth.[47]

Augustine expanded the relationship between church and Christ from simply head and body to that of marriage in *Ad catholicos fratres* in a way that brings to mind the analogy of church as mother. Inverting Paul's teaching in Ephesians, he wrote of the *totus christus*: "Head and body are the complete Christ. The head is the only-begotten Son of God the Father and the body is Christ's church, husband and wife, two in one flesh."[48]

---

45. *De quantitate animae* 33.76, translation in Alexander, *Augustine's Early Theology of the Church*, 121.

46. Cameron, "*Enarrationes in Psalmos*," 292–93.

47. *Ennaration in Psalmos* 30[2].3, translation in *Expositions of the Psalms 1–32*, 323.

48. *Ad catholicos fratres* 4.7: "Totus Christus caput et corpus est. Caput Unigenitus Dei Filius et corpus eius Ecclesia, sponsus et sponsa, duo in carne una." *Totus Christus,* particularly with *caput et corpus* rings throughout Augustine's output.

His third trinitarian analogy is between the church and the Holy Spirit. In *In Johannis evangelium tractatus* 5 and 6, Augustine began a word play that lasts through two long sermons by saying:

> After all, the dove did not teach John [the Baptizer] and then fail to teach the Church—the same Church of which it was said, *One is my dove* (Sg 6:9). Let the dove teach the Dove. Let the Dove know what John learned through the dove.[49]

The image of church and dove as well as church *as* Dove is a recurring motif in *De Baptsimo*:

> For those who come into the church, journeying to Christ after leaving the association of the devil, build upon the rock and are incorporated into the Dove, secured in the enclosed garden with a set-apart font.[50]

The church and the dove are one. *Totus Christus*, yes. But even more so, *totus Spiritus*.

Finally, Augustine expands his metaphorical repertory to include the communication of the Persons. In his response to Boniface on a number of questions about the Baptism of young children, Augustine argued that Baptism forms a society of the Holy Spirit,[51] and the child "shares in grace through the unity of the Holy Spirit."[52] This benefit is not produced through the valid faith of the parents or other caregivers, but rather through the whole body of the church. In the core of his argument, Augustine told Boniface not to be disturbed when people bring their young children, for it is the Spirit's action, not the presenters' intentionality that is primary:

> Little ones are, of course, presented to receive spiritual grace, not so much from those in whose hands they are carried, though they do also receive it from them if they are good believing people, as from the universal society of the saints and believers.[53]

---

49. *In Johannis evangelium tractatus* 5.10, translation in *Homilies on the Gospel of John*, 109, Hill attempts to clarify Augustine's rhetoric by capitalizing Dove when the referent of *columba* is the church, and leaving it in lower case when it refers to the dove of Jesus's Baptism, the Holy Spirit.

50. *De baptismo* 7.49.97. See also *De baptismo* 3.18.23, 5.13.15, and 7.45.89.

51. *Epistula* 98.2. This and other quotes from this epistle are translated in *Letters 1–99*, 427–29.

52. *Epistula* 98.2.

53. *Epistula* 92.5. As usual, Augustine refers to young children as *parvulos*, not as *infantes*.

This universal society brings them into the "community of the Holy Spirit," which receives them and provides the environment for their continuing growth:

> in the Catholic Church the grains of wheat are carried in order to be purified, even through the ministry of the chaff, in order that they may be brought through the threshing floor to the society of the mass of believers.[54]

The *massa societatem*—the society of the totality of believers—into which the baptized person is brought is the true solution for the problem of human fallenness (the much more well-known *massa peccatum*). This universal society of saints and believers—not parents, not caregivers—brings a candidate to Baptism, and it is this society into which the candidate is grafted:

> For they are correctly understood to be presented by all who are pleased that they are presented and by whose holy and undivided love they are helped to come into the communion of the Holy Spirit. The whole Church, our mother, which exists in the saints, does this, because the whole Church gives birth to each and every one.[55]

Baptism is incorporation into the community of the Holy Spirit. It is the journey from the *massa peccatum* to the *massa societatum*. Forgiveness of sins is an important side effect, but Baptism does not end there. As Augustine's sermons around Easter thunder, Baptism is resurrection—and it is the resurrection of the entire community.

Conclusion

Augustine the philosopher desired to be purified of his past so that he could continue, with more intensity and authority, his life of theological and philosophical *otium*—the leisure of the retired academic. Instead, Augustine the catechumen was enrolled, exorcised, washed, anointed, and clothed, and with that Baptism, his theology and philosophy opened out to the church and world around him. Forgiveness of sins and washing away of the past is means, and means only, to participation in the mission of God, to union with God,[56] and to incorporation into the community of the Spirit.

Luis Vela summarized Augustine's baptismal ecclesiology:

54. *Epistula* 98.5.
55. Ibid.
56. See Meconi, "Becoming Gods."

> St. Augustine's doctrine of Baptism as a sacrament of regeneration
> and incorporation is wonderful and extraordinarily beautiful. . . .
> According to the marvelous will of God the Father through the
> Word, in an action of both the Spirit and the Word, God incorpo-
> rates humanity [into the life of the Trinity]. . . . Through Baptism,
> the church incorporates us into the great family of Christians, and
> she is our loving mother, who through Christ, the living head,
> structures our life and shares our ministry.[57]

Augustine's theology of Baptism is not primarily about the "sinful individual," but rather the building up of the church. Salvation of the believer
is not the goal, as it was with Augustine, the Manichean hanger-on, but
salvation is what is effected on the way as the church is renewed and resurrected in the resurrection of Christ and in the resurrection of Christ's
brothers and sisters. Our theology of Baptism and our life as Christian
and Christians is impoverished by a theology and practice of Baptism
that sees Baptism as moment, not process; individual, not corporate; and
soteriological rather than ecclesiological. The power of Baptism should
be grounded, for us, as it was for Augustine, in catechumenal growing in
Christ and in a process of Baptism which effects the conversion of those
who can truly answer "Do you turn to Christ?" Their "Yes" unleashes
the power of the Holy Spirit to rejuvenate the community of the faithful
through the example of the *infantes'* own resurrection.

---

57. Vela, "La incorporación a la Iglesia por el Bautismo en San Agustín," 175–76.

Bibliography

Alexander, David C. *Augustine's Early Theology of the Church: Emergence and Implications, 386–91*. New York: Lang, 2008.

Ambrose. "The Mysteries." In *Saint Ambrose: Theological and Dogmatic Works*, translated by Roy J. Deferrari, 5–28. Washington, DC: Catholic University of America Press, 1963.

Augustine. *Answer to the Pelagians. III*. Translated by Roland J. Teske. Works of St. Augustine I/25 25. Hyde Park, NY: New City, 1999.

———. *Confessions*. Translated by Garry Wills. New York: Penguin, 2006.

———. *Expositions of the Psalms 1–32*. Translated by Maria Boulding. Works of St. Augustine III/15. Hyde Park, NY: New City, 2004.

———. *Homilies on the Gospel of John, 1–40*. Translated by Edmund Hill. Works of St. Augustine I/12. Hyde Park, NY: New City, 2009.

———. *Letters 1–99*. Edited by John E. Rotelle. Translated by Roland J. Teske. Works of St. Augustine II/1. Hyde Park, NY: New City, 2001.

———. *On Genesis: A Refutation of the Manichees*. Translated by Edmund Hill. Works of St. Augustine I/13. Hyde Park, NY: New City, 2002.

———. *Sermons (230–272B) on the Liturgical Seasons*. Translated by Edmund Hill. Works of St. Augustine III/7. Brooklyn, NY: New City, 1991.

———. *Sermons, (184–229Z) on the Liturgical Seasons*. Translated by Edmund Hill. Works of St. Augustine III/6. Brooklyn, NY: New City, 1991.

———. *Sermons: Newly Discovered Sermons*. Translated by Edmund Hill. Works of St. Augustine III/11. Brooklyn, NY: New City, 1991.

———. *Soliloquies: Augustine's Inner Dialogue*. Translated by Kim Paffenroth. Hyde Park, NY: New City, 2000.

———. *Vingt-six sermons au peuple d'Afrique: retrouves à Mayence*. Edited by François Dolbeau. Paris, FR: Institut d'Études Augustiniennes, 2009.

Cameron, Michael. "*Enarrationes in Psalmos*." Edited by Allan Fitzgerald. *Augustine through the Ages: An Encyclopedia*. Grand Rapids: Eerdmans, 1999.

Diehl, Ernst, editor. *Inscriptiones Latinae Christianae Veteres*. 4 vols. Berlin: Apud Weidmannos, 1961.

Ferguson, Everett. "Inscriptions and the Origin of Infant Baptism." *Journal of Theological Studies* n.s. 30 (1979) 37–46.

Ferrari, Leo C. "Young Augustine: Both Catholic and Manichee." *Augustinian Studies* 26 (1995) 109–28.

Harmless, William. "Christ the Pediatrician: Infant Baptism and Christological Imagery in the Pelagian Controversy." *Augustinian Studies* 28 (1997) 7–34.

Harrison, Carol. *Beauty and Revelation in the Thought of Saint Augustine*. Oxford: Clarendon, 1992.

———. *Rethinking Augustine's Early Theology: An Argument for Continuity*. Oxford: Oxford University Press, 2006.

Kolbet, Paul R. *Augustine and the Cure of Souls: Revising a Classical Ideal*. Notre Dame, IN: University of Notre Dame Press, 2010.

Meconi, David Vincent. "Becoming Gods by Becoming God's: Augustine's Mystagogy of Identification." *Augustinian Studies* 39.1 (2008) 61–74.

Mohlberg, Leo Cunibert, editor. *Missale Gallicanum Vetus (Cod. Vat. Palat. Lat. 493)*. Rerum Ecclesiasticarum Documenta. Series Maior 3. Rome: Herder, 1958.

————. *Missale Gothicum: (Vat. Reg. Lat. 317)*. Rerum Ecclesiasticarum Documenta: Series Maior 5. Rome: Herder, 1961.

O'Donnell, James J. *Augustine: Confessions: Commentary*. Vol. 2. Oxford: Clarendon, 1992.

Rist, John M. *Augustine: Ancient Thought Baptized*. Cambridge: Cambridge University Press, 1994.

Vela, Luis. "La incorporación a la Iglesia por el Bautismo en San Agustín." *Estudios eclasiásticos* 46 (1971) 162–82.

Wilson, Henry Austin, editor. *The Gelasian Sacramentary: Liber Sacramentorum Romanae Ecclesiae*. Oxford: Clarendon, 1894.

Wright, David F. "At What Ages Were People Baptized in the Early Centuries?" *Studia Patristica* 30 (1997) 387–92.

————. "Infant Dedication in the Early Church." In *Baptism, the New Testament, and the Church*, edited by S. E. Porter and A. R. Cross, 352–78. Sheffield, UK: Sheffield Academic Press, 1999.

3

"Putting on Christ"

Baptism as a Christological Practice

MICHAEL B. AUNE

Introduction

IN THE YEARS SINCE Vatican II, the dominant emphasis in the practice(s) and theology/ies of Baptism in many Christian communities is that of *initiation* into the church, the body of Christ. This emphasis is further unfolded theologically and ritually in terms of a *baptismal ecclesiology* and as a *baptismal covenant.* A baptismal ecclesiology, as our colleague and friend Louis Weil has written, is "an understanding of the church that defines Christian community in terms of the common ground that all the baptized members share. This understanding of the church sees Baptism as the defining sacrament of incorporation into its life."[1] Moreover, as Weil has argued, a *baptismal ecclesiology* "leads us to understand the church's life much more broadly"—as affirmative of the gifts of the Holy Spirit that are given to all members and "*shared by all of the people*, whether lay or ordained."[2] And these gifts are expressive of each Christian's and of each Christian community's relationship to the world—a relationship grounded in the church's "theology of the Incarnation, that God has in Jesus Christ shared totally in our human reality."[3] A consequence of the

1. Weil, *A Theology of Worship*, 13.
2. Ibid., 13–14.
3. Ibid., 16.

Incarnation is that each individual Christian is called to be Christ in the place where she or he lives.

These emphases in our common life, rooted in the renewal of baptismal theology and practice, have moved our understanding of "church" from primarily a collection of individuals who have been fortunate enough to be "graced" in this sacrament to an understanding of "church" as the people of God. This community of equals is to be engaged in its ministry that proclaims "the Christ whose life, death, and resurrection offer the key to the meaning of the whole creation."[4]

Certainly, these ecclesiological and missiological emphases are to be welcomed, but it seems that they have become so relentlessly dominant—to the point of "over-ecclesiologizing"—that they might obscure other time-honored emphases. I cannot help but wonder if one of the continuing (if not neuralgic) tensions in our understandings of Baptism (now almost exclusively called initiation)—that of divine initiative and human response, have become neglected. For example, *Christological* images and themes of "putting on Christ," of "appropriating divine life" that have been associated with Baptism should prompt us to attend more fully—to the *incarnational*—but also to the *soteriological*—for it is in this baptismal event that we begin to see the unfolding of the entire plan of salvation—and that is nothing less than the re-creation of the human race.[5]

In this essay, I wish to introduce a corrective to our current discussions by exploring how Baptism is a *Christological* practice. I will do so in three parts: first, a brief historical entrée in order to surface a particular baptismal image from the New Testament and from early communities of faith—that of *putting on Christ*—looking at how this theology of the incarnation was ritually "put on" in two particular traditions. This historical entrée will allow me, secondly, to attend to a rich but largely untapped resource for an understanding of Baptism as a *Christological* practice—the theology of St. Cyril of Alexandria. Then, lastly, I will conclude with some comments about how some of the insights set forth in this essay might move us to revisit the Cyrillian part of our Christological heritage, which offers a very different understanding of the economy of redemption, hence possibly strengthening and deepening our sense of what the person and work of Christ are about and what the life of faith after Baptism should be like.[6]

---

4. Ibid., 19.

5. Keating, "Baptism of Jesus," 201–222.

6. Here I mean primarily Lutherans who now seem to avoid pivotal concepts from their own tradition, like Christology, or are reluctant to even address them.

Historical Entrée: Introducing Baptism
as a Christological Practice

As we look at the development of baptismal practice(s) in the early Christian movement, we find diverse patterns, structures, and theologies from the very beginning.[7] Given that this is now the dominant scholarly understanding, it might seem foolhardy to attempt a historical overview just to uncover some common dynamics and purposes. However, I do want to place my considerations of Baptism as a Christological practice into a larger framework of historical development and this portion of my essay is a brief entrée to that development.

In his book *Early Christian Worship*, Paul F. Bradshaw of the University of Notre Dame has written, "Jesus apparently did not leave his followers with a fixed set of doctrines but rather with an experience that changed their lives, which they then tried to articulate in their own way."[8] Similarly, Edward Schillebeeckx, the great Flemish Dominican theologian, once wrote:

> It began with an experience. Some people—Aramaic—and perhaps also Greek-speaking Jews—came into contact with Jesus of Nazareth and stayed with him. This encounter, and what took place in the life of Jesus and connection with his death, gave their lives new meaning and new significance. They felt they had been born again, that they had been understood, and their new identity found expression in a similar solidarity toward others. . . . This change in the course of their lives was the result of their encounter with Jesus; for without him they would have remained what they had been (see 1 Cor 15:17). It had not come about through any initiative of their own; it had simply happened to them.[9]

This astonishing and overwhelming encounter with Jesus became the point of departure for any understanding and practice of Christian worship.[10] Even when we come across what we might call liturgical or ritual terminology (for example, St. Paul's use of words such as "liturgy," "sacrifice," "priest," or "offering"), the reference is to a life of self-giving, lived after the pattern of Christ who has personalized all of salvation history. Everything has been assumed into the person of the incarnate

---

7. A complete and up-to-date as well as clear and comprehensive study of this material is Johnson, *The Rites of Christian Initiation*. However, see also Ferguson, *Baptism*.

8. Bradshaw, *Early Christian Worship*, 2.

9. Schillebeeckx, *Christ*, 19.

10. My discussion here depends on Taft, "Toward a Theology of the Christian Feast," 21, 19.

one—he is God's eternal Word; God's new creation; the new Adam; the new Pasch and its lamb; the new covenant; the new circumcision and the heavenly manna; God's temple, the new sacrifice and its priest; the fulfillment of the Sabbath rest and the Messianic Age that was to come. Christ is quite simply "all in all," "the alpha and the omega, the first and the last, the beginning and the end."[11]

Martin Connell's recent discussion of how these Christocentric motifs may have been expressed ritually considers those texts in which actual clothing is associated with Baptism—what these earliest communities "might have been doing in those rites that involved clothing."[12] Connell notes how commentators tend to assume that the clothing references are not about actual clothing. Rather they are "metaphorical" or "figurative." For example, Protestant exegetes like Hans Dieter Betz have regarded this passage, not as expressive of perhaps a particular ritual practice involving clothing, but as having to do with faith in Christ.[13] Connell more than suspects here what he calls a "Protestant bias" toward the external works of ritual behavior that would be—horrors!—*ritus ex opere operato*. If we can rid ourselves of this particular polemic, Connell observes, we can regard Paul's description of being brought into the body of Christ "as an act of getting dressed"—an incorporation into "a new body," a new community.[14]

Cyril of Alexandria, whom we will consider more fully in Part II of this essay, refers to the neophytes' new clothing received in Baptism is this way: "It is fitting and quite reasonable to say to those who have been baptized what was said through the voice of the prophet."[15] Then, he quotes Isaiah 61:10: "I will rejoice greatly in the Lord, my soul shall exult in my God; *for he has clothed me with the garments of salvation, he has covered me with the robe of righteousness.*"[16]

---

11. Taft, "Toward a Theology of the Christian Feast," 19.

12. Connell, "Clothing the Body of Christ," 132. My discussion is following Connell.

13. J. Albert Harrill provides yet another reading of this Galatians text by arguing that this Pauline baptismal formula of "putting on Christ" can be best understood through the Gentile experience of the *toga virilis* rite—a Roman coming-of-age ceremony—in which the newly togaed young and male person is warned against succumbing to the temptations of the flesh. Paul contextualizes "putting on Christ" like a garment in order to "create meaning for gentiles of the Christ event in manner that makes immediate sense ritually and in direct contact with the Roman household experience (Harrill, "Coming of Age and Putting on Christ," 277.

14. Connell, "Clothing the Body of Christ," 134.

15. Ferguson, *Baptism*, 692.

16. Isa 61:10. Cited in Ferguson, *Baptism*, 692. My emphasis.

Some centuries later, we find a ritualized expression of "putting on" or "being clothed with Christ" in late antique Coptic Christian practices such as wearing tunics with scenes from the life of Christ. Such a "putting on" was regarded as a *Christological practice*, especially of the *Incarnation*. Stephen J. Davis, both in an essay entitled "Fashioning a Divine Body: Coptic Christology and Ritualized Dress"[17] and his study *Coptic Christology in Practice: Incarnation and Divine Participation in Late Antique and Medieval Egypt*,[18] has demonstrated how understandings of the incarnation can move beyond dogmatic questions and conceptual categories to a consideration of the implications of Christology for the ways people lived out their faith. Ritual enactments of incarnational theology provided sensory reinforcement of liturgical references to the Incarnation and of the power of the sacraments.[19] These ritual enactments of incarnational theology provided sensory reinforcement of liturgical references to the incarnation and of the power of the sacraments. Think of a community of believers, for example, "as they incline their ears to hear a sermon read[,] . . . as they stand with faces lifted upward and eyes widened to discern the painted lines of Christ's glorified body through the shadows, as they wait with bated breath to receive and taste that very body in the eucharistic meal."[20]

There is a tunic from about seventh- or eighth-century Egypt, perhaps belonging to a woman, displaying those distinctive themes found elsewhere in early Christian art such as the Nativity, the Adoration of the Magi, the Baptism of Jesus, as well as representations of Christ, the Virgin, and Saints.[21] Of particular interest here is the Baptism of Christ: "odd," perhaps to our sensibility, because John the Baptizer is absent from this representation. Instead, an angel replaces him and looks like the one baptizing Christ. Vasileios Marinis describes this representation on the tunic in the following way: "In the center there is the Baptism scene, which is flanked by figures extending their hands in proclamation. Curiously . . . both the one who baptizes and the one who is being baptized bear a cruciform halo."[22]

Wearing a tunic such as the one just described reflected and promoted Egyptian understandings of Christ "and more specifically, of the

17. Davis, "Fashioning a Divine Body."

18. Davis, *Coptic Christology in Practice*.

19. This is Davis' singularly important contribution. See also Schroeder, "Coptic Christology in Practice."

20. Davis, *Coptic Christology in Practice*, 270.

21. Marinis, "Wearing the Bible." My discussion here is based on Marinis.

22. Ibid., 102.

Incarnation as a saving event."[23] This actual "putting on Christ" more than suggests, according to Davis, that such discourses "were not always restricted to the metaphorical realm" but may actually have been a particularly embodied way in which these Christians enacted their understanding of the incarnation by actually "performing" it. Athanasius also used this kind of language of "putting on the Lord Jesus" or "being clothed" with him as an expression of God's recreation of humankind "in the image and glory of Christ."[24]

In Syriac practice and understanding from the fourth to the seventh century, we also find that one of the favorite images of writers during this period is that of clothing.[25] In fact, as Sebastian Brock has noted, "the entire span of salvation history can be expressed in terms of clothing imagery."[26] He goes on to describe how this history is unfolded in a dramatic sequence of four main scenes:

Scene 1: Adam and Eve are in Paradise where they are clothed in "robes of glory" or "of light."

Scene 2: Adam and Eve "are stripped of their 'robes of glory/light'" in the Fall

Scene 3: In the incarnation, Jesus Christ "puts on Adam" so as "to remedy the naked state of Adam/humankind" in order to "reclothe" humankind "in the robes of glory." Particularly important in this scene is Jesus's descent into the Jordan at his Baptism to deposit the "robe of glory/light" in the water, "thus making it available once again for humankind to put on in baptism."

Scene 4: The descent of Christ into the Jordan at his Baptism is, in Brock's words, "the fountainhead and source of Christian baptism." Hence, when the Spirit is invoked at Christian Baptism in the prayer of consecration of the water, the water of the individual font becomes identical "in sacred time and space with the Jordan waters." Brock notes further, "Thus, when he or she is baptized, the Christian is himself going down into the Jordan waters and from them picks up and puts on the 'robe of glory' which Christ left there."

23. Davis, *Coptic Christology in Practice*, 170.

24. Ibid., 176 ff.

25. Ferguson, *Baptism*, 497. But see especially Brock, "Clothing Metaphors," cited in Ferguson, *Baptism*, 497.

26. Brock, "Clothing Metaphors," 11–12. I employ Brock for the subsequent dramatic description of salvation history.

This metaphor of "putting on the robe of glory/light" found further expression in the well-known New Testament passage of Galatians 3, cited by Connell earlier, where the Christian "puts on Christ" at Baptism. Also, this metaphor likely calls to mind Philippians 2:7–8, where Christ Jesus has "emptied himself, taking the form of a servant, being born in the likeness of men. And being found in human form he humbled himself and became obedient unto death, even death on a cross." Although "putting on the body" is not used in the Greek New Testament, it does occur in the Syriac version of the New Testament, the Peshitta, describing Christ "being clothed in flesh" or "putting on a body." This latter expression, according to Brock, became "a standard term for the process of the Incarnation in early Syriac Christianity."[27] It was also associated with Baptism, especially as the clothing imagery likely prompted by the putting on of new clothing after Baptism. The glory lost by Adam is restored in the baptismal water and is "put on" in the white garment.[28] Hence, writes Ferguson, "Baptism is our Jordan: 'Instead of the river Jordan you have glorious Baptism,'" and Christ's Baptism, paralleling "his birth and resurrection, were 'for the restoration of the humanity to God'"—a theme that will also be found in Cyril of Alexandria, as we will soon see.[29]

Of the theological interpretations of these baptismal practices, there is one that will stand out with particular emphasis in the evolving life of the church, particularly in the Christian East, and that is specifically its *Christological* or *incarnational* character. It took its bearings from Jesus's own Baptism by John in the Jordan. This was the turning point in the process of being prepared for Baptism that involved such consequences as receiving Christ's teaching, being anointed with the Spirit which Christ had received at his Baptism in the Jordan, and being immersed in the water in the name of the Lord (later of the Trinity). The linking of Jesus's Baptism with the affirmation of Christ's divine sonship meant for fourth-century Syrian writers that Christian Baptism was a birth to new life—with corresponding images of the baptismal font as the Jordan and as womb.

These *Christological* and *incarnational* emphases were also soteriological, we might say.[30] We certainly caught such an emphasis in our

27. Brock, "Clothing Metaphors," 15.

28. Ferguson, *Baptism*, 515–16.

29. Ephrem the Syrian, *Hymns on the Epiphany* 9.2 and 10.3, cited in Ferguson, *Baptism*, 518.

30. It's important to recall here, as Lewis Ayres has pointed out, that "Christology is (for patristic authors, at least) also soteriology, sacramental theology, and hermeneutics." Ayres, "Christology as Contemplative Practice: Understanding the Union of

earlier considerations of clothing and "putting on Christ." The use of the biblical model based on Romans 6, where it is not Christ's Baptism in the Jordan, but rather his passage from death to resurrection in which believers symbolically share, introduces another emphasis. Those being baptized renounce this evil world and go down into the water, where they confess/proclaim their faith and come up again as God's priestly people, marked as God's own with the sign of the cross—and receive the Spirit of the risen Lord and enter the promised land.

This *Christological* emphasis was expressive, even revelatory of the larger divine economy, and here it is that Baptism—especially the Baptism of Jesus—played "a pivotal role . . . for a proper understanding of both the incarnation and the plan of redemption."[31] Yet we do not see these features and dynamics as always present or salient in much current baptismal discourse that is so preoccupied with ecclesiology—preoccupied with us, as it were (not that ecclesiology always has to be, however). As we turn now to a consideration of Cyril of Alexandria's understanding of Baptism and of the Christian life, we can see a particular linking of this event of putting on Christ and so to its understanding that here, the re-creation of the human race is being expressed.

Baptism in Cyril of Alexandria: The Re-Creation of the Human Race

My former teacher, Robert Taft, once wrote, "Christ came not just to save individuals, but to change the course of history by creating the leaven of a new group, a new people of God, paradigm of what all peoples must one day be."[32] Cyril of Alexandria understood Baptism similarly—an understanding that took its bearings above all from the Baptism of Jesus. It may be even equally remarkable to employ Cyril of Alexandria's understanding of Baptism, rooted as it is in Christ's Baptism, in a more contemporary discussion of the significance of the foundational Christian practice of washing, clothing, and incorporating new believers into a community of faith. We should recall,

> The patristic understanding of the Incarnation owes much more
> to Cyril of Alexandria than to any other individual theologian.

Natures in Augustine's *Letter 137*," 191. Here I am reprising material from my essay, "Practicing a Theopaschite Christology with St. Cyril of Alexandria."

31. Keating, "Baptism of Jesus," 202. See also Ferguson, *Baptism*, 688 ff.

32. Taft, *Liturgy of the Hours*, 342.

> The classic picture of Christ the God-man, as it is delineated in the formulae of the Church from the Council of Chalcedon onwards, *and as it has been presented to the heart in liturgies and hymns*, is the picture Cyril persuaded Christians was the true, the only credible, Christ.[33]

In fact, Cyril's exposition of the Baptism of Christ is situated "at the junction of his anthropology, his Christology, and his trinitarian theology.[34] Thus, it is my judgment that here is a rich, untapped resource for adding a much-needed *Christological* corrective to our contemporary discussions of what Baptism is and does.

For Cyril, "the Baptism of Christ was a major event in salvation history."[35] Prescinding for now from the Christological problems and controversies generated by this event,[36] let us consider for a moment why the Jordanian Baptism of Christ is so important. The Baptism of Jesus and the pertinent New Testament texts in John and Luke reveal for Cyril "the very purpose and strategy of the incarnation, the re-creation of the human race in the incarnate Christ as exemplified in his Baptism."[37] For example, in his exposition of Jesus's Baptism in John 1, the primary focus here is the descent of the Spirit upon Jesus in the form of a dove. However, this is no "adoptionist" Christology in Cyril's mind. Rather, according to Cyril, Christ receives the Spirit for *humanity's sake*. Keating notes, "What the Son eternally possesses as God he now receives for us *as a man*."[38] Besides, due to the emptying of the Son of which we read in Philippians 2, there was nothing additional to gain that he did not have before. This point is further underscored in Cyril's

33. Wickham, "Introduction," xi. Here again I am reprising material from my essay, "Practicing a Theopaschite Christology with St. Cyril of Alexandria."

34. Boulnois, "Le Soufflé Et l'Esprit: Exégèses Patristiques De L'insufflation Originelle De Gen. 2,7 En Lien Avec Celle De Jn 20,22," 33. Cited in Keating, "Baptism of Jesus," 152. I should mention here that I will rely heavily on the three studies by Keating: "Divinization in Cyril"; "Baptism of Jesus"; and *Appropriation of Divine Life*, for this part of my essay. For a more thorough discussion of Cyril's understanding of Baptism, the reader is advised to consult these works.

35. Ferguson, *Baptism*, 687.

36. For an account of these problems and controversies, see Wilken, *Judaism and the Early Christian Mind*, 127 ff. See also McDonnell, "Jesus' Baptism in the Jordan," 212: "Because of adoptionism, which held that Jesus received his divine sonship and became the Christ, or anointed one, at his Baptism, there are protests which touch the theology of Jesus' Baptism."

37. Keating, "Baptism of Jesus," 202. My following discussion of Jesus's Baptism is indebted to Keating, *Appropriation of Divine Life*, 21 ff.

38. Keating, "Divinization in Cyril," 153. My emphasis.

citation of 2 Corinthians 8: 9, "that though he was rich, yet for your sake he became poor, so that by his poverty you might become rich."

With the Arian objection out of the way, Cyril can turn to Jesus's Baptism once again. In beginning with the Creation, he can remind his readers/hearers that a person is made in God's image, in God's likeness. That creative gift of the image is, further, sealed by the Spirit—"the breath of life"—and is also expressed in the gift of the "saving commandment" or better, the "preserving commandment" by living in a particular way. By including this aspect of the creation, Cyril can underline the moral element that is given that then brings with it a moral capacity. All of this is the divine image, "guaranteed by the indwelling of the Holy Spirit, a gift that needs to be guarded, lest it be lost."[39]

But this gift of the Spirit was lost in the Fall and sin came to dominate the human race. Cyril wrote that "nature was stripped of the ancient grace" and "the Spirit departs altogether." Even more crucially, however, is that "the final stripping of grace is marked by the decisive departure of the Holy Spirit." As Keating notes further, "the decisive feature of this account is the acquisition and forfeiture of the Holy Spirit."[40]

What is now interesting about Cyril's exegesis is that he gives really no attention to Jesus's Baptism and its ritual details. Rather, he attends to the question: "how could or why would Jesus receive the Spirit if he is indeed the Son, the Logos?" It is because in Cyril's understanding of the Creation and the Fall, the Spirit had been lost—the ancient grace had been stripped away as we saw earlier—only to return—to be reacquired—when Jesus is baptized. "The descent of the Spirit on Christ represents *the* decisive return of the Spirit to the human race, now abiding in one who can reliably 'preserve it.'"[41] This is nothing less than a reversal, thus giving the human race "the opportunity for a new beginning, for a new man has appeared who promises to turn back what Adam had done and accomplish what none since the time of Adam was capable of doing."[42]

But this second Adam is no ordinary man, who could simply have been gifted with the Spirit. No. He is God's Son, the Word of God become human and who began the work of renewal, which was nothing less than the the re-creation of the human race. It is also important to note that the Spirit does not merely come upon Jesus; it remains upon him. Thus,

39. Keating, "Baptism of Jesus," 206.

40. Ibid., 206.

41. Keating, "Divinization in Cyril," 156.

42. Wilken, *Judaism and the Early Christian Mind*, 139.

for Cyril, the descent of the Spirit is not just a past event. It has begun something that is of "great significance for the human race"[43]—that the original grace can be rooted in humanity once again. Moreover, the Word Incarnate, in receiving the Spirit, receives it not for himself "but for us and *as one of us*, that he might preserve it in our nature, that the original grace might be rooted in us once again."[44]

It is important to remember that the larger context for reading and interpreting the Baptism of Jesus in Cyril is the Incarnation of the Word.[45] Let us consider a particular passage from one of Cyril's New Testament commentaries that provides a very condensed statement or exposition of how his understandings of the Trinity, of Creation, of the Incarnation of the Word, and of the Spirit's sanctifying work all hang together:

> It was not otherwise possible for man, being of a nature which perishes, to escape death, unless he recovered that ancient grace, and partook once more of God who holds all things together in being and preserves them in life through the Son in the Spirit. Therefore his Only-Begotten Word has become a partaker of flesh and blood (Heb. 2:14), that is, he has become man, though being life by nature, and begotten of the Life that is by nature, that is, of God the Father, so that, having united himself with the flesh which perishes according to the law of its own nature . . . he might restore to it his own life and render it through himself a partaker of God the Father. . . . And he wears our nature, refashioning it to his own life. And he himself is also in us, for we have all become partakers of him, and have him in ourselves through the Spirit. For this reason we have become "partakers of the divine nature" (2 Pet. 1:4), and are reckoned as sons, and so too have in ourselves the Father himself through the Son.[46]

As Daniel Keating observes, all these understandings cohere in a narrative of a particular kind that he calls a narrative of divine life.

While in our time we like to speak of the "shape" of a rite or of a liturgy rarely do we speak of a theology, especially a theology of Baptism, as having a narrative "shape." Cyril's theology of Baptism is best read, it seems, as a particular kind of "narrative of the economy of salvation in Christ, framed in terms of the gift of divine life to the human race, and the reception of

43. Keating, *Appropriation of Divine Life*, 22.

44. Keating, "Baptism of Jesus," 207.

45. Ibid., 209.

46. In *Joannem* 14.20, in Cyril, *Commentary on the Gospel according to S. John*, 2:485–86. Cited in Keating, *Appropriation of Divine Life*, 8.

divine life by the human race."[47] It is this narrative that reveals the shape of Cyril's theology—a theology that has a great deal to offer to our contemporary discussions of what Baptism is and what Baptism does.

The center of this theology, "a well-integrated theology,"[48] as it has been described, is a *Christology*—the Incarnation of Christ that includes the narrative and the soteriological purpose of the Word made flesh. It is in this Christ—the center—that the world is redeemed, and the human race is re-created *in him*. Moreover, the Second Adam[49] in whom the Spirit has decisively returned provides a Christological grounding and centering for the human reception of divine life. The result is a kinship that is both ontological as well as moral whereby we can live lives of faith and obedience. This re-creation of the human race in which we take part is appropriated through Baptism as well as the Eucharist. As Kilian McDonnell notes, "the voice of the Father and the descent of the Spirit lay down the boundary where the old creation ends and the new begins."[50] Thus, it is possible for Christ's humanity to become a pattern for our own.

A Christological Corrective
to Our Thinking about Baptism

And so we return to where we began in this essay—with the tension "between Baptism conceived as a human activity, and as a divine activity, and the attempt to steer a course between Baptism as a human rite and unguarded assertions which turn it into an *opus operatum*."[51] Such a tension is also present in terms of the "controlling hermeneutic" or "optic" for our articulation of a baptismal theology that is adequate to the multiple images and implications of Baptism. More recently, however, it would seem that this tension has been largely dissolved into a baptismal ecclesiology

47. Keating, *Appropriation of Divine Life,* 191.

48. Keating, "Baptism of Jesus," 221.

49. Cyril is particularly taken with the image of "Christ as the Second Adam." It enabled him to speak of Christ "as fully human, as Adam, yet to show in what way he was more than a man, as the heavenly Adam who conquered death." What is also important about the Christ-Second Adam image is that it "keeps the reader's attention focused on the Bible as a whole (Adam at the beginning, the heavenly Adam at the beginning of the end) and what gives the entire biblical narrative its meaning, the resurrection of Christ." The references here are to Wilken, "St Cyril of Alexandria," 471. See also Wilken, *Judaism and the Early Christian Mind,* 141–42.

50. McDonnell, "Jesus' Baptism in the Jordan," 222.

51. Spinks, "Luther's Timely Theology of Unilateral Baptism," 24.

that uncritically seeks to move "directly from the uniqueness of the incarnation to the life of the church."[52] However, it is necessary to first consider the life of the church as resulting from the mission of the Spirit, as there can be no "incarnational" ecclesiology, if the coming of the Logos in the particularity of Jesus of Nazareth only exemplifies a general principle. It is the mission of the Spirit to universalize the particularity of Christ—so that he is actually everything he said he is.

In addition, there is now this preoccupation with water, perhaps rightly so because of our ongoing ecological crisis. But with reference to Baptism, however, "water cannot choose for or against God."[53] We use water to express or to communicate something significant about what God, triune and holy, is up to in the baptismal event. For example, to say that Luther's so-called "flood prayer"—his *Sintflutgebet*—provides the basis for the thanksgivings over the water in the 1978 *Lutheran Book of Worship* and 2006 *Evangelical Lutheran Worship* is wishful thinking at best.[54] Luther's prayer began, not with creation, but with believing or trusting Noah, and went on to mention Jesus's Baptism in the Jordan—"the Baptism of your dear Son, our Lord Jesus Christ, who sanctified and set apart the Jordan and all waters as a blessed flood . . ." Surprisingly, to us, the *Sintflutgebet* does not mention the Baptism of Jesus's own death and resurrection, as do the prayers of *LBW* and *ELW,* as somehow foundational and/or determinative for Christian Baptism. Rather, Luther's prayer seems to suggest the larger narrative, and hence broader scope of the economy of salvation such as we find in Cyril of Alexandria, that it is the Baptism of Jesus that "uniquely captures and reveals . . . the entire economy of salvation."[55] Moreover, the Baptism of Jesus "comes to

52. Yeago, "Theological Renewal in Communion: What Anglicans and Lutherans Can Learn from One Another," 209. My comments in the remainder of this paragraph are based on Yeago.

53. Riggs, *Baptism in the Reformed Tradition,* 14.

54. Here is the text of the first part of that prayer:

> Almighty eternal God, according to your righteous judgment you condemned the untrusting world through the flood, yet in your great mercy preserved trusting Noah and his family, eight souls in all. You drowned hard-hearted Pharaoh and all his host in the Red Sea, you led your people Israel through the water on dry ground, foreshadowing this washing of Your Holy Baptism. *Through the Baptism of your dear Son, our Lord Jesus Christ, you sanctified and set apart the Jordan and all waters as a blessed flood and a rich and full washing away of sin.*

(Luther, "The Order of Baptism 1523," 97.)

55. Keating, "Divinization in Cyril," 152. The remaining citations in this paragraph are from this essay and can be found on pp. 152, 153, and 159.

signify the re-creation of the human race, pointing back, as it were, to the creation of Adam, and pointing forward to the completion of humanity in the resurrection and ascension of Christ."

A more deeply developed Cyrillian perspective on Baptism would need to articulate more fully, one might think, a pneumatology. For Cyril, however, the Spirit plays a prominent role because the Spirit is the agent who accomplishes in us the fruits of Christ's redemption. Such an understanding is grounded in both the Scripture and is seen in "the entire economy of salvation."[56] This "agency of the Spirit is not other than the Spirit of Christ" and it is this "gift of the indwelling Spirit [that] is the means by which Christ now accomplishes our cleansing and sanctification and imparts to us new life."[57]

It is the descent of the Spirit upon Christ, then, that fills out the soteriological frame of Cyril's narrative of divine life as a whole. Its significance, as we have seen, is for the manifestation of the plan of redemption through the Incarnation. This decisive return of the Spirit to the human race in the Baptism of Jesus is no momentary event. Rather, the Spirit now abides in him—"remains" on him who can reliably "preserve it" because this Jesus is the Incarnate Word who carries out the work of redemption and re-creation in himself and as such "reveals the end intended for the whole human race" and "inaugurates a renewed human life on earth through the gift of the Spirit." This is the gift from the Incarnate Christ to us. Here is a corrective that an understanding of Baptism as a *Christological* practice can provide where in putting on Christ we receive "the grace of God the Word, Christ the Lord, the Son of God, who became one with us."[58]

---

56. Keating, *Appropriation of Divine Life*, 63.

57. Ibid., 63.

58. From the reading for Epiphany (11 Tubah), Forget, *Synaxarium Alexandrinum*, i. 204, cited in Davis, *Coptic Christology in Practice*, 99.

Bibliography

Aune, Michael B. "Practicing a Theopaschite Christology with St. Cyril of Alexandria." *Lutheran Forum* 45.4 (2011) 23–34.

Ayres, Lewis. "Christology as Contemplative Practice: Understanding the Union of Natures in Augustine's *Letter 137*." In *In the Shadow of the Incarnation: Essays on Jesus Christ in the Early Church in Honor of Brian E. Daley, S.J.*, edited by Peter W. Martens, 190–211. Notre Dame, IN: University of Notre Dame Press, 2008.

Boulnois, Marie-Odile. "Le Soufflé Et l'Esprit: Exégèses Patristiques De L'insufflation Originelle De Gen. 2,7 En Lien Avec Celle De Jn 20,22." *Recherches Augustiniennes* 24 (1989) 20–38.

Bradshaw, Paul F. *Early Christian Worship: A Basic Introduction to Ideas and Practice.* London: SPCK, 1996.

Brock, Sebastian P. "Clothing Metaphors as a Means of Theological Expression in Syriac Tradition." In *Studies in Syriac Christianity: History, Literature, and Theology,* XI:11–38. Collected Studies Series CS357. Hampshire, UK: Variorum, 1992.

Connell, Martin F. "Clothing the Body of Christ: An Inquiry about the Letters of Paul." *Worship* 85 (2011) 128–46.

Cyril. *Commentary on the Gospel according to S. John.* Translated by Philip Edward Pusey and Thomas Randell. Vol. 2. A Library of Fathers of the Holy Catholic Church 43, 48. Oxford: Parker, 1874.

Davis, Stephen J. *Coptic Christology in Practice: Incarnation and Divine Participation in Late Antique and Medieval Egypt.* Oxford: Oxford University Press, 2008.

———. "Fashioning a Divine Body: Coptic Christology and Ritualized Dress." *Harvard Theological Review* 98 (2005) 335–62.

Ferguson, Everett. *Baptism in the Early Church: History, Theology, and Liturgy in the First Five Centuries.* Grand Rapids: Eerdmans, 2008.

Forget, Jacobus, editor. *Synaxarium Alexandrinum.* Corpus Scriptorum Christianorum Orientalium 47–49. Louvain: Durbecq, 1953.

Harrill, J. Albert. "Coming of Age and Putting on Christ: The Toga Virilis Ceremony, Its Paraenesis, and Paul's Interpretation of Baptism in Galatians." *Novum Testamentum* 44 (2002) 252–77.

Johnson, Maxwell E. *The Rites of Christian Initiation: Their Evolution and Interpretation.* Collegeville, MN: Liturgical, 2007.

Keating, Daniel A. *The Appropriation of Divine Life in Cyril of Alexandria.* Oxford: Oxford University Press, 2004.

Keating, Daniel A. "The Baptism of Jesus in Cyril of Alexandria: The Re-creation of the Human Race." *Pro Ecclesia* 8 (1999) 201–22.

———. "Divinization in Cyril: The Appropriation of Divine Life." In *The Theology of Cyril of Alexandria: A Critical Appreciation*, edited by Thomas Weinandy and Daniel A. Keating, 149–85. London: T. & T. Clark, 2003.

Luther, Martin. "The Order of Baptism 1523." In *Liturgy & Hymns.* Luther's Works 53. St. Louis, MO: Concordia, 1955.

Marinis, Vasileios. "Wearing the Bible: An Early Christian Tunic with New Testament Scenes." *Journal of Coptic Studies* 9 (2007) 95–109.

McDonnell, Kilian. "Jesus' Baptism in the Jordan." *Theological Studies* 56 (1995) 209–36.

Riggs, John W. *Baptism in the Reformed Tradition: A Historical and Practical Theology.* Louisville, KY: Westminster John Knox, 2002.

Schillebeeckx, Edward. *Christ: The Experience of Jesus as Lord*. New York: Crossroad, 1980.

Schroeder, Caroline T. "Review: Coptic Christology in Practice: Incarnation and Divine Participation in Late Antique and Medieval Egypt." *Church History* 78 (2009) 884–86.

Spinks, Bryan D. "Luther's Timely Theology of Unilateral Baptism." *Lutheran Quarterly* 9.1 (1995) 23–45.

Taft, Robert F. *The Liturgy of the Hours in East and West: The Origins of the Divine Office and Its Meaning for Today*. Collegeville, MN: Liturgical, 1986.

————. "Toward a Theology of the Christian Feast." In *Beyond East and West: Problems in Liturgical Understanding*, 2nd ed., 15–29. Rome: Edizioni Orientalia Christiana, Pontifical Oriental Institute, 1997.

Weil, Louis. *A Theology of Worship*. New Church's Teaching Series 12. Cambridge, MA: Cowley, 2001.

Wickham, Lionel R. "Introduction." In *Cyril of Alexandria, Select Letters*. Oxford Early Christian Texts. Oxford: Clarendon, 1983.

Wilken, Robert Louis. *Judaism and the Early Christian Mind: A Study of Cyril of Alexandria's Exegesis and Theology*. New Haven: Yale University Press, 1971.

————. "St Cyril of Alexandria: The Mystery of Christ in the Bible." *Pro Ecclesia* 4 (1995) 454–78.

Yeago, David S. "Theological Renewal in Communion: What Anglicans and Lutherans Can Learn from One Another." In *Inhabiting Unity: Theological Perspectives on the Proposed Lutheran-Episcopal Concordat*, edited by Ephraim Radner and Russell R. Reno, 206–23. Grand Rapids: Eerdmans, 1995.

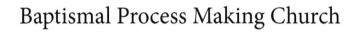

Baptismal Process Making Church

4

Baptism and the Journey
of Christian Initiation

Paul Avis

As a leading exponent of liturgical theology, Louis Weil has been
a catalyst for deeper theological reflection on Baptism and its place in
Christian initiation, especially among Anglicans. Professor Weil is identified in the minds of many of us with the stance of The Episcopal Church's
1979 Book of Common Prayer, namely that Baptism is complete sacramental initiation. However, in my view he should not be typecast on this
matter—his thought has continued to develop. In his recent article in the
Anglican Theological Review, "Baptism as the Model for a Sacramental
Aesthetic," Weil repeatedly draws attention to the fact that, for the early
church, Baptism led on to the Eucharist and that these two sacraments
were regarded as the beginning and the end of the journey of initiation. He
shows that Baptism belongs within a sacramental dynamic of induction
into the life of grace in the church. In this recent reflection, Weil has come
close to the position that I and other Anglicans have been arguing for in
the *The Journey of Christian Initiation* and elsewhere.

In this contribution, which I feel honored to offer as a tribute to a
friend and a colleague in ecclesiological research and reflection, I want to
examine, in a spirit of fraternal dialogue, the claim that Baptism is complete sacramental initiation and to propose an alternative way of looking at the question of Christian initiation.[1] I want to challenge a view of

1. Here I draw on my contributions to *The Journey of Christian Initiation*, which
in turn reflects my paper "Is Baptism 'Complete Sacramental Initiation'?." Another
version of the paper was given at the Fifth Theological Conference under the Meissen

initiation that enjoys wide currency at an unofficial level in the Church of England and other churches of the Anglican Communion and which has been officially adopted by The Episcopal Church in its Book of Common Prayer of 1979.

Baptism as Complete Sacramental Initiation?

It is sometimes said that Baptism comprises the whole of sacramental initiation. This view, which I designate as "BACSI"—"Baptism as Complete Sacramental Initiation"—seems to have achieved the status of unquestioned orthodoxy in some circles. I am interested in the question of where it has come from, because it does not have support in the Eastern or Western traditions or in the Book of Common Prayer, 1662, and is in fact a late twentieth-century innovation.

The 1979 Book of Common Prayer of the Episcopal Church of the USA formally endorsed BACSI. "Holy Baptism is full initiation by water and the Holy Spirit into Christ's Body the Church" (p. 298). The American prayer book attempted to achieve a unified rite of initiation—a laudable aim—but in the context of infant Baptism, which is resistant to that aim (unless one is an Orthodox). In the American prayer book there is provision for chrismation, administered by a priest, at Baptism, and the bishop often gives a second chrismation at "confirmation." Confirmation is seen as the first occasion of "mature public affirmation" (p. 412) of the baptismal commitments made by those baptized at an early age. The emphasis seems to be on the human response, rather than the divine gift, which seems to me to be the wrong way round. The baptismal promises are affirmed, but what does the Holy Spirit give? The rite may be affirming for those who undergo it, but it has created a predicament for Episcopalians—What exactly is happening in "confirmation"? This question has generated intense scholarly debate, notably in the pages of the *Anglican Theological Review*. [2]

Agreement between the Church of England and the Evangelische Kirche in Deutschland (EKD) at Fox Hill, near Chester, in September 2005 and will be published in German. For further discussion of the Anglican understanding of Baptism see Avis, *The Identity of Anglicanism*, chapter VI, "Anglicanism and Baptismal Ecclesiology."

2. See Burnett, "Reconsidering a Bold Proposal," which re-affirms BACSI and sees confirmation as an opportunity for the affirmation of faith, and Tanner, "Towards a New Theology of Confirmation," which attempts to retrieve confirmation in the classical sense as a sacrament of strengthening by the Holy Spirit, not simply as an affirmation of faith, but wants to do this without relinquishing BACSI. In my view, these two aims are incompatible. See also Podmore, "The Baptismal Covenant in the American Church."

In contrast to the American prayer book, I see Christian initiation as a process or journey—we could say an event that is extended over time for pastoral reasons—one that involves several sacramental milestones, including, crucially and fundamentally, Baptism. Baptism takes its place as the foundational sacrament of initiation within a sacramental continuum. Baptism unites us through the Holy Spirit to Christ in his death and resurrection and incorporates us into his mystical body. But all that is contained in Baptism is received over time and Baptism does not stand alone as a means of inducting us into the life of grace in the church.

So I believe that confirmation is also an act of a sacramental nature. Even though it is not a dominical sacrament—that is, one directly instituted by our Lord—on the same level as Baptism and the Eucharist, confirmation has a fundamentally sacramental character as "an outward and visible sign of an inward and spiritual grace, given unto us," as the Catechism, following an ancient Christian tradition, puts it. I believe that confirmation has an important place in Christian initiation, and that participating in the celebration of the Eucharist and receiving Holy Communion, normally for the first time, which are indisputably sacramental matters, are also an essential part of initiation and the culmination of the process.

I find helpful what the report *Doctrine in the Church of England* (1938), the work of a commission set up by the Archbishops of Canterbury and York in 1922 and chaired by William Temple, says about initiation (though of course this report was addressed to the two Archbishops and does not have any status in the Episcopal Church). It affirms the need for confirmation and states that confirmation should precede admission to Holy Communion. Confirmation, according to the report, consists of prayer for the Holy Spirit (the form) and the laying on of hands of the bishop (the matter). The renewal of baptismal promises by the candidate, while normal, "is not an essential element in the rite." It is not about affirming our faith. The Holy Spirit is given to strengthen the Christian and "all theologians agree" on this. The Spirit brings the sevenfold messianic gifts mentioned in Isaiah 11, so that, in confirmation, the candidate, "already incorporated into Christ in Baptism, is made a partaker in the gifts proper to the messianic community and its mission to the world." The report is clear that "there is a real gift of grace bestowed in Confirmation." It argues that "it is appropriate that the rite wherein the gift of the Holy Spirit is bestowed in its fulness should normally precede admission to participation in the rite which expresses the completeness of Church-membership and of its obligations." Thus there is a clear sense in this report that initiation is a process and that it is completed in the Eucharist. Within that process additional grace is given through confirmation.[3]

It is interesting that *Common Worship*, the Church of England's current set of liturgical texts—which does not, again, have any authority in the Episcopal Church, but I mention here for purposes of comparison—has not embraced BACSI. In the *Common Worship* initiation services the theme of initiation as a process and a journey is clearly brought out, both in the rite itself and in the notes. In this respect, it continues the tradition of the English Book of Common Prayer through its various editions.[4] A service of confirmation was included in the successive editions of the *BCP* from 1549 to 1662. Although it was not regarded as necessary to salvation, confirmation was a vital part of Christian initiation. It was a means of grace that gave strength to resist temptation and to live the Christian life. This provision obviously made sense when virtually all Baptisms were of infants. But confirmation was still required in 1662 when for the first time a service of Baptism was provided for those who were "of riper years and able to answer for themselves" (especially those who had missed out on Baptism during the upheavals of the English Civil War and the Commonwealth period under Oliver Cromwell). It seems clear, from the requirement that those adults who were baptized should be confirmed by the bishop as soon as convenient, that Baptism and confirmation were seen as parts of a process of Christian initiation. Thus there is considerable continuity and consistency in the practice of initiation in the English Church from medieval times, through the Reformation to the present day. Of course, that does not necessarily make it right!

Why has BACSI gathered support; why is it quite widely accepted, not least in the Episcopal Church? Given that BACSI has not been endorsed by a Lambeth Conference and is in tension with the liturgical tradition (owned by The Episcopal Church), that stems from the English Book of Common Prayer, why has it made headway among Anglicans? I tell myself that there must surely be more to BACSI than meets the eye!

In one sense, if "Baptism" is taken to include the whole cluster of initiatory events that—either at the time in the case of adults or at a later stage in the case of infants—accompany it, it can be seen as complete initiation. Thus a Baptism in the Orthodox churches is complete sacramental initiation, because it includes chrismation and first communion, among other elements. But I do not think that that is what defenders of BACSI mean. They do not

3. Church of England, *Doctrine in the Church of England*, 186–89.
4. A useful composite edition is Cummings, *The Book of Common Prayer*.

mean that chrismation, the laying on of hands for the strengthening of the Holy Spirit, participating in the celebration of the Eucharist and receiving Holy Communion for the first time are included in Baptism. They apparently do not see these elements as part of initiation at all.

Affirming Initiation as a Process

In response to BACSI, I want to make several theological affirmations about Christian initiation.

Baptism Is at the Heart of Christian Initiation

We cannot praise Baptism too highly. The proponents of BACSI are right to the extent that we cannot take too high a view of Baptism or exaggerate its importance. Baptism unites us with Jesus Christ in his death and resurrection (Rom 6:1ff). Baptism is an action of the Holy Spirit, incorporating us into the body of Christ (1 Cor 12:13). The Catechism that is included in the Book of Common Prayer, 1662, says that Baptism makes each of us "a member of Christ, the child of God, and an inheritor of the kingdom of heaven." But it does not follow from the truth that Baptism is the foundation and heart of initiation that Baptism comprises the whole of initiation. Baptism does not stand alone.

Baptism Cannot Be Repeated

All churches agree that water Baptism can be received only once. It is not possible, theologically, to be re-baptized. It belongs to the nature of Baptism that it is unrepeatable. Where Baptists appear to "re-baptize" a person who has previously been baptized in infancy, they believe that the candidate is undergoing (true) Baptism for the first time. The unrepeatability of Baptism appears to lend some support to the BACSI position, because it suggests the finality of the sacrament. But what is unrepeatable may be part of a larger whole, as Baptism is part of Christian initiation.

Baptism Cannot Be Incomplete Or Partial

Defenders of BACSI are right to say that Baptism cannot be "completed" or "topped up" in any way. Baptism "contains," sacramentally, Christ and all that is his: in Baptism we receive Christ and all his benefits. This points to the difficulty with the language of "perfecting" or completing applied to confirmation, which goes back to St. Ambrose and was used by Richard Hooker in the sixteenth century and by Lionel Thornton, CR, in the twentieth. What is being "perfected"? For Hooker, it is the work of grace, begun in us by Baptism; for Thornton, it seems to be our vocation as disciples. Neither of these seems objectionable, provided it is not Baptism itself that is said to be perfected in confirmation, but perhaps the language is unfortunate.[5] Baptism is complete as Baptism, but not complete as initiation into the life of grace in the church.

Baptism Is Normally Necessary for Salvation

The traditions shaped by the Reformation insist that the conditions of salvation are clearly revealed in Scripture.[6] It has been common ground between the mainstream churches that Baptism is normally necessary for salvation. This is taught in both the Lutheran Augsburg Confession of 1530 and the English Book of Common Prayer.[7] It is a teaching that can appeal to Scripture in Matthew 28:19, Mark 16:16 (the longer ending), John 3:5, and Acts 2:38. However, as the early Church recognized, this requirement of church discipline needs to be tempered with flexibility. So the early fathers acknowledged that there could be a Baptism of desire and a Baptism of blood (martyrdom), as well as water Baptism. In modern times, several churches have reflected on the possibility of those of other faiths being saved through the work of Christ, even though in his life they may have no knowledge of him.[8]

5. R. Hooker, *Of the Laws of Ecclesiastical Polity*, V, lxvi, 1: "to confirm and perfect that which the grace of the same Spirit had already begun in Baptism." Hooker also endorses the language of "strengthening" in virtue and against temptation (4, 9). Thornton, *Confirmation; Its Place in the Baptismal Mystery*, derives the language of "perfecting" from the Epistle to the Hebrews.

6. E.g., Article VI of the Church of England's Thirty-nine Articles of Religion, 1562–71: "*Of the Sufficiency of the Holy Scriptures for salvation*: "Holy Scripture containeth all things necessary to salvation: so that whatsoever is not read therein, nor may be proved thereby, is not to be required of any man, that it should be believed as an article of the Faith, or be thought requisite or necessary to salvation."

7. Augsburg Confession IX (translation of Latin text) "Our churches teach that Baptism is necessary for salvation . . ."; Book of Common Prayer, Catechism: the two dominical sacraments are "generally necessary to salvation."

8. Vatican 2: *Nostra aetate: Declaration on the Relations of the Church to Non-Christian Religions*: Flannery, *Vatican Council II, the Conciliar and Post Conciliar*

Confirmation Is a Means of Grace

The Reformers did not regard confirmation as a sacrament and therefore as necessary to salvation. Thus they rejected the popular medieval belief (though it was not the official teaching of the Western church) that confirmation or chrism was necessary to salvation.[9] Nevertheless, in the Reformation and post-Reformation periods confirmation is seen as a means of grace, not as a human work. It meets the first criterion (derived from Peter Lombard) of a sacrament in the Catechism: an outward visible sign of an inward spiritual grace (the second criterion being dominical institution). The Book of Common Prayer, 1662, sees confirmation as a sacramental action concerned with strengthening the Christian. This view reflects the medieval tradition that is also upheld by the Roman Catholic Church. The Second Vatican Council says of those who have been baptized: "Reborn as sons of God, they must confess before men the faith which they have received from God through the Church. Bound more intimately to the Church by the sacrament of confirmation, they are endowed by the Holy Spirit with special strength".[10]

The Rites of Christian Initiation Should Be as Unified as Possible

Medieval and Reformation views of confirmation did not make the connection between Baptism, confirmation, and the Eucharist as strongly as they should have done. The disjunction between them gives some credibility to BACSI. However, there is a theological, if not always a chronological, unity to the rite or rites of initiation. Initiation is the induction of new Christians into the mystical body of Christ. Initiation is precisely into the salvation process, that is to say, the process of the reception of God's gift of salvation in Jesus Christ. If Baptism is one focal point of the

---

Documents, 1:738–42; Doctrine Commision of the Church of England, *The Mystery of Salvation*.

9. Melanchthon, "Apology of the Augsburg Confession," sec. 13, p. 212; Tyndale, "Obedience of a Christian Man," 277. Jewel, "A Treatise of the Sacraments," 1126: "They said he was no proper Christian, that was not anointed with this holy oil chrism. This was another abuse. For whosoever is baptized receiveth thereby the full name of a perfect Christian, and hath the full and perfect covenant and assurance of salvation." See also Bromiley, *Baptism and the Anglican Reformers*; for the Reformed family of churches, Riggs, *Baptism in the Reformed Tradition*.

10. *Lumen Gentium*, 11. Abbott, *The Documents of Vatican II*, 28.

salvation process, the Eucharist is another. Both dominical sacraments, Baptism and the Eucharist (more correctly, participation in the celebration of the Eucharist and first Communion) take their place within the totality of Christian initiation because both of them induct us into the salvation process, into the mystery of Christ. To make one's communion is the culmination of sacramental initiation, which remains incomplete if this point is not reached. Could one say that a person was fully initiated and inducted into the life and worship of the mystical body of Christ if that person had never received the sacramental body of Christ? Full participation in the Eucharist, including receiving the sacrament, is a means of grace that completes the process of initiation.[11]

Initiation Is an Articulated, Extended Event

It is sometimes said that initiation is not a process but an event. I am happy to consider initiation as an event, provided we think in terms of an *extended* or *unfolding* event, an event that has several stages. When a play is performed, that is an event, but there are usually several "acts" and probably even more "scenes" within the play. When a symphony, concerto, or sonata is performed, that too is an event, but there are usually several "movements" within the piece of music. An event may be composite, composed of several parts which are linked together, and it may take place over an extended period. Christian initiation can be described as an extended, articulated event.

Baptism Needs a Process of Reception

Initiation is a process of receiving and Baptism is the heart and the paradigm of this.[12] God's whole gift of salvation is contained in Baptism (just as it is in the Eucharist), but we need a process, including other sacramental occasions, in order to receive the gift to the full extent. Baptism is an "ef-

---

11. Cf. Benedict XVI, Post Synodal Exhortation, *Sacramentum Caritatis* (2007) "If the Eucharist is truly the source and summit of the Church's life and mission, it follows that the process of Christian initiation must constantly be directed to the reception of this sacrament . . . our reception of Baptism and Confirmation is ordered to the Eucharist. Accordingly, our pastoral practice should reflect a more unitary understanding of the process of Christian initiation. . . . The Holy Eucharist, then, brings Christian initiation to completion."

12. See on this theme Sykes, *Unashamed Anglicanism*, 13ff. Sykes suggestively analyses the themes of reception and divine promise in the Book of Common Prayer service for the Baptism of children.

fectual" means of grace. It conveys what it signifies. Baptism is the sacra-ment of rebirth or regeneration by the Holy Spirit, through which the gift of the Spirit is received. We are born into a new relational world. Because Baptism makes one a member of the body of Christ, it is both ontological and relational: in fact, the ontology itself is essentially relational. How-ever, it is equally important to emphasize that Baptism requires a human response of faith and of committed discipleship and (as Martin Luther particularly emphasized) Baptism should be appropriated and entered into again and again, more and more, throughout one's life.

Initiation Changes Us

The Anglican doctrine of initiation is philosophically realist. That is to say, the sacraments are not basically about our human response to God's grace; they are about receiving a gift. A sacrament truly effects what it signifies—provided that the collateral conditions regarding the formal intention and the disposition of faith are fulfilled. Sacraments are not magic, but neither are they emotive gestures on our part. The central idea in the Thirty-nine Articles and in Richard Hooker is that Baptism is an "effectual sign," but one that functions only in the context of prayer, faith, and the life of the Christian community. Baptism is also eschatological, in the sense that its meaning and effect are only partially realized in this life: we hope to receive within our-selves the definitive experience of union with Christ at the consummation of God's saving purposes, in heaven. Baptism needs to be seen in personalist and relational terms—its theological content is God's covenant. Baptism, we may say, is a relational transaction in the personal mode.

Baptism Does Not Stand Alone

Baptism is the focal sacramental event in a process of Christian initiation that includes several other vital steps. Although Baptism is the pivotal event of this process, other elements are integral to it. As an unfolding process by which the grace of God, decisively and definitively given in Baptism, is received and appropriated, Christian initiation is necessarily extended in time, even if certain crucial moments are sometimes compressed together. As St. John of the Cross put it, God gives his gift of grace at God's own pace, that is to say, all at once; but we receive that gift at our human pace, little by little. Initiation comprises a journey into Christ and his church. The initia-tion is not complete until the journey has been completed and the process has run its full course. In addition to Baptism, initiation includes instruction in the faith, personal profession of faith, strengthening for service by the Holy Spirit, and admission to Holy Communion. Baptism and the Eucharist are the Alpha and Omega of Christian initiation.[13]

Confirmation Is Charismatic

Although Baptism takes place in the milieu of the Holy Spirit, there is a further work of the Spirit in confirmation. Is it "strengthening" for discipleship, witness and spiritual conflict, or is it something even more than this, a fuller participation in the event of Pentecost and a receiving of the sevenfold gifts of the Spirit (Isa 11:2–3), as the traditional Anglican liturgies suggest? The Book of Common Prayer, 1662, rite of confirmation explicitly affirms both the strengthening *and* the sevenfold gifts (as does *Common Worship*, though not quite as explicitly) in the same breath and without seeing any tension between the two. After all, to confirm simply means to strengthen.[14] Surely both aspects can be held together. In the Acts of the Apostles, the Holy Spirit came repeatedly upon the apostolic community. We can never say that we do not need fresh anointing of the Spirit and we can never say that we do not need more strength for Christian life, witness, and ministry.

Initiation Is a Holistic Reality

In this process account of Christian initiation, initiation involves several inter-related elements: Baptism with water in the name of the Holy Trinity; instruction in the faith and formation for discipleship; a liturgical opportunity for the individual to profess the faith for themselves; the laying on of hands with prayer for the confirming and strengthening power of the Holy Spirit; and participating in the Eucharist and receiving Holy Communion.[15]

13. See Fiddes, "Baptism and the Process of Christian Initiation."

14. "The Order of Confirmation" (1662) "Almighty and everliving God, who hast vouchsafed to regenerate these thy servants by water and the Holy Ghost, and hast given unto them forgiveness of all their sins: Strengthen them, we beseech thee, O Lord, with the Holy Ghost the Comforter, and daily increase in them thy manifold gifts of grace; the spirit of wisdom and understanding; the spirit of counsel and ghostly strength; the spirit of knowledge and true godliness; and fill them, O Lord, with the spirit of thy holy fear, now and for ever."

15. The Book of Common Prayer (1662) takes the Baptism of adults very seriously. The rubrics for the service for "The Public Baptism to such as are of Riper Years

Conclusion

I have a good deal of sympathy with the idea that nothing but nothing should detract from Baptism. It is a bit paradoxical to say that Baptism unites us with Christ in his body, but there is still more to receive. However, to me it does not follow from the momentous significance of Baptism that Baptism is complete sacramental initiation. It is complete as Baptism (when it is administered with water, in the name of the Father and of the Son and of the Holy Spirit, and with the intention to do what the church does). But that does not mean that Baptism is complete as Christian initiation. Initiation requires several elements in addition to Baptism, and some of them are clearly sacramental. Can we be initiated into Christ and his Body without receiving instruction about the faith into which we are to be (or have been) baptized? Does it make sense to say that we have been completely initiated as Christ's disciples if we have not yet had an opportunity publicly to confess our faith in him? Have we received all that God has to give us if we have not received the strengthening of the Holy Spirit for discipleship through the laying on of hands and prayer, following the apostolic pattern? Finally, is it credible to insist that we have been fully and completely initiated into the life of the body of Christ when we have not participated in the celebration of the Eucharist and, as part of that celebration, received sacramentally his Body and Blood?

In the light of the above discussion, I want to affirm certain truths about Christian initiation. First, Christian initiation is a journey, a process, an extended event. Second, the Holy Spirit is the agent at work throughout Christian initiation. Third, the sacramental dimension of initiation is not exhausted by Baptism. Fourth, confirmation brings a further gift of grace, a strengthening and equipping by the Holy Spirit. Fifth, initiation cannot be complete until the individual has had the opportunity to confess the faith for themselves in a liturgical setting, and in the case of those baptized in infancy, to make their baptismal promises their own. Sixth, initiation into the life and worship of the body of Christ comes to completion only at first communion, through participation in the Eucharist, when we are drawn into the movement of Christ's self-offering to the Father, and receive sacramentally his body and blood, his divine life and strength. Then and only then have we been fully inducted into the life of grace that God has provided in the church. Then and only then are we fully fledged disciples,

---

and able to Answer for Themselves," echoed in Canon B. 24, stress that examination and instruction of the candidates shall take place in good time and that they shall be exhorted to prepare themselves *by prayer and fasting* to receive this sacrament.

spiritually equipped and prepared for witness and ministry. As Winston Churchill said after the victory of the Battle of El Alamein in November 1942: "Now this is not the end. It is not even the beginning of the end. But it is, perhaps, the end of the beginning."[16]

---

16. Gilbert, *Road to Victory*, 254. This was also the famous "blood, tears, toil and sweat" speech, given at the Lord Mayor of London's luncheon at the Mansion House.

Bibliography

Abbott, Walter M., editor. *The Documents of Vatican II*. London: Chapman, 1966.

Avis, Paul. *The Identity of Anglicanism: Essentials of Anglican Ecclesiology*. London: T. & T. Clark, 2007.

———. "Is Baptism 'Complete Sacramental Initiation'?" *Theology* 111.861 (2008) 163–69.

———, editor. *The Journey of Christian Initiation: Theological and Pastoral Perspectives*. London: Church House, 2011.

Bromiley, Geoffrey William. *Baptism and the Anglican Reformers*. London: Lutterworth, 1953.

Burnett, Joe G. "Reconsidering a Bold Proposal: Reflections, Questions, and Concerns Regarding a Theology of Confirmation." *Anglican Theological Review* 88 (2006) 69–83.

Church of England. *Doctrine in the Church of England: The Report of the Commission on Christian Doctrine Appointed by the Archbishops of Canterbury and York in 1922*. London: SPCK, 1938.

Cummings, Brian. *The Book of Common Prayer: the Texts of 1549, 1559, and 1662*. Oxford: Oxford University Press, 2011.

Doctrine Commision of the Church of England. *The Mystery of Salvation: The Story of God's Gift: A Report*. London: Church House, 1995.

Fiddes, Paul S. "Baptism and the Process of Christian Initiation." *Ecumenical Review* 54.1 (2002) 49–65.

Flannery, Austin, editor. *Vatican Council II, the Conciliar and Post Conciliar Documents*. Vol. 1. Northport, NY: Costello, 1975.

Gilbert, Martin. *Road to Victory: Winston S. Churchill 1941–1945*. London: Heinemann, 1986.

Jewel, John. "A Treatise of the Sacraments." In *The Works of John Jewel*, Vol. 2, edited by John Ayre, 1098–1139. Parker Society 24. Cambridge: Cambridge University Press, 1847.

Melanchthon, Philip. "Apology of the Augsburg Confession." In *The Book of Concord: The Confessions of the Evangelical Lutheran Church*, edited by Theodore G. Tappert, 97–285. Philadelphia: Mühlenberg, 1959.

Podmore, C. J. "The Baptismal Covenant in the American Church." *Ecclesiology* 6.1 (2010) 8–38.

Riggs, John W. *Baptism in the Reformed Tradition: A Historical and Practical Theology*. Columbia Series in Reformed Theology. Louisville, KY: Westminster John Knox, 2002.

Sykes, Stephen. *Unashamed Anglicanism*. Nashville, TN: Abingdon, 1995.

Tanner, Kathryn. "Towards a New Theology of Confirmation." *Anglican Theological Review* 88 (2006) 85–94.

Thornton, Lionel Spencer. *Confirmation: Its Place in the Baptismal Mystery*. Westminster, UK: Dacre, 1954.

Tyndale, William. "Obedience of a Christian Man." In *Doctrinal Treatises and Introductions to Different Portions of the Holy Scripture*, edited by Henry Walter, 131–344. Tyndale Publications 1. Cambridge: Cambridge University Press, 1848.

Weil, Louis. "Baptism as the Model for a Sacramental Aesthetic." *Anglican Theological Review* 92 (2010) 259–70.

5

Confirmation

*Completion of Baptism
and Gateway to the Eucharist*[1]

PAUL DE CLERCK

THE RITE OF CONFIRMATION raises many complex questions. In it, various elements are combined; if too strong an emphasis is placed on one aspect, there is often a neglect of others so that, in the end, one may arrive at a perspective that is incomplete. One may scarcely speak of confirmation without taking into account historical data, Trinitarian and sacramental theology, and developments in pastoral practice, and we cannot overlook the larger context of secularization which has taken place over a long period and which affects the way one solves the problems which inhere in confirmation. It thus becomes the responsibility of theologians to engage this subject with great rigor in order to avoid developing perspectives which have no underpinning, nor to propose pastoral solutions in the short term which in the end prove to be of little value, and which exhaust those who have the responsibility for leading people forward in the mystery of faith. Thus, I shall also try to present a systematic approach to these questions.

I have organized this essay in two sections. At first, I shall present three points of reference: the history of confirmation, the understandings of confirmation in the wider church, and the doctrinal and pastoral contributions of Vatican II to our subject. With these resources, we shall be

---

1. Originally published as De Clerck, "La confirmation, parachèvement du baptême, porche de l'Eucharistie." Translated by Louis Weil.

able to take up, in the second section, reflections and future perspectives on the pastoral practice of confirmation.

History of Confirmation

The Early Church

We all know that, for adult catechumens in antiquity, the celebration of Christian initiation took place most often at Easter—at least in the Western church—with the bishop presiding. These rites included the water rite, post-baptismal rites, and the concluding celebration of the Eucharist. This pattern was no longer possible from the mid-fourth century because of the greatly increased number of candidates. After this time, with regard to the practice of initiation, the East and the West began to move along two different paths that for a while did not conflict.

In the Eastern church, the responsibility for presiding over initiatory practice passed from the bishop[2] to his presbyters. It was they, the local pastors, who from that time on fulfilled this ministry which previously had been performed by the bishop. The connection of the bishop to initiation practice was maintained, however, by means of the use of holy chrism, which was always blessed by the bishop.

The Western church did the same for both the water rite and the Eucharist, henceforth celebrated by the presbyters, but reserved to the episcopal ministry both unction and the laying-on-of-hands which followed the water rite. Contrary to what one may read, it is thus not true that only the Eastern church maintained the ancient tradition; it is indeed true that the East preserved the ancient ritual sequence, but this was done at the cost of a change in the minister of the sacrament. The only elements which have been maintained until the present day are the blessing of chrism by the bishop both in the East and in the West, and, in the West, reservation of the post-baptismal rites to the bishop. Later, in both East and West, there was a gradual shift from a majority of adults as candidates for Baptism to a predominant number of infant candidates. Because of these changes, we may highlight three related developments in the West: separation of rites, the change of the meaning of "Baptism," and the movement toward three distinct sacramental stages.

---

2. Translator's note: Because of the evolving eucharistic practice in the early church, De Clerck uses "bishop," "presbyter," "deacon," rather than "bishop," "priest," and "deacon."

The Gradual Separation of Baptism and Confirmation

Ministerial delegation was total in the East, but only partial in the West. The rubrics in the sacramentaries state this clearly: "If the bishop is present, he confirms with chrism at once; if he is absent, the presbyter will give communion."[3] It is this absence of the bishop which created the problem, and which led to the delay of the post-baptismal rites until a later time. This led to a kind of disassociation of the latter rites from the complete ritual in which they would normally have found their place. No theological justification was developed at the time for the delay of these post-baptismal rites until a time after the first communion.[4] The disjunction, however, became habitual.

The dislocation of the ancient pattern is thus due, in the West, to the delay of the post-baptismal rites until the bishop could perform them. Why? At the time this change was scarcely explained. We find writers such as Jerome or Pope Innocent I emphasizing the "honor of the episcopate"[5] from a hierarchical perspective. Two important theological perspectives are being emphasized: the first underscores the relation of Christian initiation to the local church, which avoids making it a private action, and seeks the theological context of confirmation, as occasionally is done today, in pastoral ministry with young persons. The second casts light on the relation of the Holy Spirit, of which the post-baptismal rites speak, to the church, as represented by the bishop of the diocese. It is the Spirit that

---

3. Deshusses, *Le sacramentaire grégorien*.1088–89.

4. See De Clerck, "La dissociation du baptême et de la confirmation au haut Moyen Age."

5. This expression is found in Jerome in his *Altercatio luciferiani et orthodoxi*, 9, written at Rome in 382. He wrote to his opponents (Jerome, *Débat entre un luciférien et un orthodoxe*, 118–23, trans: "The Dialogue against the Luciferians," 319–34) :

> If you now ask how it is that a person baptized in the Church does not receive the Holy Ghost, Whom we declare to be given in true Baptism, except by the hands of the bishop, let me tell you that our authority for the rule is the fact that after our Lord's ascension the Holy Ghost descended upon the Apostles. And in many places we find it the practice, more by way of honouring the episcopate than from any compulsory law.

It is necessary to place this within the context of the Jerome's well-known presbyteral bias. See also, *The Letter of Innocent I to Decentius of Gubbio* (Innocent, *Church and Worship in Fifth-Century Rome*, 28). Here the pope rests his argument upon Acts 8 to affirm that only the bishop may anoint. "The presbyters, although they share in the priesthood, do not have the highest degree of the episcopate."

brings the church to birth, as the order of affirmations in the Apostles Creed shows: "I believe in the Holy Spirit, the holy catholic Church . . ." It is the Holy Spirit which is the source of the three "bodies of Christ": the earthly body "conceived by the Holy Spirit, born of the Virgin Mary," the eucharistic body made present by the invocation of the Holy Spirit in the epiclesis, and the ecclesial body in which we are made members by the post-baptismal anointing, performed by the bishop.

Because the post-baptismal rites were delayed until they might be performed by the bishop, there developed a progressive division between the water rite which was led by the presbyters and the later rites which the bishop performed. Let us note, however, that already in antiquity, a distinction was introduced between these two parts. For example, when a newborn infant in danger of death was baptized, the water rite was performed by a presbyter in a baptistery, without gathering the whole community. Later, if the person survived, the newly-baptized "would enter the church," physically and theologically.[6] Even if the two buildings were not far from each other, this movement from the baptistery to the cathedral introduced a distinction between the water rite and what followed in the celebration.

The Appearance of the Term "confirmation"

Since the presbyteral water rite and the episcopal anointing had now become separated, it is not surprising that gradually a specific name was applied to the episcopal rite. In Gaul, towards the middle of the fifth century, the term *confirmatio* appeared for the first time, but this term never achieved universal usage. According to his linguistic analysis of the term, Dom Bernard Botte suggested that

> The terms *perficere, perfectio, confirmare,* and *confirmatio* express the conviction that the rite of confirmation adds a sort of perfection to Baptism. . . . It is probably a mistake to draw from the word confirmation the idea of a sacramental grace with its own meaning. It is worth noting here another use of the verb *confirmare.* When one of the faithful has received the Body of Christ, this act is "confirmed" with the reception of the chalice. The wine adds, we might say, a nutritive value to the meal; it is a normal complement. It is in this sense, I believe, that we must understand the word in the rites of Initiation.[7]

---

6. See, for example, Cyprian, *Epistle* 73.9.1.

7. Botte, "Le vocabulaire ancien de la confirmation," 21–22.

Thus a new term appeared: confirmation. It did not arise because of the invention of a new sacramental reality, but simply because of the separation in time of two dimensions of a rite that had formerly been united.

"Baptism" Changes Its Meaning with the Separation of "Confirmation"

At the time of its appearance, confirmation cannot be defined as a complement to Baptism. It does not add additional meeting, but appears rather as a part of the ancient baptismal celebration now divided into two distinct parts. This can be represented schematically as:

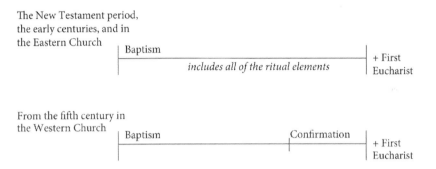

The New Testament period, the early centuries, and in the Eastern Church

Baptism	
includes all of the ritual elements	+ First Eucharist

From the fifth century in the Western Church

Baptism	Confirmation	
		+ First Eucharist

In other words, the meaning of the term "Baptism" had changed: previously it had referred to the totality of the rites that preceded the Eucharist, but now it had come to be distinguished from confirmation. From that time onward, Christians in the West no longer used the word "Baptism" in the same sense that it is used in the New Testament where, in fact, the term "confirmation" does not appear.

So we find that in the West, from the fifth century onward, we have a unity made up of two elements, a unity comparable, in its own way, to the polarity between the altar and the ambo in the sanctuary of a church which form, as it were, the unique "Table both of the Word of God and of the Body of Christ."[8] This unity is also comparable to the relation between Easter and Pentecost, two feasts which accentuate, each in its own way, a dimension of the paschal mystery. If Acts presents the resurrection of Jesus and the gift of the Spirit as two events that are chronologically distinct, the Gospel of John unites them on Easter Day (John 20:1–23). As Louis-Marie Chauvet has written:

---

8. *Dei verbum*, 21.

> This does not mean that Baptism would be placed in relation
> to Easter and confirmation in relation to Pentecost, but rather
> that the Baptism-confirmation connection may be understood
> as analogous to that between Easter and Pentecost. What is
> relevant here is, one might say, *a connection of connections.*
> In this perspective, confirmation adds nothing to Baptism: it
> gives it fulfillment.[9]

Movement toward Three Distinct Sacramental Stages

Later in the West, there developed a separation of Baptism from confirmation, and eventually as well from first communion, which was delayed until the age of reason. Thus the original unity of Christian initiation became separated into three stages. It is at this period in the twelfth century that theologians began to debate the number of the principal sacraments and determined that there were seven. The purpose of the sevenfold numbering was to emphasize the importance of the fundamental Christian rites, those that are generally intended for all people because they are linked to salvation.

This determination was made at a particular time in the history of the church, and the numbering thus depends upon the theological and liturgical developments at that time in the West. Thus the sevenfold model counted three separate sacraments as initiation, but only one for the sacrament of holy orders, with no significant distinction between the episcopate, the presbyterate and the diaconate.

In summary, the church in the West preserved the role of the bishop in performing the rites that followed the water rite which, from the end of the fourth century, was performed by presbyters. This distinction of ministers brought with it a distinction of the rites, which had now become separated into two stages named "Baptism" and "confirmation," unlike the terminology of the New Testament.

Initiation Practice in Our Time

In order to develop a theology of confirmation which might be received ecumenically, it is necessary to take into account both the history of initiation, and also the practice and understanding of initiation amongst the

---

9. Chauvet, "La confirmation séparée du baptême," 284.

Eastern churches, the churches of the sixteenth-century Reformation and the Roman Catholic Church.[10]

The Orthodox

As we have seen above, the East continued the practice of the ancient church, modified, however, on two points: the usual minister of Christian Initiation is now the presbyter, who anoints the newly-baptized with chrism blessed by the bishop, and the great majority of the candidates for Baptism are now infants. At its meeting in Bari, Italy, in 1987, the International Commission for dialogue between the Roman Catholic Church and the Orthodox Church addressed the theme *Faith, Sacraments and the Unity of the Church.* At no. 46 of its report, the Commission declares that:

> This pattern [of the early church] remains the ideal for both churches since it corresponds the most exactly possible to the appropriation of the scriptural and apostolic tradition accomplished by the early Christian churches which lived in full communion with each other.[11]

The difficult issue is stated at no. 51:

> Moreover, in certain Latin Churches, for pastoral reasons, for example in order to better prepare confirmands at the beginning of adolescence, the practice has become more and more common of admitting to first communion baptized persons who have not yet received confirmation, even though the disciplinary directives which called for the traditional order of the sacraments of Christian initiation have never been abrogated. This inversion, which provokes objections or understandable reservations both by Orthodox and Roman Catholics, calls for deep theological and pastoral reflection because pastoral practice should never lose sight of the meaning of the early tradition and its doctrinal importance. It is also necessary to recall here that Baptism conferred after the age of reason in the Latin Church is now always followed by confirmation and participation in the Eucharist.[12]

10. De Clerck, "Towards a Consensus on Confirmation?"; revised and expanded in "La confirmation: vers un consensus oecuménique?".

11. Joint Commission for the Theological Dialogue between the Roman Catholic Church and the Orthodox Church, *Faith, Sacraments and Unity*, 46.

12. Joint Commission for the Theological Dialogue between the Roman Catholic Church and the Orthodox Church, *Faith, Sacraments and Unity*, 51.

Here we may observe that the confirmation of adolescents who have previously been admitted to communion raises questions for the Orthodox. The restoration by Vatican II of the complete initiation of adults, in its three aspects during the Paschal Vigil, offers reassurance of the theological understanding among Roman Catholics. The problem is how to harmonize the two different practices.

The Sixteenth-Century Reforms

The principal reaction among the reformers was to suppress confirmation, to question its sacramental character, or both, since, for them, it lacked a biblical foundation. Today historical studies permit us to assess the given facts differently, but the habits of the past remain deeply ingrained.

LUTHERANISM

In 1990 the Lutheran World Federation launched a large-scale international inquiry on the subject of confirmation, which yielded a global report published in 1995,[13] however, the conclusions of that document are not entirely clear. In the introduction we read:

> Confirmation ministry has been widely used by Lutheran churches and they have adapted it to the various situations in which they carry out their activities. It is a combination of at least three factors:
>
> - a yearning for future generations to experience faith;
>
> - a passing on of the faith tradition of the Bible as summarized in the catechism;
>
> - a sense of authorization by the community.[14]

Later the document attempts to limit confirmation in these terms:

> As confirmation ministry takes its rightful place in relation to the sacraments, it is freed to once again become the educational and pastoral effort of the church to encourage the baptized to rekindle the gifts already received so that Christian identity with God's mission, baptismal vocation, and discipleship are deepened.[15]

13. Lutheran World Federation, *Confirmation Ministry Study.*

14. Ibid., 11.

15. Ibid., 45.

In other words, most Lutheran communities celebrate confirmation, but without acknowledging in it a sacramental character. A catechetical approach clearly dominates, and thus draws our attention to a tendency found in the Western theology of confirmation.[16]

CALVINISM

Calvinists remain deeply influenced by the teaching of their master in which he affirmed that confirmation is "an overt outrage against Baptism, which obscures and abolishes its function."[17] Their reaction was based upon Calvin's understanding that confirmation was an addition to Baptism, although we know today that it began as a detached part of the baptismal rite. Their starting point for the question was thus clearly anti-sacramental. The Reformed Church of France did not hesitate to remove confirmation from its Discipline in 1995. The liturgy officially adopted at the Synod of Mazamet in 1996 does not even mention it.[18]

If Calvin did away with confirmation in the name of *sola scriptura,* it was restored in the eighteenth century for cultural reasons, notably by Frédéric Ostervald, a Swiss pastor.[19] By the Age of Enlightenment, it had become impossible to rest the entirety of Christian commitment upon a baptismal rite received in infancy. If one supports the Baptism of small children, it is necessary to compensate for its disadvantages when children have reached an age when they may consciously make the promises for themselves. This act Ostervald calls both *ratification* and *confirmation.*[20] Yet if the word "confirmation" has been retained, ambiguities have not been avoided. The problem comes from the use of the same word for both the act and its reaffirmation. Such confusion was not a promising solution.

In a word, confirmation was defined as a personal ratification of a commitment made in infancy when the child was unconscious of this action. This focus on conscious intention was characteristic of early modernity. This draws our attention to a fundamental cultural characteristic of

16. Johnson, "Shape of Christian Initiation."

17. Calvin, *Institutes,* 4.19.8 (p. 127).

18. Eglise réformée de France, *Liturgie de l'Eglise réformée de France.*

19. Ostervald, *Traité des sources,* v. 2, 109. Quoted by Allmen, *Pastorale du baptême,* 108–9.

20. In Ostervald's liturgy of 1713, admission to communion is preceded by vows which state that: "We ratify and confirm the baptismal vow . . . " (Allmen, *Pastorale du baptême,* 109, see Ostervald, *La liturgie*).

the West. In this view, a Christian is not confirmed, but rather it is Christians who confirm their baptismal vows.[21]

ANGLICANISM

The Anglican tradition takes a middle path on this issue. Its traditional practice presumes the Baptism of small children, with confirmation to follow at around the age of twelve years giving access to eucharistic communion. The Lambeth Conference of 1968 concluded confirmation prior to communion was no longer to be required, perhaps because of developments in the liturgy of Baptism so that it was now understood to include all of the elements of Christian initiation in the early church. At the fourth meeting of the International Anglican Liturgical Consultation, held at Toronto in 1991, this was affirmed as follows:

> Baptism is complete sacramental initiation and leads to participation in the Eucharist. Confirmation and other rites of affirmation have a continuing pastoral role in the renewal of faith among baptized, but are in no way to be seen as a completion of baptism or as necessary for admission to communion.[22]

Vatican II and Contemporary Roman Catholic Understanding

THE IDEA OF CHRISTIAN INITIATION

Although confirmation had been the object of numerous studies beginning in the late nineteenth century in both Anglicanism and Roman Catholicism, it cannot be claimed that by the time of the Vatican Council a consensus on the question had been achieved. Questions about Christian initiation remained; *Sacrosanctum Concilium* states:

> The rite of confirmation is to be revised and the intimate connection which this sacrament has with the whole of Christian initiation is to be more clearly set forth; for this reason it is

21. One can see here the distance between this theological concept and the epicletic dimension which Nathan Mitchell sees as essential in Christian initiation. See Mitchell, "Dissolution of the Rite of Christian Initiation," 65–69. See also his essay "Confirmation in the Second Millennium: A Sacrament in Search of a Meaning."

22. International Anglican Liturgical Consultation, "Growing in Newness of Life," 229.

fitting for candidates to renew their baptismal promises just before they are confirmed.[23]

Consequent to the decisions found in the Constitution, two categories of rites were prepared. Although this work began with the rite for adults, it was the rites for the Baptism of small children and for confirmation that were published first, in 1969 and 1971. The fact that the Rite of Christian Initiation of Adults did not appear until 1972 made it seem that the rituals for children were the more important. This delayed the realization in the church of significant changes in the understanding of Christian Initiation.[24]

PASTORAL IMPERATIVES

The revisions place the rite of confirmation of children within the context of Initiation, but with some strains. The canon law of 1917 authorized, in keeping with ancient discipline, the delay of confirmation until the age of seven years, but the *Prenotanda* to confirmation suggested that it be placed at a more mature age. This was a victory for the point of view of Cipriano Vagaggini, supported by the personal opinion of Pope Paul VI, over the teaching of Dom Bernard Botte, who was the chair *(relator)* of the study group *(coetus)*.[25] This tendency to delay confirmation was motivated, at the time of the council, by the pressures of secularization. The delay of confirmation was seen as an opportunity to counteract this development by demanding a longer period of catechesis with the hope of assuring a stronger commitment on the part of more mature confirmands. This pastoral view was also based upon the rediscovery of Christian initiation, more precisely of the catechumenate. Many felt that a form of catechumenal preparation of young people for confirmation was required as the only means by which their future perseverance in the faith might be assured. We see here the conflict between pastoral imperatives and the historical understanding of Christian initiation.

---

23. *Sacrosanctum Concilium*, 71.

24. J. Lamberts laments this fact forcefully in his article, "Les sacrements de l'initiation," 233: "it is an unfortunate fact which distorts to some degree the scope of the intention of the revision which Vatican II wished to achieve."

25. Botte, "A propos de l'âge de la confirmation"; Vagaggini, "L'età della confermazione"; Botte, "L'età della confermazione. Riposta a Padre Cipriano Vagaggini." For the debates provoked by these publications, see Bugnini, *The Reform of the Liturgy, 1948–1975*, 613–25; one may find the personal perspective of Dom Botte in his book *From Silence to Participation*, 153–61.

Summary of the Historical Evidence

Faced with this body of facts and its contradictions, a theologian cannot remain unconcerned, but is obliged to take a position, or rather to weigh the arguments so as to decide between the opposing views. It is for this reason that I have maintained a strictly historical and critical orientation to this point. History, theology, and pastoral concerns permeate the discussion of the place of confirmation in the arc of Christian initiation. In my view, there are three main points: first, the importance of Christian initiation as theological acts, not simply rites of passage; second, the sequence of water Baptism, anointing, and reception of the Eucharist is of great significance; and third, there has been flexibility in the way various churches have celebrated initiation throughout history, but that flexibility must be bounded by theological reflection.

Reflection and Perspective

The first part of this essay proposed theological points of reference for reflection on confirmation. This second part will do the same with regard to pastoral practice, since it is on the basis of pastoral concerns that decisions about confirmation are being made today. Let us examine these concerns in the context of the theological perspective that has been presented above. Since Vatican II, the Roman Catholic Church has had two classes of rites of Christian initiation: one intended for use with infants and children, and the other for adults. Theologically it was agreed to give priority to that for adults, not because it was new, but because it provided the normative context for persons coming to faith, that is to say, to the making of a free choice and a personal response in coming to faith, which lies at the heart of the meaning of Baptism. The churches that perform only believer-Baptism remind us of the derivative character of the Baptism of small children, even if it can be justified theologically.

These two sets of rituals correspond to two different understandings of initiation that reflect the circumstances of their subjects.[26] The Rite of Christian Initiation of Adults corresponds to *a logic of conversion*; it defines a before and after, and a break between a life without Christ and a life with him—it presumes a discontinuity, a new reality. The Baptism of an infant, on the other hand, rests upon a different foundation, one of *forma-*

---

26. I have tried to contrast these two understandings in an article, "Un seul baptême? Le baptême des adultes et celui des petits enfants."

tion, and is based upon the hope of future growth in the faith, supported by the family and Christian community. In a profoundly human way, it presumes continuity and development. Whether the three sacraments are celebrated in a single rite, as in the East, or spread out over time, as in the West, does not greatly change the logic of either of these two structures.

There are consequences to the Western pattern in which the rites are spread out over time. From a psychological point of view, the insistence upon confirmation as a definitive commitment can arouse in some persons the anxiety that they may never be truly ready, and among the persons in charge an expectation for strong signs that the candidate is a "true Christian." And from a theological point of view, the Western pattern of separated rites causes a kind of "excommunication" of the children between their Baptism and first communion. Secondly, continual access to the Eucharist before confirmation creates the idea that personal commitment in the Eucharist is less important than that at the time of confirmation, which causes in the long run a devaluing of the Eucharist. This problem is particularly blatant when confirmation is postponed to a later time at the Baptism of adults. Finally, the delay of confirmation means that young people have not received the seal of the Holy Spirit during an important period of their Christian life, which may contribute to the lack of interest shown by many Western Christians with regard to the Holy Spirit.[27]

In the face of the evidence that adolescents and young adults no longer practice the faith as did their parents and have a hard time finding a place for themselves in the church, the pastoral tendency since the eighteenth century has been to try to achieve a greater maturity of Christian commitment. Since this is not possible at the time of the Baptism of a small child, nor at the time of first communion, this commitment is sought in the context of confirmation. In my opinion, the most serious cause for the delay of confirmation is found in the secularization of the Western world since the eighteenth century, and in the crisis in the transmission of Christian values, and thus of the faith itself, since the second half of the twentieth century. It is in this context without doubt that we must understand the appearance of such theologies of confirmation which

---

27. One may find other examples of this theological carelessness in the absence of an epiclesis in the Roman Canon, in the weak valorization of the epicleses in the new eucharistic prayers, or yet in the fact that theologians have scarcely taken into account the epicleses found in the ordination prayers in the development of a theology of ministry. On this subject, see De Clerck, "Les épiclèses des nouvelles prières Eucharistiques du rite romain."

define it as "the ordination of the laity,"[28] or as "admission to the ministries of the church, like the sacrament of ordination, but different,"[29] or as a "commissioning for ministry."[30]

These remedies do not produce all the hoped-for results. From the point of view of sacramental sense, this pastoral approach can lead to surprising consequences. If Christian initiation consists of three sacraments, two of which are not repeatable, whereas the third is celebrated normally at least each Sunday, is it not surprising that clergy wish to ensure the perseverance of young Christians by concentrating pastoral effort on a sacrament that is not repeated, and is thus a one-time celebration? Would it not be more fruitful to base these hopes on the Eucharist?

In the face of this analysis, it may be claimed that pastors have chosen to extend the catechetical process and to delay confirmation because they had no other choice. Neither the occasion of (infant) Baptism, nor of first communion have proven capable of yielding the hoped-for mature commitment. Thus confirmation with its flexible theology offered a means to accomplish this goal. But this led inevitably to the idea that after this great moment, one graduates from church and is free to leave. However, the same preoccupation regarding continuity in the Christian life also arises with regard to those baptized as adults, since they, too, are affected by the same spirit of the times. But the possibility today is that the Christian initiation of adults will consist in reversing the reflex: rather than saying that with the celebration of confirmation, "it is finished," one might hope that, at the end of the Paschal Vigil, the newly baptized would cry, "now it begins!" The time of the mystagogical catechesis is moreover in its place an attempt to offer a basis for this hope.[31]

A crucial problem appears when the educational sense of confirmation, in the Western context, does not bear sufficient fruit and does not produce adult Christians, but rather produces a significant number of people who cease to practice their faith. What is to be done when the journey begun at the Baptism of a small child, celebrated in the context of a secularized society, constantly fails to produce mature Christians who take their place in the life of the church, even when the effort has been

28. Thurian, *Consecration of the Layman.*

29. Moingt, *Le devenir chrétien,* 135.

30. Wess, "Der wechselseitige Zusammenhang von Initiation und Gemeinde." The author makes a distinction between *Tauf-Firmung* (baptismal confirmation) and *Sendungs-Firmung* (missional confirmation).

31. See De Clerck, "La mystagogie, entrée progressive dans le mystère." The volume is titled *Catéchèse et liturgie, une conversion réciproque.*

made to counteract this situation through a strategy of training for perseverance at the time of confirmation? There are two possible answers: If persons baptized in infancy do not achieve mature faith, they might be invited, at an appropriate time, to renew the process by undertaking some new kind of catechumenal journey.[32] The other is to strengthen initiation through celebrating Baptism of infants at the Easter worship of the Christian community, and with that, celebrating confirmation and the first Eucharist. These proposals would have the advantage of radically healing the situation, for they would avoid confusing the sacraments with life stages, or to expecting sacraments to bear catechetical expectations for which they are not suited.

Conclusion

The title of this essay is "Confirmation: Completion of Baptism and Gateway to the Eucharist." We acknowledge that this affirmation has not always been respected in pastoral practice, but as soon as one begins the study of this question, the conviction emerges that this is the most reliable approach. Indeed, it is the only understanding of the Eastern church, and the dominant view in the West. The critique voiced by the Reformers of the sixteenth century does not retain its force when we expand our historical framework, and pastoral efforts concentrated on confirmation and the delay to a more mature age have not been crowned with success.

In the context of the secularization of our time, it thus seems urgent to develop a pastoral practice based upon a commitment to a life in faith, and to do everything possible, above all with young people, to assure their growth in that faith. From the theological perspective, this can be most effectively realized in the context of the Sunday Eucharist, more effective because of its weekly rhythm and at a celebration at which all are gathered, following in the path of the Lord and along with one's fellow-Christians, renewing their Christian commitment as fully as possible in their daily lives.

32. See Bourgeois, *Redécouvrir la foi.*

Bibliography

Allmen, Jean-Jacques von. *Pastorale du baptême*. Fribourg: Editions Universitaires Fribourg, 1978.

Botte, Bernard. "A propos de l'âge de la confirmation." *Nouvelle revue théologique* 88 (1966) 848–52.

————. *From Silence to Participation: An Insider's View of Liturgical Renewal*. Translated by John Sullivan. Washington, DC: Pastoral, 1988.

————. "L'età della confermazione. Riposta a Padre Cipriano Vagaggini." *La scuola cattolica* 95 (1967) 270–74.

————. "Le vocabulaire ancien de la confirmation." *La Maison-Dieu* 54 (1958) 5–22.

Bourgeois, Henri. *Redécouvrir la foi: les recommençants*. Paris: Desclée de Brouwer, 1993.

Bugnini, Annibale. *The Reform of the Liturgy, 1948–1975*. Translated by Matthew J. O'Connell. Collegeville, MN: Liturgical, 1990.

Calvin, John. *Institutes of the Christian Religion*. Translated by Ford Lewis Battles. Grand Rapids: Eerdmans, 1986.

Chauvet, Louis-Marie. "La confirmation séparée du baptême." In *Dans vos assemblées: Manuel de pastorale liturgique*, edited by Joseph Gelineau, 281–92. Paris: Desclée, 1998.

De Clerck, Paul. "La confirmation, parachèvement du baptême, porche de l'Eucharistie." In *La cresima*, 144:205–25. Rome: Studia anselmiana, 2004.

————. "La confirmation: vers un consensus oecuménique?" *La Maison-Dieu* 211 (1997) 81–98.

————. "La dissociation du baptême et de la confirmation au haut Moyen Age." *La Maison Dieu* 168 (1986) 45–75.

————. "La mystagogie, entrée progressive dans le mystère." *Lumen Vitae* 59 (2004) 267–74.

————. "Les épiclèses des nouvelles prières eucharistiques du rite romain." *Ecclesia Orans* 16 (1999) 189–208.

————. "Towards a Consensus on Confirmation?" *Studia Liturgica* 26 (1996) 190–201.

————. "Un seul baptême? Le baptême des adultes et celui des petits enfants." *La Maison-Dieu* 185 (1991) 7–33.

Deshusses, Jean, editor. *Le sacramentaire grégorien: ses principales formes d'après les plus anciens manuscrits*. Fribourg: Editions Universitaires, 1979.

Eglise réformée de France. *Liturgie de l'Eglise réformée de France*. Paris: Les Bergers et les Mages, 1996.

Innocent. *Church and Worship in Fifth-Century Rome: The Letter of Innocent I to Decentius of Gubbio: Text with Introduction, translation and Notes*. Translated by Martin F Connell. Joint Liturgical Studies 52. Cambridge: Grove, 2002.

International Anglican Liturgical Consultation. "The Toronto Statement: Walk in Newness of Life." In *Growing in Newness of Life: Christian Initiation in Anglicanism Today*, edited by David Holeton, 227–53. Toronto: Anglican Book Centre, 1993.

Jerome. *Débat entre un lucifèrien et un orthodoxe*. Edited by Aline Canellis. Sources chrétiennes 473. Paris: Le Cerf, 2003.

————. "The Dialogue against the Luciferians." In *The Principal Works of St. Jerome*, edited by Philip Schaff, translated by W. H. Freemantle, 6:319–34. A Select Library of the Nicene and post-Nicene Fathers of the Christian Church 2. Edinburgh: T. & T. Clark, 1989.

Johnson, Maxwell. "The Shape of Christian Initiation in the Lutheran Churches: Liturgical Texts and Future Directions." *Studia Liturgica* 27 (1997) 33–60.

Joint Commission for the Theological Dialogue between the Roman Catholic Church and the Orthodox Church. *Faith, Sacraments and the Unity of the Church.* Bari, IT, n.d. http://www.vatican.va/roman_curia/pontifical_councils/chrstuni/ch_orthodox_docs/rc_pc_chrstuni_doc_19870616_bari_en.html.

Lamberts, J. "Les sacrements de l'Initiation chrétienne dans l'esprit de Vatican II." *Questions Liturgiques* 79 (1988) 229–48.

Lutheran World Federation. *Confirmation Ministry Study: Global Report, 4–8 September 1995.* Geneva, Switzerland: Lutheran World Federation, 1995.

Mitchell, Nathan D. "Confirmation in the Second Millennium: A Sacrament in Search of a Meaning." In *La Cresima*, edited by Ephrem Carr, 133–75. Studia Anselmiana 144. Rome: Studia anselmiana, 2004.

———. "Dissolution of the Rite of Christian Initiation." In *Made, Not Born: New Perspectives on Christian Initiation and the Catechumenate*, edited by Murphy Center for Liturgical Research, 50–74. Notre Dame, IN: University of Notre Dame Press, 1976.

Moingt, Joseph. *Le devenir chrétien. Initiation chrétienne des jeunes.* Paris: Desclee de Brouwer, 1973.

Ostervald, Jean Frédéric. *Traité des sources de la corruption qui régne aujourd'huy parmi les Chrétiens.* Amsterdam: Desbordes, 1700.

Ostervald, Jean-Frédéric. *La liturgie, ou La manière de célébrer le service divin, qui est établie dans les Eglises de la Principauté de Neufchatel et Vallangin.* Basel: Pistorius, 1713.

Thurian, Max. *Consecration of the Layman: New Approaches to the Sacrament of Confirmation.* Translated by W. J. Kerrigan. Baltimore, MD: Helicon, 1963.

Vagaggini, Cipriano. "L'età della confermazione." *Rivista liturgica* 54 (1967) 110–18.

Wess, Paul. "Der wechselseitige Zusammenhang von Initiation und Gemeinde." *Heiliger Dienst* 56 (2002) 138–53.

6

Baptismal Ecclesiology without Baptism?

Conflicting Trends in Contemporary Sacramental Theology

LIZETTE LARSON-MILLER

IN HIS SEVERAL BOOKS, Anglican ecclesiologist Paul Avis reminds his readers that Anglicanism is not rooted solely or even primarily in the reformations of the sixteenth century, but rather in the depth and breadth of the early church.[1] One would hope that the Anglican communion of churches is ultimately rooted in Jesus the Christ, but the reminder that Anglicanism professes its identity as the one, holy, catholic, and apostolic church calls us to look to the whole of Christian tradition for our roots. Who, then, are Anglicans in the twenty-first century? What does it mean to be catholic and apostolic, trinitarian and sacramental, scriptural and reformed, especially as these marks have developed over the past four hundred years, and, in some cases, have radically changed in the last century? Throughout our ecclesial history, we have often situated these theological mega-descriptions in the essentiality of the church, the very body of Christ, in order to hold diversity in unity. How individuals become a part of the whole, and how that process gives expression to the meaning of the whole in initiation rites is, therefore, a central aspect of the diverse articulations of who we are within the church. The rites of initiation—how we are grafted onto the vine that is Christ and made members of the household of God—are of the essence of what it is to be Christian, and

---

1. See, for example, Avis, *The Identity of Anglicanism*, 84.

secondarily, of what it means to express that new identity in Christ within a particular ecclesial community.

If we were to take a sampling of early and medieval church reflections on the rites of initiation, we might see, among other emphases, the movement of the diversity of rites towards the Eucharist, the culmination of the rites of initiation and the font of ongoing life in and as the body of Christ. This surprising consistency—enduring for centuries—must tell us something both about the individual's journey into the body of Christ as well as the ongoing identification of the church in its constant remaking. As small streams of liturgical practice flowed into larger and diverse rivers of sources leading to contemporary Anglican practice and interpretation, the same impetus toward the table remains visible:

From the first century: "And let no one eat or drink from your Eucharist except those baptized in the name of [the] Lord, for the Lord has likewise said concerning this, 'Do not give what is holy to the dogs.'"[2]

From the second century: "After thus baptizing those who have believed and given their assent, we escort them to the place where are assembled those whom we call brothers and sisters, to offer up sincere prayers in common for ourselves[;] . . . at the conclusion of prayer we greet one another with a kiss. Then, bread and chalice containing wine mixed with water are presented to the one presiding over the brothers and sisters."[3]

From the third century: "the flesh is washed that the soul may be made spotless; the flesh is anointed that the soul may be consecrated; the flesh is signed that the soul too may be protected; the flesh is overshadowed by the imposition of the hand that the soul also may be illumined by the Spirit; the flesh feeds on the Body and Blood of Christ so that the soul as well may be filled with God."[4]

From the fourth century: "As soon as they come up from those sacred waters all present embrace them, greet them, kiss them, congratulate and rejoice with them, because those who before were slaves and prisoners have all at once become free—invited to the royal table. For as soon as they come up from the font, they are led to the awesome table

---

2. *The Didache*, 9.5, in Milavec, *The Didache*, 23.

3. Justin Martyr, *First Apology*, 65, in Whitaker and Johnson, *Documents*, 3.

4. Tertullian, *De resurrectione carnis*, 8, in Whitaker and Johnson, *Documents*, 11.

which is laden with all good things. They taste the body and blood of the Lord and become the dwelling place of the Spirit . . ."[5]

From the sixth century: "the Hierarch dips him three times, invoking the threefold Subsistence of the Divine Blessedness, at the three immersions and emersions of him that is being perfected . . . they lead him again to the Hierarch, who when he has sealed the man with the most divinely operating Chrism pronounces him to be from now on a partaker of the most divinely perfecting Eucharist."[6]

We could repeat this pattern through centuries of Christian tradition and find similar statements—initiation, in all its pluralistic wonder in the early and early medieval church, finds its summation in bread and cup, in the celebration of the Eucharist and/or reception of communion. Even in the second millennium of Western (Latin) Christianity, the delay of the post-baptismal chrismation, because of the perceived necessity of episcopal confirmation in some geographical areas, often meant the delay of the reception of communion. Here the temporal framework shifted, with a shortening length of time between birth and Baptism, and a prolongation of time between Baptism and the completion of the rites of initiation.[7] But even those substantial changes in the timing of the rites of initiation generally did not change the ultimate position of communion reception. As late as the Sarum Rite (from the latest manuscript, the *Manual of Rouen,* 1543), the presence of a bishop at Baptism meant that all three rites of initiation could be observed together: "If a bishop is present he [the newly baptized] must immediately be confirmed and next communicated, if his age require it, the priest saying: the body of our Lord Jesus Christ preserve your body and your soul unto eternal life."[8] That tradition, that rich inheritance, leads Avis to say that a church claiming a practice of complete initiation into the body of Christ without participation in the Eucharist "is a bizarre idea."[9] "That church," of course, is the American Episcopal

5. John Chrysostom, *Baptismal Instructions* 27 (*Stavronikita Series.* 2), in Whitaker and Johnson, *Documents*, 47.

6. Pseudo-Dionysius the Areopagite, *On the Ecclesiastical Hierarchy* 2:7, in Whitaker and Johnson, *Documents*, 61.

7. See Fisher, *Christian Initiation*, chap. 7–8.

8. *The Sarum Rite,* in Whitaker and Johnson, *Documents*, 302.

9. Avis, *The Identity of Anglicanism*, 114. He is referencing the American prayer book, "Holy Baptism is full initiation by water and the Holy Spirit into Christ's Body the Church. The bond which God establishes in Baptism is indissoluble." Book of Common Prayer (1979), 298.

Church, which states clearly in the Book of Common Prayer (1979), "Holy Baptism is full initiation by water and the Holy Spirit into Christ's body the church."

This statement is one of several which appear to lead us down a problematic theological path. In a church with no magisterium or Augsburg Confession, we claim, both popularly and academically, that the prayer book and its actual liturgies are primary sources for theological understanding. Here we find an initiatory rite that never mentions the reception of communion as part of initiation, but one that is frequently cited as both source of, and result of, a much more substantial shift in describing who we are. That new description is "baptismal ecclesiology," understood to mean much more than simply a focus on Baptism itself, but still presumably linked in crucial ways to the sacrament of Baptism.

It is a venerable Christian tradition to shape one's identity and one's arguments against a counter argument, as a polemical articulation. Part of baptismal ecclesiology's contemporary origins were polemical, intended to challenge a view of the church perceived as clerical and rigidly hierarchical, where, either deliberately led to it or not, its members perceived ordination as elevating "the status of the ordained above the laity."[10] Louis Weil called for a return to an understanding of church in which all the baptized, not just those ordained, understood themselves as sharing in the priesthood of Christ. Faithful to Scripture, to tradition, and to ecumenical dialogue and developments in light of the liturgical movement and its fruitfulness in the documents of Vatican II, a return to Baptism as the foundational sacrament of identity, rather than to ordination, seemed far more faithful to the early church than a later hierarchical ecclesiology where "every aspect of the church's life [was understood] through the prism of holy orders."[11] In the charged atmosphere surrounding ordination in the 1970s, it also raised the unavoidable question that if a church baptizes women, how could it not ordain them? Ruth Meyers's summary of baptismal ecclesiology describes the result of this and other inconsistencies as requiring "an understanding of the Church as a community formed by Baptism and empowered by Baptism and the Eucharist to carry out the reconciling ministry of Christ in the world."[12]

Certainly these theological reflections on the part of Weil and Meyers, as well as those on the part of other writers concerned with Baptism

10. Weil, "Baptismal Ecclesiology," 25.

11. Ibid., 27–28.

12. Meyers, *Continuing the Reformation*, xvi.

and ordination, make no presumptions about a "Baptism-less" baptismal ecclesiology. But, as the Episcopal Church's Book of Common Prayer (1979) was reaching its final shape, there were many other issues surrounding the articulation of baptismal ecclesiology in which overt links between the actual liturgies of the prayer book and the assumptions of baptismal ecclesiology are found far more often in an ongoing secondary body of literature than in actual texts of the prayer book. This conversation surrounding the prayer book may very well be the source of the inadvertent shift to initiation without eucharistic summation, or, for some, of eucharistic participation without Baptism. Of the many questions that this shift raises, the first—"how did we get to a place where we blithely espouse a baptismal ecclesiology without Baptism?"—in turn raises the possibility that the formative conversation may have been so focused on the immediate polemics that it missed other important threads. While hindsight is always sharper, I would like to propose two necessary parts of a single conversation—an ecclesiological conversation that is first theological, not cultural, and a cultural conversation that is catholic, not tribal.

Ecclesiology: The Theology of Church

A great deal of what is central in discussions of "ecclesiology" in Anglican circles is really about identity, but is Anglican identity the same thing as Anglican ecclesiology? The identity conversation often draws us immediately into the national origins of Anglicanism in the Church of England and to what it might possibly mean to be a non-anglo Anglican. Or, it draws us into the overused *via media* location of Anglicanism—whether audaciously claiming to be *the* bridge church (bridging all other churches together by being all things to all people) or to the middle way as expression of a church that has no particular beliefs, articulations, or gifts to bring to the ecumenical table. It may bring us to the particular difficulty of the Episcopal Church in the United States, namely, being both catholic and protestant in a sociology-of-religion-culture that demands Christians be one or the other, not both.[13] This is not to say that there are not Anglicans who reflect, write, and challenge the church to talk about the theology of the church, but rather that their voices are difficult to discern in

13. This has been particularly prominent since the 1960s. Note the use of the term "Catholic," without the adjective "Roman" in most American studies, from Robert Bellah's classic study, *Habits of the Heart*, through the work of Wade Clark Roof, such as his *Spiritual Marketplace*, to Anthony J. Blasi's edited volume, *American Sociology of Religion: Histories*.

the media-grabbing ecclesial arguments surrounding controversial issues, especially in North America.

One approach has been a pastoral and catechetical reflection on church rooted in creedal statements known to parish educators: as *one church*, we must be the one body of Christ—the real body and the mystical body—born from the side of the real body, the historical body of Christ. We are a church conceived in creation, incarnation, human life, suffering, death, resurrection, and glorification, and we are one, because Christ has just one body, made up of many members, and its members must be diverse—because without diversity there is no functioning body.[14] Part of the Anglican understanding of the essentials of this unity has been that the fullness of the church does not abide solely in the Anglican communion, nor is it complete in any manifestation of the body; that fullness is an eschatological reality.[15] Another Anglican dimension of the one body is in its diversity of members, visibly signified in the threefold order of ordained ministry, or perhaps better, in the fourfold order of baptized Christians: lay, deacon, priest, and bishop.

As *one holy church*, we find ourselves in the holiness of God, not through anything we do or think or say or believe, but rather in a Trinitarian faith and a Trinitarian ecclesiology. We are made in the image of God, a Trinitarian God, and therefore we are most the image of God *together*, not as individuals. Baptized into Christ, whether we understand that Baptism as a *mimesis* of Christ's own Baptism, reborn in waters fertile with sanctity, or dying and rising sacramentally with Christ, we put on Christ, he dwelling in us and we in him in a life-long (and perhaps lifes-long) journey into the very heart of God as response to God's initiative. God's holy body, with members both holy and sinful, is the mystery of becoming what we already are by means of sacramental grace, divine gift, and the ongoing self-communication of God in encounter with the ecclesial actions of the whole church.

As *one holy catholic church*, we know ourselves to include more than meets the eye; the church is not this community here in this room, but in all the rooms of the gathered church throughout the world, from the rising of the sun to its setting, and in each individual Christian isolated for a time, but part of the corporate body. Catholic is not tribal; there is no particular ethnic identity that is essential, no preferred culture, no essential modern

14. Freely paraphrasing the Apostle Paul, 1 Cor 12, in which a body is only a body because of its essential diversity.

15. See Archbishop of Canterbury William Temple, *Christianity and Social Order*.

language that is above all others.[16] Catholic is also not limited to this world; it is the church in heaven and on earth, the centuries of Christians before us and those yet to come. Universal and inclusive, in Anglican understanding this is often revealed in the insistence that upon joining an Anglican congregation one does not join a denomination, but rather commits to following Jesus the Christ in the one, holy, catholic, and apostolic church.

As *one holy catholic apostolic church*, we find ourselves always in remembrance of the unbreakable bonds of the whole church catholic, and particularly the responsibility and joy of being both guardians and transmitters of the articulation of faith that comes through Scripture and tradition, from the apostles and from the saints, and in communities and individuals. This is not tradition frozen in a particular cultural expression, but tradition ever constant and ever reforming. The scriptural, traditional, reasonable, and experiential means of apostolic continuity again turn us toward sacramental actions; what is received is handed on in and through the church, "The mystical body of thy Son, which is the blessed company of all faithful people."[17]

A Cultural Conversion to Catholicity

This approach is consistent with much historical and contemporary Anglican writing in its use of the four creedal attributes of the church, but this is a description of church that can remain external to us as individuals and as communities; it is a *nominalist* understanding of church.[18] Even the biblical and liturgical language of indwelling, or putting on Christ, or the sacramental action of eating the body and drinking the blood as both external and physical, as well as internal and spiritual, is up against extraordinary cultural pressures. How does the essential Christian dimension of "we" trump a culture of radical individualism? How is "real" and "true" comprehended in a culture of affective relativism supported by postmodern theories? Here is the danger of doing ecclesiology that ignores cultural location. We can neither delude ourselves into thinking church can or should be pure from culture, or assume that all cultural practices can uncritically be incorporated into liturgical and ethical practices. We are inculturated beings, and that re-

16. See Bell, "Ritual Tensions: Tribal and Catholic," in which she draws partially on Turner, "Ritual, Tribal and Catholic."

17. Postcommunion prayer, Book of Common Prayer (1979), 339.

18. Here *nominalist* is used in the classic theological sense of something being such in name only. This was, in particular, a theological approach in the writings of William of Ockham (c. 1287–1347) where, among other things, nominalism was a naming of reality opposed to metaphysical universals.

ality requires a more critical analysis of insidious cultural assumptions in order to discern more wisely what is consistent with our best understanding of gospel tradition, faith, and future. M. Francis Mannion's seminal article of twenty-five years ago contains one of the most helpful descriptions of fundamental cultural stumbling blocks related to the supremacy of the individual. He titles the first section of his article on inculturation, "The Subjectification of Reality,"[19] which he describes as "the widespread assumption in modern American culture that the individual person rather than institutions or traditions is the locus and origin of meaning and values."[20] I would simply call it "the conviction that there is no greater reality than me." Out of this cultural assumption flows both "the abandonment of the social and cultural arenas to consumerism and the propaganda of mass advertising,"[21] as well as a shift in the location of the sacred, from "its traditional location in the Church gathered at public worship . . . to 'inside,' in the personal history and geography of the self."[22] The impact on liturgy is problematic, for liturgy ends up as a "resource for getting in touch with the inward God,"[23] a God sufficiently domesticated to meet personal needs. John Drane helps place this tendency when he writes that "reliance on oneself is the inevitable outcome of a world view that in the last two or three centuries has systematically removed the possibility of transcendence from our lives, leaving us with nothing but ourselves as the touchstone of authenticity."[24]

If church, the body of Christ, is "we together" and our cultural practices prevent us from recognizing anything real about "we," what are we to do beyond functioning as another club, support group, or comfortable affinity group, acting in order to reconfirm one's own centrality in all reality? Rowan Williams presents a challenge to speak of the community of *ecclesia* in its differences from other communities. He says that "what constitutes our belonging together, morally and spiritually, is our corporate relation to God."[25] Just as "the sacraments faithfully performed hold up a mirror to other forms of sociality and say that these [forms] are at risk and under judgement . . . [so also] . . . the Church declares, symbolically if all too seldom in its own

---

19. Mannion, "Liturgy and the Present Crisis of Culture."

20. Ibid., 102.

21. Ibid., 103.

22. Ibid., 105.

23. Ibid., 106.

24. Drane, "Contemporary Culture and the Reinvention of Sacramental Spirituality," 42.

25. Williams, "Sacraments of the New Society," 93.

social concreteness, that there is a form of common human life that 'means' or communicates the meanings of God, and it is a form of life in which unchosen solidarities are more significant than 'elective affinities.'"[26]

This realness, the reality of Christ, of salvation, of the sacraments, and of the church, is the other ecclesiological issue which tangles with an inability to see through the cultural haze. Last year, I was at a presentation by a visiting Irish scholar, and at one point, as she was speaking about the primary difficulty she faces in being a missionary sister, she said that when she preaches the gospel, "Jesus is Lord," the automatic response is not for or against, it is rather, "How nice for you. Your reality is not my reality, there is no real reality, therefore no definitive truth."[27] But this encounter between a version of postmodern thought and the Christological heart that is Christ as "the way, the truth, and the life"[28] is meeting a resurgence of new life in the world of sacraments and sacramental theology arising in the past ten to fifteen years. The present Archbishop of Canterbury reminds us that the "new" sacramentality is not a vague new-age approach, such as "a general principle that the world is full of 'sacredness': [but rather] it is the very specific conviction that the world is full of the life of a God whose nature is known in Christ and the Spirit."[29] At the heart of much sacramental theological discussion is an ecumenical return to a key question: how are the human and divine, earth and heaven, human and spirit joined, united, bridged? Hans Boersma, writing as one of several evangelical Christians convinced of the necessity of sacramental theology, says that, counter to much contemporary teaching and preaching, we need to be clear regarding what he calls a "sacramental ontology" which "insists that not only does the created world point to God as its source and 'point of reference,' but that it also subsists or participates in God. A participatory or sacramental ontology will look to passages such as Acts 17:28 ('for in him we live and move and have our being . . . '), and will conclude that our being participates in the being of God."[30] This sacramental theology resists a perspective that keeps God external, *nominal*, to our 'real' lives. In a complementary way, Anglican theologian David Brown reminds us that "Christianity has had a

---

26. Ibid., 100.

27. Sr. Maeve Heaney, Bannon Scholar at Santa Clara University and the Jesuit School of Theology, Spring 2012.

28. John 14:6.

29. Williams, "Foreword," xiii.

30. Boersma, *Heavenly Participation*, 24.

long history of seeing the world as God's 'second book' [after Scripture],"[31] and this is a "form of perception that has largely been lost in our utilitarian age, experiencing the natural world and human imitations of it not just as means to some further end but as themselves the vehicle that makes possible an encounter with God, discovering an enchantment, an absorption that like worship requires no further justification."[32]

The church is centered in radical *communitas*: a real body of Christ, the real presence, the real body, the mystical body, living Christians, putting on Christ, being Christed, now forever dwelling in God and God in them. Being community unlike other communities, being sacrament and symbol of the reign of God, to themselves and for others, are the essential dimensions of a real ecclesiology of the real body of Christ. Seeing the prayer and the mission of the church as both radically material (matter "matters" in Christianity),[33] yet not a matter of consumption or end product, is part of the necessary tension of being church in the world, not of the world. Marked by activities like "useless prayer"[34] that do not produce a product at the end or result in a material purpose, the countercultural stance of the church is signified and symbolized as inculturated, even while it is counter to much surrounding culture. In addition, in finding words for a reality that is not dependent on our feeling, it is essential to dispute the all-too-common assumption that if it doesn't make me feel good, it doesn't work, and therefore is not real. Being really the body of Christ, participating—actually unable to not participate through our being in the being of God—is an essential theological teaching that needs to be rewoven into pastoral understandings of ecclesiology.[35] We have too often been caught at a very shallow level of perception of what participation means, concerned with whether everyone is saying all the prayers together in every liturgy, or following every word in print, rather than remembering—or better, knowing—that in Baptism we have put on Christ and Christ dwells in us. Participation in its deepest sense is not an option, for not to do so would be to deny our very selves. Knowing that this participation is dynamic—never done—and that we are never done, it is also important to recognize that participation and ecclesiology are ultimately eschatological realities. Indeed, participation in Christ, in the

31. Brown, *God and Enchantment of Place*, 33.

32. Ibid., 36.

33. Rowell, "The Significance of Sacramentality," 4.

34. Nathan Mitchell's description of the liturgy of the hours—"we don't get anything!"—in "Useless Prayer."

35. Searle, *Called to Participate*, especially chapter 2.

Trinity, is the link between ecclesiology and eschatology in many ways. It is through this common participation in Christ, begun in the waters of Baptism, that we do church, a dynamic activity that leads to only one purpose, only one "product": the fullness of the reign of God.

Conclusions

These ecclesial and cultural considerations develop in response to an articulation of church, whose identity and mission is defined by baptismal ecclesiology. This theology was conceived for concrete and very good reasons, but often slipped into a more self-serving articulation. In many conversations, the focus seems to have shifted from being a response to a call to discipleship to a demand for the democratic and inculturated rights of all American Christians to a ministerial "position," a move mired in confusion about cultural expectations, emerging from a radical individualism anathema to the body of Christ.

Given a baptismal ecclesiology grounded in participation in the life of the Trinity, why is Baptism a necessity, and necessary as a prerequisite to communion? No one has said it more succinctly in the last century than Henri de Lubac: "the church makes the Eucharist and the Eucharist makes the church."[36] If you are not yet church, not yet within the body of Christ, not yet really—ontologically and relationally—part of the real and mystical body, then you cannot make Eucharist; the church makes Eucharist, the body of Christ makes Eucharist, the body that has Christ as its head and the diverse members of the one, holy, catholic, and apostolic church "offers this sacrifice of praise and thanksgiving . . . " The church, born of water and blood, sees these two dominical sacraments as the primordial foundations of the church. A baptismal ecclesiology must include Eucharist, a eucharistic ecclesiology must include Baptism, so perhaps what we mean might be better labeled a sacramental ecclesiology. Colin Podmore and other Anglican theologians find John Zizioulas, a leading orthodox Christian theologian, helpful in putting meat on these sacramental bones. Zizioulas sees Baptism as "the process by which God grants the fullness of personhood to humans,"[37] and the church plays a pivotal role in this process. As each baptized person participates fully and deeply in the body, the eucharistic

---

36. Lubac, *Corpus Mysticum*, 13.

37. Cited in Durheim, "The Possibility of Eucharistic Sharing," 296.

celebration constitutes the communion of the whole church; "the church becomes the church when it celebrates the Eucharist"[38] in its catholicity.

This catholic—universal, inclusive—nature of true ecclesiology is approached from a different perspective by Nathan Mitchell:

> We can understand why the Eucharist is always the culminating act in the sacramental sequence of Christian initiation. Having been plunged into the waters and sealed with the Spirit's gifts, neophytes are led to the table where the community of believers *becomes* the visible presence of God's grace, becomes food and drink *for the world's life*. For the church is not simply "grace made visible" for its own sake; it is ... the *sacramentum mundi*—the visible, effective embodiment of the whole world's destiny to become "people of God."[39]

It is in the font that we are made what we will become, and it is from the table that we are sent to feed the hungers of the world.

Inclusion in the waters of Baptism and *then* joining in the breaking of bread and pouring of wine into the breaking of body and pouring of blood is *radical* hospitality: to be this for the world, to do this for the world, and to dare to enter the liturgy of the world, having known Christ in the breaking of bread, in order to be broken and poured out for the good of the world. It is *generous* hospitality, catholic, not tribal, to be this for the whole church and for the whole world and to have the wisdom to discern the difference between necessary inculturation and cultural practices antithetical to the gospel. It is *efficacious* hospitality: to invite the non-baptized to come and see, to listen as the strangers tell their stories and to weave those stories together with the stories of the gospel, and to show the catechumens the way in which the church opens our eyes to the presence of God who is always before us. This is *hospitality*: to return to a graceful and gracious catechumenate, not to react to some of the more insidious cultural assumptions regarding instant gratification. Discipleship, Baptism, Eucharist—in this time between the Ascension and the Parousia—are something we all strive toward, but strive with cost, supporting one another as we together move deeper into the mystery of God's *oikonomia*.

38. Durheim, "The Possibility of Eucharistic Sharing," 297.
39. Mitchell, *Eucharist as Sacrament of Initiation*, 110.

Bibliography

Avis, Paul. *The Identity of Anglicanism: Essentials of Anglican Ecclesiology.* London: T. & T. Clark, 2007.

Bell, Catherine. "Ritual Tensions: Tribal and Catholic." *Studia Liturgica* 32 (2002) 15–28.

Bellah, Robert N. *Habits of the Heart: Individualism and Commitment in American Life.* Berkeley: University of California Press, 1985.

Blasi, Anthony J., editor. *American Sociology of Religion: Histories.* Leiden: Brill, 2007.

Boersma, Hans. *Heavenly Participation: The Weaving of a Sacramental Tapestry.* Grand Rapids: Eerdmans, 2011.

Brown, David. *God and Enchantment of Place: Reclaiming Human Experience.* Oxford: Oxford University Press, 2004.

Drane, John. "Contemporary Culture and the Reinvention of Sacramental Spirituality." In *The Gestures of God: Explorations in Sacramentality*, edited by Geoffrey Rowell and Christine Hall, 37–55. London: Continuum, 2004.

Durheim, Benjamin. "The Possibility of Eucharistic Sharing: An Application of John Zizioulas's Theology." *Worship* 85 (2011) 290–305.

Fisher, J. D. C. *Christian Initiation: Baptism in the Medieval West.* Alcuin Club Collections 47. London: SPCK, 1965.

Lubac, Henri de. *Corpus Mysticum: The Eucharist and the Church in the Middle Ages.* Translated by Gemma Simmonds. London: SCM, 2006.

Mannion, M. Francis. "Liturgy and the Present Crisis of Culture." *Worship* 62 (1988) 98–123.

Meyers, Ruth A. *Continuing the Reformation: Re-visioning Baptism in the Episcopal Church.* New York: Church, 1997.

Milavec, Aaron. *The Didache: Text, Translation, Analysis, and Commentary.* Collegeville, MN: Liturgical, 2004.

Mitchell, Nathan. *Eucharist as Sacrament of Initiation.* Chicago: Liturgy Training, 1994.

Mitchell, Nathan D. "Useless Prayer." In *Christians at Prayer*, edited by John Gallen, 1–25. Notre Dame, IN: University of Notre Dame Press, 1977.

Roof, Wade Clark. *Spiritual Marketplace: Baby Boomers and the Remaking of American Religion.* Princeton: Princeton University Press, 1999.

Rowell, Geoffrey. "The Significance of Sacramentality." In *Gestures of God: Explorations in Sacramentality*, edited by Geoffrey Rowell and Christine Hall, 1–20. London: Continuum, 2004.

Searle, Mark. *Called to Participate: Theological, Ritual, and Social Perspectives.* Edited by Barbara Schmich Searle and Anne Y. Koester. Collegeville, MN: Liturgical, 2006.

Temple, William. *Christianity and Social Order.* London: SCM, 1950.

Turner, Victor W. "Ritual, Tribal and Catholic." *Worship* 50 (1976) 504–26.

Weil, Louis. "Baptismal Ecclesiology: Uncovering a Paradigm." In *Equipping the Saints: Ordination in Anglicanism Today*, edited by Ronald L. Dowling and David Holeton, 18–34. Blackrock, IE: Columba, 2006.

Whitaker, E. C., and Maxwell E. Johnson, editors. *Documents of the Baptismal Liturgy.* 3rd ed. Collegeville, MN: Liturgical, 2003.

Williams, Rowan. "Foreword." In *The Gestures of God: Explorations in Sacramentality*, edited by Geoffrey Rowell and Christine Hall, xiii–xiv. London: Continuum, 2004.

———. "Sacraments of the New Society." In *Christ: The Sacramental Word*, edited by David Brown and Ann Loades, 89–102. London: SPCK, 1996.

7

"Be Joyful . . . All You Little Children Are Invited to the Feast."

Children at the Table in Liturgical Song

DAVID HOLETON

The Evolution of a Eucharistic Movement

THREE YEARS AFTER THE general restoration of the lay chalice in Bohemia, the year 1417 saw the re-establishment of the communion of all the baptized, including infants. This was the culmination of a remarkable eucharistic movement that had begun in the 1370s.[1] The restoration of frequent communion (at least weekly but best daily) was the first step—a practice which seems to have become widespread in Bohemia by the beginning of the fifteenth century. By the second decade of that century, repeated reflection on the biblical, patristic, scholastic, liturgical, and canonical texts which had been used to justify frequent communion (often in the context of ongoing academic debate), eventually were understood to justify communion *sub utraque*—under both bread and wine.[2] After Jan Hus's death at the stake on July 6, 1415, the chalice quickly became a principal symbol

1. A more detailed rehearsal of this movement can be found in Holeton, "The Bohemian Eucharistic Movement in Its European Context."

2. The proponents of the lay chalice came to be known as the party *sub utraque* or Utraquists both neutral, descriptive, terms. The term "Hussite" was bestowed on them by their opponents, the party *sub una*, and was never used of themselves.

of the reform movement which he had led. The texts used for frequent communion, and then for communion under both kinds had, within a relatively short time, come to be read in much larger sense, and were taken to include all the baptized, regardless of age.

Perhaps it is not surprising that, in a medieval context in which the practice of general Baptism was accepted without question,[3] the move to restore the communion of all the baptized did not emerge out of a renewed theology of Baptism; rather it came from the conviction that communion *sub utraque* was part of "the Law of God" and is thus binding on all. Utraquist theologians had no patience for the scholastic gymnastics which had come to be used to rationalize the clear conflict between the traditional teaching of the church and what had become the all-but-universal pastoral practice in the Latin church: the abandonment of the historic practice of giving communion to infants from the time of their Baptism.

The Johannine text, "Unless you eat the flesh of the Son of Man and drink his blood, you have no life in you," (John 6:53) which had played such a prominent role in the dossier on frequent communion came to be read in a literal sense—all who were to be saved must receive communion.[4]

As a direct consequence of this theological belief in the necessity of communion reception for salvation, children and their place in the life of the church soon came to play an important role in Utraquist reflection on both the Eucharist and the church. In part, this was generated by the ongoing need to justify the practice in the face of the minority *sub unist* (Roman) party within Bohemia, which rejected both communion *sub utraque* and communion for the young. These debates saw the development of long florilegia of texts similar to those justifying frequent communion and the chalice.[5]

3. This was soon to be challenged by the radical reformer Petr Chelčický (see: Wagner, *Petr Chelčický*, 114) who saw general Baptism as a perpetuation of the Constantinian church. Chelčický's spiritual heirs the Jednotá Bratrska (*Unitas Fratrum*) put his theories into practice and rejected general Baptism choosing to baptize only the progeny of their followers who were certain to be brought up in their tradition and "confirming" them upon a profession of faith as adolescents. See Holeton, "The Fifteenth Century Bohemian Origins of the Reformation Understanding of Confirmation."

4. The "Four Articles of Prague," (communion *sub utraque* for all the baptized, free preaching of the word, clerical poverty and the punishment of public sin), dating to 1419, were the Utraquist "bottom line" and were the demands taken by them for debate to the Council of Basel. Of these, communion *sub utraque* for all, was the one article that saw no compromise in its implementation until the very end of Utraquism in 1620.

5. These debates and the formulation of the Utraquist dossier can be found in Holeton, "The Communion of Infants," and *La communion des tout-petits enfants*. The texts make a case which, even today, would be regarded as exhaustive. When the case

The Place of Children in Liturgical Song

The *Jistebnický Kancionál* (JK)[6], from around 1420, is an important document in the history of the Western liturgy as a whole, as it is the earliest extant witness of an attempt to translate the Roman eucharistic rite and office into a vernacular for regular pastoral use. Along with musically notated Czech translations of texts for the proper for the Eucharist and Office, this codex contains a collection of over sixty vernacular hymns and songs. In thirteen of them (eight of which I will examine in this essay), children play an important role. They figure under a variety of themes, ranging from catechetical texts, to hymns on children's place at the Eucharist to the eschatological role played by children in both imaging the heavenly Jerusalem on earth and leading the praises of the assembly of the redeemed in heaven. While it is difficult to attribute exact dates to the all of the hymns and songs in the JK, those concerning children were most likely composed between about 1417, when the communion of infants and small children was restored, and the early 1420s when the compilers of the codex finished their work.

From the beginning of the Bohemian sacramental and liturgical renewal movement in the fourteenth century, apologies for the practice of frequent communion often referred to the *parvuli in Christo* (the little ones in Christ) as being those to whom particular care should be paid, and to whom it was important to give the Eucharist frequently. At first, these "little ones" were understood to be the poor, the simple, and the socially marginalized, who could not fulfill the rigorous requirements that were imposed on would-be communicants, and who were thus kept from regular reception of the sacrament.[7] By the fifteenth century, the term ap-

---

was put before the Council of Basel, the council "fathers" did not dispute the texts themselves but, rather, argued anachronistically that the texts were descriptive of the practice of the church in ages past and none of them were binding for the present age e.g. the injunction to "drink this *all* of you" was spoken to the disciples alone.

6. *Kolár, Vidmanová-Schmidtová, and Vlhová-Wörner, Jistebnický kancionál.* Only the first volume, *Graduale,* has been published. Volume 2, *Cantionale* is currently in preparation. The entire manuscript, Prague, National Museum Library, Ms. II C 7 (Jistebnický Kancionál), can be studied in digital form at http://www.manuscriptorium.com. The manuscript was paginated by hand in the nineteenth century (recto, upper right corner); the webpage has foliated the text. I will cite hymns from JK by their sequential numbers as well as by pages and folios. Excerpts are provided in the appendix to this article.

7. See Rubin, "Elevation, Communion and Substitutes"; Holeton, "Les conditions de la communion fréquante," 58–61; Holeton, "The Bohemian Eucharistic Movement in Its European Context," 30ff.; Holeton, "The Sacramental Theology of Tomáš Štítný of Štítné," 66ff.

pears to have come to include those who were more literally the "little ones in Christ"—infants and children. Just as Jesus had invited the poor and socially marginalized to occupy seats at his banquet, so too he also invited children and infants to his table—for had he not held up a child as the model of the ideal inheritor of his kingdom? Thus, infants and children came to hold a particular place in Utraquist ecclesiology and eucharistic theology and, accordingly, found an important place in their rapidly growing corpus of vernacular hymnody.

Popular song had played an important role in the Bohemian reform movement from the first years of the fifteenth century. Proponents of reform as well as its opponents had long used vernacular song in their public demonstrations. Neither the efforts of the Archbishop of Prague, Zbyněk Zajíc of Hasenburk, nor the injunctions of Pope Martin V had much success in suppressing the use of vernacular hymnody. While some of the hymns were intended to be provocative and polemical, most were clearly intended to play a catechetical role, so that those who sang them appropriated the fundamental rational for a particular party's position. In a world in which most were illiterate, there could be few better ways of communicating important teachings than song in the vernacular.

Singing about Communion Sub Utraque
and Communion for All the Baptized

Two hymns in particular, "First, opening the Bible" (JK 73, Appendix 1) and "Let us belong to the wise God," (JK 78, Appendix 2) provide a fundamental catechesis on the biblical and patristic foundations for giving the Eucharist *sub utraque* to all, including children. The hymn "First, opening the Bible" is a rehearsal of what were held to be some of the important Old and New Testament injunctions for the reception of the Eucharist *sub utraque*. While children are at first absent from the hymn, they appear in the final strophe adding their "amens" of approbation to the catena of texts. The final phrase reminds the community that *all* have been called to the Supper. The second hymn, "Let us belong to the wise God," devotes itself entirely to presenting a catena of versified patristic texts on why infants and children are given communion.

As florilegia of biblical and (what were thought to be) patristic texts, the hymns present the most commonly cited authors used in the defense of giving communion to infants and children. By the time the hymns were written, communion *sub utraque* was well established in Bohemia and, with it, two of its foundational biblical texts, John 3:5, "Unless one is born of water and the Spirit," and John 6:53, "Unless you eat the flesh of the Son of Man and drink his blood, you have no life in you," had come be accepted as a part of "the Law of God," adherence to which was believed by Utraquists to be required of all Christians. More than any other, it was these two texts (read along with the command from the synoptic institution narratives, "drink you *all* of this") that had brought Utraquists to hold that the dominical commands applied to all, regardless of age.

Together, these two hymns provided adult Utraquists with an *aide mémoire* of the basic scriptural and patristic exemplars for their practice, and which they could use when called upon to make an apology for the rightness of their practices should they fall into dispute with the diminishing minority of the population opposed to their stance. As children grew old enough to sing and to remember the words of these hymns, they would begin to understand why they had been brought to be fed *sub utraque* at the Lord's Table from the time of their Baptism. As such, these hymns are fine examples of liturgical mystagogia in which experience is supported with biblical, patristic, and theological rationale.

Children and the Eucharist: A Theology in Song

Not surprisingly, a significant number of hymns in the Kancionál were written to encourage all the faithful to come to the eucharistic banquet. In the hymn "In his time God gives his marvelous gifts" (JK 76, Appendix 3) the faithful are reminded of how God fed the people of Israel in the wilderness, how he feeds them now, and they are then warned of the dangers of refusing such a generous gift. In this hymn, we find two important themes of Utraquist theology which differed significantly from the current theology and piety of the time. Theology here is highly communitarian—in an age in which preparation for communion had been highly individualistic. Adults, along with their children, are reminded in the refrain after every verse "to hurry to the feast."

This reflects the "movement to the hills," during the summer of 1419, when Wenceslaus IV, under pressure from Pope Martin V, expelled many Utraquist priests from their parishes and replaced them with *sub unists*. This expulsion was the principle catalyst for the "Hussite Revolution" which began that summer. With their church buildings no longer available for their use, priests and people loyal to the chalice made their way to local hilltops where there was preaching, opportunity to confess, and celebrations of the Eucharist at which *all* received communion *sub utraque*, followed by shared meals.[8] The general atmosphere was eschatologically charged and, because these events included the whole family of God, they were perceived as a re-creation of the community meals found in the Acts of the Apostles. In addition, as communities expelled from their buildings they developed a strong sense of having become a pilgrim people, and they identified with the people of Israel in Exodus.

In this hymn, it is clear that God's invitation to the banquet includes both the good and the wicked. This inclusiveness reflects Bohemian eucharistic theology as it developed during the last quarter of the fourteenth century. Matěj of Janov (ca.1350/5–93), the greatest contemporary advocate of frequent communion, found himself faced with a medieval theological tradition—and its accompanying popular piety—which supported eucharistic abstinence as the better practice for the average (imperfect) Christian. Matěj and his theological allies took the opposite point of view. For them, the sacrament was, first and foremost, for eating. In so doing, communicants were changed and slowly perfected by the One they consumed, becoming in turn, more worthy of receiving the sacrament. The apocalyptically charged atmosphere of the time heightened the sense of urgency—frequent communion fortified the individual for the immanent last battle.

Another hymn, "Let us praise God, who is ever good" (JK 77, Appendix 4) also contains a rich tapestry of themes. The hymn is a call to all the faithful to give praise for God's goodness given to all—both old and young alike. This thanksgiving quickly focuses on the Eucharist and almost immediately turns to the importance of children's participation in the sacrament. The hymn then takes a polemical turn, addressing those priests who seem to be uncertain about giving communion to infants and children. John 6:53 is invoked after which the children themselves ask the priest accusingly how he could possibly obstruct their salvation by refusing them the sacrament. Here we encounter the recurring theme of children as inheritors of the kingdom of God, to whom the sacrament cannot be denied. The hymn then returns to the necessity of the sacrament for the salvation of all, particularly the young.

The rebuke to those who deny communion to infants can be found in a yet stronger form in the hymn "King Jesus Christ, beloved Lord" (JK 88, Appendix 5). The vehemence of this rebuke to those who would not give

---

8. Several accounts of these events can be found in Kaminsky, *A History of the Hussite Revolution*, 279–80.

communion to children and infants may well reflect the hymn's origins during the days when the communion of all the baptized was being introduced, and disputed even within Utraquist quarters.[9] Here the stress is on the importance of all baptized children being present at the eucharistic table by right and not by sufferance.

"Christians, let us rise from our sins" (JK 89, Appendix 6) also includes an extended exhortation on the importance of including children at the Eucharist. Beginning as a call to repentance, the hymn then turns to giving thanks for God's goodness in sending Jesus, and above all, for the gift of the Eucharist. Thereupon follows an exhortation not to prevent children from coming to the Eucharist, and a reminder of the things Jesus said about children. The hymn then returns to a call to repentance and prays for God's mercy at the time of judgment and concludes with a series of bitterly anticlerical verses, in which the clergy are rebuked for deceiving and misleading the people. In these verses we find a reflection of the last of the Four Articles of Prague which enjoins clerical poverty and an assurance that the clergy maintain a lifestyle in conformity with the gospel.

Singing about Children During the Liturgical Seasons

There are two hymns in which children figure in an important role during the celebration of the liturgical year. The first, "All children, young and old" (JK 122, Appendix 7), was composed for Advent and Christmas and in it, the community as a whole, is called upon to celebrate the coming Jesus, whom the prophets foretold. The development of the hymn then follows a somewhat unexpected path. After all are bidden to be joyful, along with infants, for "the king of angels wished to be a little infant to dwell among us," the hymn segues into a series of verses on Jesus's acceptance of children and his promise of the kingdom to them followed by a reminder of his solemn warnings to those who would reject children and not repent of their own sins.

Here, during the season when we are hardly surprised to encounter infants in hymnody, we encounter language that is certainly not that of children's passive obedience and emulation of a sentimentalized Jesus. Instead, the hymnodist turns quickly from Jesus's will to take the form of an infant in humility to warnings to adults who would try and prevent children's access to his person, and who do not recognize children's primacy of place as citizens in God's kingdom. As elsewhere, the hymn ends with

9. Holeton, *La communion des tout-petits enfants*, 112ff.

the voices of children leading the praises of the community, joining with the heavenly host and singing the angelic hymn.

The feast of the Presentation of the Lord in the Temple, forty days after Jesus's birth, was initially celebrated as a Christological feast which, over time came to be increasingly understood as a Marian feast, and kept under the title the Purification of the Blessed Virgin Mary. The JK has a hymn under each title. "According to God's law" (JK 101d, Appendix 8) is headed "De purificatione," and begins by recounting the story of Joseph and Mary taking the infant Jesus to the temple (Luke 2:22–40). It goes on to suggest that Jesus's presentation in the temple was a model for others that they, too, might bring their children with them as they go to the temple to make sacrifice. The last lines turn from the biblical event and interprets the meaning of the historic events for those now singing the hymn: they are to bring children to Jesus, "little ones to the little one—equals to an equal." This phrase gives a status to children otherwise unheard of in the large corpus of hymns composed for the Presentation.[10]

Conclusion

In the collection of just over sixty vernacular hymns in the JK, over a dozen give prominent place to infants and children. Some of these hymns are clearly intended to be catechetical and both adults and children are taught why communion *sub utraque* was requisite for the salvation of all. In other hymns, children play important roles in the transformation of both church and society. Held up by Jesus as the ideal citizens in God's reign, children served as models for a new world in which human norms are turned upside down. Thus, their rightful place at the eucharistic table is to be defended, and those who would deny it risk their own souls as well as those of the children.

In these hymns, we observe a popular theology, developed during an exceptional period in the history of Western Christianity—a late medieval renewal movement which first saw the widespread restoration of frequent

---

10. The second hymn, headed "*De presentacione Iesu Cristi in templum*" (JK no. 101e p. 79, f. 46r.), is devoted to three events in Jesus's life associated with the temple or synagogue: first, the story of Jesus going to the temple with his parents when he was twelve and being left behind (Luke 2:41–51); second Jesus's visit to the synagogue in Nazareth and his prophetic interpretation of a passage from Isaiah (Luke 4:16ff.) and a final, collective strophe, in which various acts of salvation were performed on feast days, including driving demons from the temple. The hymn makes no mention of the events usually commemorated at the feast of the Presentation.

communion, then the chalice for the laity and then communion for all the baptized. This movement had no parallels in the "Second Reformation" of the sixteenth century, where the major reformers did little to renew early patterns of Christian initiation. When the question of restoring the communion of all the baptized was raised during this period, it was generally in a polemical context and served as a tool for the emerging "believers' baptist" (anabaptist) attacks on the inconsistency of the paedobaptist practice of infant Baptism but not infant communion.[11]

Until the second half of the twentieth century, the restoration of the pastoral practice of communicating all the baptized was unheard of in the mainline western churches, and appeared only in small separated churches such as the Usagers among the Non-Jurors in the eighteenth century and the Catholic Apostolic Church beginning in the nineteenth. It was only after World War II, in light of the evident failure of inherited patterns of Christian Initiation in the major Western churches, and the subsequent renewal of the theology and practice of earlier initiation patterns, that the question of the communion of all the baptized began to be posed afresh. First, it appeared as a matter of theological consistency; the various commissions charged with the task of examining baptismal practice usually reviewed the historical evolution of initiation practices, and generally acknowledged that baptismal communion for all candidates was the universal practice of the undivided church, noting the reasons for its dissolution in the West. The reports of these commissions also made clear that there was no theological reason why all those who were baptized should not also be communicants, regardless of age.[12]

At first, few churches drew pastoral consequences from these commission reports. Over time, however, they realized that if the practice of infant Baptism was to continue with integrity, the restoration of baptismal communion and the regular communion of all the baptized ought to follow. In some churches this took place tentatively and experimentally while in others it became a normal part of renewed baptismal practice. Today, it is common to see infants and children regularly receiving communion alongside adults. However, contemporary young communicants have had little impact on what their communities sing, unlike in the Utraquist experience. Contemporary hymnals show virtually no impact from this major change in pastoral practice.

11. Holeton, "Communion of All the Baptized and Anglican Tradition," 21–28; Holeton, *Infant Communion*, 16–20; Dalby, *Infant Communion: Post-Reformation*, 8–10.

12. Holeton, "Christian Initiation in Some Anglican Provinces."

Seeing adults as regular candidates for Baptism has helped transform communities' understanding of the meaning of Baptism and has often given them a new vision of baptismal life. It is natural that this finds itself reflected in baptismal hymnody. Seeing children and infants as regular communicants should have presented an even greater stimulus to the Christian imagination, so that it, too, would have found its way into hymnody, especially in those churches that had traditionally insisted on confirmation before admission to communion. Seeing the very young as communicants challenges our assumption of the established order of things as they have been, and this new thing is certainly something to sing about. We should make it clear in our hymnody that children are valued and equal members of the church, and that their status as communicants is by right of their Baptism and not because of the generosity of adults. Singing of the priority of place given to children in God's reign would provide a vision that could only be salutary. It is curious that in churches engaged in heated discussions over the admission of the unbaptized to the Eucharist, little heed seems to be paid to the importance of welcoming all the baptized to the Lord's Table. Just as it was necessary to encourage hymn writers to compose hymns to be used at Baptisms where adults are candidates, we would do well to encourage the creation of hymns that celebrate the presence and rightful place of children at the Lord's Table.

"Be joyful . . . all you little children are invited to the feast."

Appendix: Hymns from the Jistebnický Kancionál (JK)

1. JK 73: "First, opening the Bible" [13]

> First opening the Bible at Kings chapter nineteen,[14]
> and reading, we discover together in a parable what
> we are expected to fulfill.
> The angel said to Elijah: "Get up and fortify yourself.
> The long journey you must travel will be an upwards journey,
> if you fortify yourself with bread and then with drink from
> the cup."
> This bread is now the body of God,[15] prepared for Christians.
> Here is Godhead and humanity in both kinds.
> Both of them are the entire sacrament, ordained for people for
> their happiness.
> . . .
> Let us bear in mind the New Testament, given by Christ.
> The evangelists bear witness to what Christ, through his power,
> bequeathed in his memory, so that he might sanctify humanity
> thereby.
> Saint Paul also writes to the people of Corinth:[16]
> "I received from Jesus for your salvation.
> The Lord Jesus declared thus and I followed him in this.
> When Christ was to be betrayed, after the ceremonial supper,
> he took bread, blessed it and broke it saying: 'This is my body:
> Do this in memory of me, whenever you receive it.'
> Then he also took the chalice, the supper being ended:
> 'Drink of it, all of you. This is my blood of the New Testament.
> Eat my body and drink my blood and thus you will fulfill my
> testament.'"
> . . .
> Let us accept with grace the Scripture concerning both testa-
> ments,
> a sacred thing given to all the faithful, and not seek to alter it.
> In this way we will appease God's anger.
> Let us return to the custom agreed by God,
> if we desire the peace of eternal life afterwards,
> to live for ever and rejoice with Jesus.
> . . .

13. JK no. 73: "Biblí najprv otevrúcei," 52–53, ff.32v–33r.

14. 1 Kgs 19:5ff.

15. To this day the "Body of God" (*Boží tělo*) is the usual Czech formulation of the English "Body of Christ."

16. 1 Cor 11:23ff.

2. JK 78: "Let Us Belong to the Wise God,"[17]

. . .

Christ commands Baptism, and no one is exempt,
either by estate or age, saying, "he who is not born of the Holy Spirit
and of water will not get to heaven."[18]
Likewise no one is exempt, neither young nor old, saying,
"if you do not receive the body of the Son of Man and his blood,
you will not enter into life."[19]
Before all true Christians, the saints of olden day,
such as Timothy, and after him Dyonisius, taught by Paul the Apostle.[20]
Let us see what God's great martyr Cyprian
affirms about children, and also abide by
Saints Augustine, John Chrysostom, and Remigius.
Timothy, that saint who was mocked by non-believers,
who gave to children the body of Jesus Christ, as well as Baptism,
wrote to Dyonisius asking what he was to do.
Dyonisius wrote back to Timothy,
telling him that he should continue
to give [communion] to children in both kinds,
and not be downhearted, despite the mockery
and errors of non-believers.[21]
. . . *The hymn-writer then cites Cyprian, Augustine, and John Chrysostom.*
St Remigius also declares that the body and blood of God
is to be given to those in need for their fortification.[22]

---

17. JK no. 78: "Patřmež k Bohu tak múdrému," 56–57, ff. 34v–35r.

18. John 3:5.

19. John 6:53.

20. At the time the hymn was written, the corpus of texts now known under the name of Pseudo-Dionysius were still universally regarded to be the works of Dionysius, converted by Paul on the Areopagus. The gloss by Peter of Spain (then understood to be part of the original) played a fundamental role in the Utraquist case for baptismal communion presented at the Council of Basel as "Dionysius" states that no sacrament is complete unless it is fulfilled in the Eucharist—*De ecclesiastica hierarchia* III, Title, gloss.

21. Pseudo-Dionysius, *De ecclesiastica hierarchia* VII,11.

22. The works of Remegius, the last of the "patristic" witnesses cited was believed to have been the Remigius who baptized Clovis, king of the Franks and who was also identified with the Carolingian scholar Remigius of Auxerre. The texts referred to are,

"Be joyful . . . all you little children are invited to the feast."

So here you have six courageous witnesses,
with which let us be content.

. . .

3. JK 76: "In His Time God Gives His Marvelous Gifts"[23]

Refrain: So invited, hurry to the feast;
prepare yourselves with your children, for everything is ready,
with one heart prepared to go to his table.
Who has invited all to himself, both good and wicked,
the good as his friends, but as a command to the wicked. *Refrain.*
Eat the body and drink the blood, all who wish to have life,
and not to die from snakes in the desert. *Refrain*
For with this bread and bread of the Father,
they went from Egypt to the Promised Land, along with their
children
taking everything with them and not wanting to leave anything
behind. *Refrain*
This sacrament also has the virtue of taking away the evil of
our sins,
but because we always sin, we always take communion. *Refrain*
*The hymn continues with a reminder that the first Christians
received communion daily, that God wishes to feed his people
with "daily bread" and that those who refuse this invitation will
face divine punishment.*

4. JK 77: "Let Us Praise God, Who Is Ever Good"[24]

Let us praise God, who is ever good and merciful to sinners:
the heavenly Father;
let us praise also his Son, blessed for ever and ever,
and the Holy Spirit.
Refrain: Who out of his divine goodness
dispenses his bounty from heaven to each of the faithful.
To old and young alike, he opens straight way his treasures,
and gives to all. *Refrain*

---

in fact, the work of Haymo of Halberstadt, *Homilia* 43.

23. JK no. 76, " Časy svými jistými," 54–55, ff. 33v–34r.

24. JK no. 77, "Chvalmž Boha vždy dobrého," 54–55, ff. 34r–35v.

. . .

You gave us him here on this earth, blood and body in dual essence
for eternal life *Refrain*
So that we may consume him, eating and drinking and thanking
our Lord in heaven. *Refrain*
Through his holy body and the blood that flowed from him,
prepare us for goodness. *Refrain*
O elders, start to sing, lest your children escape you,
hastening to God. *Refrain*
Wishing to feast with God, children must accomplish
a worthy supper. *Refrain*

. . .

Do not take offence, O priest, the words of Christ apply
to all and sundry. *Refrain*
Saying: "You will not enter into life unless you all eat of me
and drink of my blood." *Refrain*
And how will you now explain why you obstruct our salvation
although we are innocent? *Refrain*

. . .

The kingdom of God belongs to children, to whom the holy
treasure of the church
must not be denied. *Refrain*
The body of God, and Baptism, that double general sacrament
must be given to all. *Refrain*
Wherever they are able to go, both the elderly and children
should take both. *Refrain*
(If you old ones do not wish to [receive] for fear of God's face
allow the little ones at least!) *Refrain*
. . . But let the body of your Son give the blood of eternal life.
And let us all say: Amen. *Refrain*

5. JK 88: "King Jesus Christ, Beloved Lord" [25]

King Jesus Christ, beloved Lord,
glorified with God the Father and the Holy Spirit:
In supplication we pray to you: help your family,
and do not let the small children die.

25. JK no. 88, "Iesu Christe králí. Pane zmilelý," 67–68, ff. 40r–v.

Having suffered violence for generations,
the care of the first sins without relenting.
Having through you a second birth
of your holy Baptism and renewal.
. . .
Be pleased to cheer children brought to you,
and quickly free them from the sin of blasphemy.
Just as you freed the enslaved children,
greatly afflicted by the pagans from Egypt, when they had to go
into the desert with their elders
to sacrifice to God with the adults.
Wanting to admit the men but not the children;
wanting to separate them from God's sacrifices.
The same is done now with children,
who are separated from God
not wanting to admit them to God's sacraments,
putting the children off with cunning reasons.
And so, children continue to suffer violence,
having obstacles and difficulties placed in their path to God.
. . .
So now let Christian children be released,
and the holy prophecy be fulfilled.
That they will bring to you their sons in their arms,
and also their daughters on their shoulders and their backs.
May God be praised for ever and ever
that you revealed to us the Scriptures of the holy prophets.
Amen.

6. JK 89: "Christians, Let Us Rise from Our Sins"[26]

Christians, let us rise from our sins
and accept true repentance, and we shall not die for ever.
Let us ask God's grace,
and let us try to avoid sin calling on him to help us.
. . .
You gave us his body to eat and his holy blood to drink.
What more could you do for us?
If we fail to be grateful for you great mercy, woe to us wretched sinners,
because the inhabitants of Sodom will be better off than us.

26. JK no. 89, "Křesťané, z hřiechóv povstaňme," 68–70; ff. 40v–41v.

Let us not prevent little children—or oppose them—
when they eat the body of Jesus.
Theirs is the kingdom of heaven, as Christ himself said,
and holy David also wrote:
"From the lips of children and infants
you have ordained praise to silence the foe."
For do not look upon persons, or judge by faces,
but by justice.
No one is rejected, as he died for all—
for old and young alike.
Praise God, little children, you little infants,
because he doesn't drive you away from him,
but feeds you with his holy body.
. . .
O you priests, who have lost your way
and rejected Jesus's law in favor of a life of wealth,
having preferred human creations
to God's ordinances and always opposing his truth.
. . .
You praise God in vain when you teach human injunctions;
you will not please him thereby.
You have greatly misled the people and blinded them with
erroneous talk,
so that they cannot recognize the truth.
Were they to discover the truth, they would admonish you
themselves,
and tell you to lead a life of poverty as holy Scripture commands.

7. JK 122: "All Children, Young and Old"[27]

All children, young and old, virgins, young men,
and all Christians, let us celebrate this moment
when we gladly await our Savior,
the Lord Jesus Christ, the King, our Savior.
. . .
Especially, may there be gladness and merrymaking
for us, all your children, because the king of angels
wished to be a little infant to dwell among us.
He loved us greatly, he showed us his humility
embracing us.

27. JK no. 122, "Dietky mladé i staré," 94–95, ff. 53v–54r.

For us, he chastened his disciples—taught them—
because they would not allow parents
to bring us [children] to him.
And Jesus said to them, to all of his disciples:
"Suffer little children to come to me,
for the kingdom of heaven is theirs."
. . .
For he loved us and laid his hands upon us.
He embraced us and gave us his blessing.
He spoke to the lawyers and explained the Scripture concerning us,
that through young babes begins God's praise.
He promised the kingdom to us the little ones and said to the
old:
"Unless you turn about, you will not enter the kingdom,"
and so don't hesitate to return to him,
and leave your anger behind if you wish to dwell with him.
Children, let us give praise to him, the mighty Father,
to his wise Son, to the good Holy Spirit:
singing joyfully, with our hearts throbbing,
let us praise him, children, with our whole hearts—
and in speech as well.
Of him always joyfully let us sing and say:
The Savior is born the redeemer of all sinners.
Glory to God in the highest and peace be on earth
to all people of good will, let there be joy and gladness.

8. JK 101d: "According to God's Law"[28]

According to God's law when they went to the temple,
Joseph and Mary took the child with them.
Then they sacrificed and paid for [the sacrifice].
. . .
That they go to the temple taking children with them
and making pious sacrifice, they took children to [the temple].
Let us take small children to Jesus, that dear child:
little ones to the little one—equals to an equal.

28. JK no. 101D, "Podlé božieho zákona," 79, f. 46r.

Bibliography

Dalby, Mark. *Infant Communion: Post-Reformation to Present Day.* Joint Liturgical Studies 67. Norwich, UK: Hymns Ancient and Modern, 2009.

Holeton, David R. "The Bohemian Eucharistic Movement in Its European Context." In *Bohemian Reformation and Religious Practice*, 1:23–48. Prague: Academy of Sciences of the Czech Republic, 1996. http://www.brrp.org/proceedings/brrp1/holeton.pdf.

————. "Christian Initiation in Some Anglican Provinces." *Studia Liturgica* 12 (1977) 129–50.

————. "Communion of All the Baptized and Anglican Tradition." *Anglican Theological Review* 69 (1987) 13–28.

————. "The Communion of Infants: The Basel Years." *Communio Viatorum* 29.4 (1986) 15–40.

————. "The Fifteenth-Century Bohemian Origins of the Reformation Understanding of Confirmation." In *With Ever Joyful Hearts: Essays on Liturgy and Music Honoring Marion J. Hatchett*, edited by J. Neil Alexander, 82–102. New York: Church, 1999.

————. *Infant Communion—Then and Now.* Grove Liturgical Studies 27. Bramcote, UK: Grove, 1981.

————. *La communion des tout-petits enfants: Étude du mouvement Eucharistique en Bohême vers la fin du Moyen-Age.* Subsidia 50. Rome: Bibliotheca Ephemerides Liturgicae, 1989.

————. "Les conditions de la communion fréquante." In *La communion des tout-petits enfants: Étude du mouvement Eucharistique en Bohême vers la fin du Moyen-Age.* 58th–61st ed. Subsidia 50. Rome: Bibliotheca Ephemerides Liturgicae, 1989.

————. "The Sacramental Theology of Tomáš Štítný of Štítné." In *Bohemian Reformation and Religious Practice*, 4:57–79. Prague: Academy of Sciences of the Czech Republic, 2002. http://www.brrp.org/proceedings/brrp1/holeton.pdf.

Kaminsky, Howard. *A History of the Hussite Revolution.* Berkeley: University of California Press, 1967.

Kolár, Jaroslav, Anezka Vidmanová-Schmidtová, and Hana Vlhová-Wörner, editors. *Jistebnice Kancionál: MS. Prague, National Museum Library II C 7: Critical Edition.* Monumenta liturgica Bohemica 2. Brno, CZ: Marek, 2005.

Rubin, Miri. "Elevation, Communion and Substitutes." In *Corpus Christi: The Eucharist in Late Medieval Culture*, 63–82. Cambridge: Cambridge University Press, 1991.

Wagner, Murray L. *Petr Chelčický: A Radical Separatist in Hussite Bohemia.* Scottdale, PA: Herald, 1983.

National Museum Library, Ms. II C 7 (Jistebnický Kancionál). Prague, c. 1420. http://www.manuscriptorium.com.

Baptismal Faith Healing Division

8

Morgan Dix and the Catholic Revival in the Episcopal Church

Donald Gerardi

THE DECADE AFTER THE Civil War was pivotal for shaping the Episcopal Church in the last quarter of the nineteenth century and beyond, presenting issues that remain challenging. Twenty years earlier the ideas of the Oxford Movement had exacerbated long-standing tensions between high church and low church partisans. Issues of baptismal regeneration, Protestant identity, and the Anglican pre-Reformation heritage were in contention on both sides of the Atlantic. In the United States the Civil War provided a distraction from religious differences, but after 1865 divisions were renewed when ritualism became the war cry preoccupying General Conventions from 1868 to 1874. Behind the sound and fury over ritual were profound differences over the Church's identity, ecclesiology, approaches to ecumenism, and the place and role of the Episcopal Church in American life.[1]

The Episcopal Church grappled with these issues at a time when currents within wider Christianity were moving in new and sometimes contradictory directions. While denominational competition continued, there were signs of ecumenical initiatives. In 1857 some English clergy founded the Association for Promoting the Unity of Christendom to overcome divisions among Anglicans, Roman Catholics, and Orthodox by pledging to offer regular masses for reunion. On a different front, Protestants in Europe and America looked for ways to promote cooperative

1. DeMille, *The Catholic Movement in the American Episcopal Church*; Chorley, *Men and Movements in the American Episcopal Church*, chapters XII, XIII; Reed, *Glorious Battle*; Nockles, *The Oxford Movement in Context*.

ventures on behalf of the gospel through an Evangelical Alliance. Greater unity, they believed, could be effective in dealing with what they perceived as growing threats from the Papacy and Infidelity.[2]

At the same time the Roman Catholic Church was facing challenges of a new age. The Papacy was under siege from the emergence of a united Italy, the loss of its political power, and reformers calling for a "free church in a free state." By 1870, the Vatican Council's dogma of papal infallibility led to an even greater concentration of ecclesiastical authority. If Rome's direction by the end of the decade confirmed Protestant anxiety about the Papacy, intellectual trends appeared to validate their alarm over the threat to religious belief. Biblical criticism by German scholars like David Friedrich Strauss in the second third of the century and the influence of Charles Darwin and Herbert Spencer after 1860 provoked spirited reactions from traditional religious thinkers, particularly when seven Anglican clergy, attempting to come to terms with decades of challenging scholarship, published *Essays and Reviews* in 1860 just five months after the appearance of *Origin of Species*. During the last half of the nineteenth century the confrontation between science and religious faith became a major issue for traditional Christianity.

The Catholic Revival in the Episcopal Church, one of various responses to these challenges, was the work of many hands. Morgan Dix, Rector of New York's influential Trinity Church from 1862 until his death in 1908, was part of a new generation that transformed the American high church tradition into Anglo Catholicism. Dix came to be known as a model of the New York pulpit for his elegant sermons, rich musical voice, and a gift for combining tightly reasoned argument with an irenical tone. Prominent in diocesan and national church affairs, he served as an adroit President of the House of Deputies from 1886 to 1898. Promoting a renewed Catholicism as an alternative to Protestant fragmentation and the Papacy's dogmatic innovation and centralization of authority, he advocated an American Catholic Church as a path to Christian unity to meet the challenges of an increasingly secular, materialistic age.[3]

In 1863 ministers from several prominent New York Protestant denominations invited Dix to participate in a sermon series in support of

---

2. The Association for Promoting the Unity of Christendom is precursor to the movement leading to the Week for Christian Unity. The Evangelical Alliance was formed in England in 1846 and spread to the Continent. In 1866 an American branch was organized in New York.

3. DeMille, *The Catholic Movement in the American Episcopal Church*, chap. 6; Chorley, *Men and Movements in the American Episcopal Church*, chaps. 7, 8; Holifield, *God's Ambassadors*, chap. 5.

Christian unity. They asked Trinity's new rector to repeat a sermon he had recently preached on the Nicene Creed as a foundation of Christian faith, a topic that showed Christians shared an essential though invisible unity. When Dix declined, explaining he considered the idea of invisible unity to be a dangerous chimera, they assured him they would welcome a sermon of his choosing and "everything in our power shall be done to suit your form of worship." Responding to their generous gesture, Dix arrived at the Broadway Tabernacle on March 13, 1864, to deliver *Thoughts on the Lost Unity of the Christian World*. Despite "suffering intensively from headache and nervous anxiety," the young rector did not mince words. Speaking on behalf "of that outward and visible unity, which once was; which now is not; for which we pray that it may be given us again," Dix said ecumenism based on unity of mind and heart amidst ecclesiastical diversity masked the cancer of disunity, the causes of which were "self-will" and individualism. The remedy was unity institutionally embodied with polity and rites going back to the first Christian centuries.[4]

Denominational pluralism, Dix asserted, impeded the spread of Christianity, abetted the spread of freethinking, and wasted resources in communities that could not adequately support several pulpits. "The Church may exist, notwithstanding her disrupt condition. But she is not in a state to put forth her power." Going to the heart of the evangelical focus on individual salvation, he granted that souls were saved despite Christian divisions. "But there is an immense selfishness in the idea that the one work for each of us to do here is to save his soul." To heal a sinful world the church should be united not just in the eye of God but also in human eyes.

In attacking individualism and private judgment Dix knew he was indicting basic features of American Protestant culture. He set aside the sensitive issue of the Reformation as the source of the splintered church and focused on "self-will" reinforced by the idea of private judgment which "in this country is carried to its extremist point." Individualism and private judgment undercut the concept of ministry with a divine commission, reinforcing Deism and Free Thought. "The moment you admit that each man may interpret the Bible as he likes, that moment its Authority is gone. The claim to Individual Infallibility is as gross an error as of that of Papal Infallibility." Both weakened organized religion, advancing the view that one could have a rewarding life without ever entering a church. The several thousand New Yorkers enjoying the adjacent park that Sunday, he suggested, doubtless shared that idea.

4. Dix, "Diary," March 13, 1964; Dix, *Thoughts on the Lost Unity*.

Dix suggested a remedy for the divided and wounded church by explaining, "Let me tell you how we think where I came from: . . . Christ made a Body for His Church when He gave her a Soul; so that it was not left to men to determine under what form she should exist." Christ or the Apostles acting under his authority endowed the church with a polity, ministry, and rites integral to the scheme of salvation. Since history shows the fundamentals of the church had remained the same, effective ecumenism should look to existing institutions for keys to unity. Foreshadowing the Chicago/Lambeth Quadrilateral, he pointed to three essential characteristics to gather one household of faith: the ancient creeds expressing the real sense of Scripture; a three-fold ministry prevalent among the majority of Christians going back to apostolic times; and rites with transcendent power for initiation into Christ's body, strengthening the Christian life, and commemorating the Redeemer's sacrifice.

Dix assured his listeners he was not suggesting the Episcopal Church supplied the precise model for each point of doctrine, discipline, and worship. He urged two things strenuously. Avoid individualism in religion, "the breeder of internal discord," and look to history. "In the Past let us seek what in the Future we may enjoy. We must come together upon a historic platform, or we shall not come together at all." Claiming the principles he advocated would not produce uniformity, he asserted "in the Catholic Church of Christ there has been from the first, Diversity in Unity." He asked for patience, study, and prayer, trusting the work of reconstruction to God. The church to emerge "will not be a new body but a body arisen from sleep." The historic creeds, ministry, and sacraments will not be new. "But changes there will be. How much of ours will be swept away when the great flood comes, no man can foretell. But whatsoever is merely local and peculiar, will probably go. The specialities of the Presbyterian, of the Baptist, of the Episcopalian, of the Romanists, of the Congregationalist, will burn, beyond all hope of rescue. That only which is Catholic and primitive will stand . . ." Encouraged by signs of transformations underway as the nation experienced the convulsions of Civil War and people yearned for peace, cohesion and renewal, Dix put his hope for Christian unity in the emergence of an American Catholic church for a new age.

Dix found the congregation attentive and the Tabernacle's pastor gracious, but he knew his message was alien to most of the 2,000 people in the pews. One reaction was probably typical. Praising Dix's lucid style and sincere tone, a reviewer "heard him with intense interest and with a respect bordering upon admiration, doubting whether Dr. Newman could have been abler, or Dr. Pusey more devoutly earnest in pleading the claims of an historical, Catholic, Apostolic Church to form the nucleus of Christian unity." But he was not persuaded, finding no trace of Dix's ecclesiology in the New Testament and the earliest Christian era. Nor had Dix explained "the phenomenon of the Church of England, with its 'Apostolic' creeds, orders and sacraments, which is today the most pestiferous nest of Rationalism in Christendom,"[5] perhaps a reference to *Essays and Reviews*.

Dix understood he was at the beginning of a long campaign, but Anglo-Catholics of his generation were energized by a conviction that the tide of history was running in their favor. With the end of the Civil War the Episcopal Church seemed poised for growth. It escaped the continued divisions of other Protestant denominations when General Convention in 1865 restored the unity of the Church by seating southern bishops. The following year New York's diocesan convention enjoyed favorable attention in the press. *The New York Times* called it the leading diocese of a denomination becoming increasingly important because of its wealth, social standing and rapidly growing membership in the Northeast and the West. *The Times* also pointed to contacts between the Episcopal and Eastern Orthodox churches as evidence of "its claims as the truly Catholic Church of America." Dix, in fact, opened the convention with a rousing sermon in which he sketched a Catholic vision to empower the Church for its mission to shape a new American era.[6]

That vision was already generating opposition in New York. Ritual enrichments at St. Alban's Chapel provoked vigorous protest, prompting Dix and several others to ask the Presiding Bishop, John Henry Hopkins, for comment on the issue of ritualism. Hopkins' response, *The Law of Ritualism*, a balanced treatment that gave the movement some encouragement, distressed low church critics. A meeting of the House of Bishops in October 1866, just a month after Dix's diocesan convention sermon, provided the opportunity for opponents to organize plans to stop ritualism at the 1868 General Convention.[7]

Anglo-Catholic proponents, Dix prominent among them, also organized. In April 1867 he preached *A Sermon for the Times*, placing ceremonial enrichments into historical context with a survey of changes in

5. "Review of Morgan Dix, 'Thoughts.'"

6. "Review of Morgan Dix, 'Sermon Preached for Diocesan Convention'"; Dix, "Sermon Preached for Diocesan Convention (I John 3:23)."

7. Hopkins, *The Law of Ritualism*; DeMille, *The Catholic Movement in the American Episcopal Church*, 66–67; Chorley, *Men and Movements in the American Episcopal Church*, 373–76.

church life since the early nineteenth century. Full of amusing anecdotes, it stressed that, "Progress is the law in a living Church." Thanks to the freedom from restraining liturgical rubrics in the formation of the Episcopal Church, embellishments over a quarter of a century had made the Church a more effective teacher, attracting "the wandering children of this miscellaneous society which surrounds us." Ranging over architecture, music, floral decorations, vestments, and liturgical forms, Dix insisted various liturgical and ornamental adaptations had enabled his clerical generation to minister more effectively to a changing city. In a time of rapid developments in technology, industry, and society "there are some who seem to think that the Church alone must . . . show no signs of growth." Moving to forestall attempts to enact rubric restrictions, he insisted "the year 1867 is no better able to legislate for 1967 upon details of rite and ceremony then 1767 was for 1867." The following year he elaborated on these ideas by publishing an essay on ritualism.[8]

Two months later Dix carried his spirited message to Episcopal students at Brown University with an enthusiastic call to join the Catholic revival. "We are in the midst of a great movement . . . towards a pure and true Catholicism. We have the realization that the body of which we are members is not a sect but a branch of the holy Catholic Church. Men who believe that cannot sit still." Calling for leadership in a new age, he discussed three models of churchmanship: Individualism, Sectarianism, and Catholicism, each represented to varying degrees in their church. Individualism saw redemption as a simple transaction between a soul and Christ, making priests and sacraments inconsequential. Against this Protestant legacy, the corporate worship of the Book of Common Prayer provided some protection. Sectarianism, with a higher conception of the church's role, was more prevalent in the Episcopal Church. But its limited vision identified Christ's work with one denomination marked by a constricted theological perspective and a tendency to complacency.[9]

Catholicism was the model for a new age, its global perspective an antidote to the Episcopal Church's insularity and self-satisfaction. People were beginning to see God at work outside the boundaries of their own denomination and beyond the United States. Americans were predisposed to see their country as the only model for excellence, but foreign travel cured this notion, making the traveler love his country not less but

8. Dix, "A Sermon for the Times, Feast of St. Mark"; Dix, "Ritualism."

9. Dix, "Individualism, Sectarianism, Catholicism: A Sermon Preached on the Fourth Sunday After Easter."

more wisely. With a Catholic global vision the Episcopal Church would seem more precious as an integral part of that larger kingdom of Christ. There were presently encouraging signs of broadening perspectives. The Episcopal Church had been establishing relations "with the Anglo-Saxon branches of the Reformed Catholic Church," and in September their bishops would meet with other Anglican bishops at Lambeth Palace for the first time "to deliberate on the affairs of a communion which they regard as essentially one." Steps were also underway for more communication with Eastern Orthodox branches of the "Holy Catholic Church."[10]

As Dix was boosting an Anglo-Catholic future, heightened Protestant activity for Christian unity both outside and within the Episcopal Church was generating a strong cross-current. Early in 1867 members of several denominations in New York had established an American branch of the Evangelical Alliance, an organization founded in London in 1846 to promote closer Protestant ties. Several Episcopal clergy, sympathetic to this pan-Protestant movement and hostile to the growth of ritualism in New York, held meetings to support cooperation with Protestant clergy.[11] When a member of the group, Stephen H. Tyng, Jr., accepted an invitation to preach at a Methodist Church in New Jersey without the permission of the local Episcopal bishop, charges were brought against him in his own diocese. In early 1868 he faced an ecclesiastical trial and a formal admonition from Bishop Horatio Potter. The flaunting of canonical restrictions on the exchange of ministerial functions with other Protestant clergy became a major issue dividing Evangelical and Catholic advocates in the Episcopal Church.[12]

In the ensuing crisis Dix was at the center of Anglo-Catholic advocacy, addressing issues of church order, sacramental ministry, and Catholicism. One response was the formation of the American Church Union "to secure the integrity of [the Church's] Catholic position and to uphold the canonical authority of the bishops." Dix drafted its constitution. Its first meeting in January 1868 criticized the exchange of pulpits by Episcopal

10. Dix, "Individualism, Sectarianism, Catholicism: A Sermon Preached on the Fourth Sunday After Easter."

11. Among them were John Cotton Smith (Ascension Church), Stephen H. Tyng (St. George's Church), Stephen H. Tyng, Jr. (Holy Trinity Church), H. Newton Heber (Anthon Memorial Church).

12. In Dix's day Evangelicals stood for basic Protestant principles, the theologically most significant touching on objections to baptismal regeneration, stressing conversion experiences rather than sacramental acts. Some wanted to change the baptismal service to reflect their views. In addition, theologically liberal broad church ministers, like H. N. Heber, also alarmed Catholics like Dix.

and Protestant ministers. Two months earlier Dix had attacked open pulpits, forbidden by canon law, as a practice that subverted the principle of ordained ministry. "The Episcopal Church holds that God has chosen to call men into ministry in one way, that they be ordained by one who succeeds to the apostolic office, namely the Bishop. Some people consider this theory uncharitable or even monstrous. But I ask such people if they consider any ordination necessary." The idea that anyone preaching from an open Bible had a right to preach anywhere threatened all denominational traditions of ordained ministry. If clerical calling was a matter of individual conviction, ecclesiastical structure and discipline were irrelevant. Critics of Episcopal ordination should consider how that system had served to preserve the idea of a divinely constituted ministry. "A high Episcopal theory and the idea of a real ordination go together."[13]

The theological stakes became higher five years later, when the Evangelical Alliance held its first American convention in New York. Dix believed Episcopal clergy had every right to participate out of their desire for Christian unity, a hope he shared. He insisted it was an altogether different matter to take part in sacramental rites with ministers not ordained as priests. George Cummins, Assistant Bishop of Kentucky, joined in officiating at an Evangelical Alliance Communion, causing a crisis that led a few weeks later to his withdrawal from the Episcopal Church and a schism that created the Reformed Episcopal Church. If schism came, Dix counseled, no real harm would be done: "if few go, the thing soon dies out; if many go, they will free the Church from what is a source of weakness." The real danger was: "To pretend to celebrate divine mysteries, which none but priests are permitted to handle, among us, with men whose ordinations our canonical law does not recognize, was to strike at the whole system of Catholic Christianity. . . . If that was right, we are all wrong." The prohibition had nothing to do with personal qualities. "Amongst the Protestant clergy are some of the best men now alive." Compromise was impossible on the basic issue, Apostolic Succession. "We have a system in which priesthood, sacraments, and mysteries form the principal part. The apostolic succession and the sacramental system imply each other. We could not admit the validity of non-Episcopal orders without letting go everything in our religion which vitally symbolizes and realizes to us the Supernatural Order with which we are linked." In a materialist and

---

13. Dix, "On Church Order (I Thessalonians 2:4)." Ecclesiology was the topic for a two-part Lenten lecture series in 1868 and 1869, "The System of the Church."

skeptical age, Dix emphasized that the church not only affirmed spiritual reality; it was the meeting point of the visible and invisible worlds.[14]

Behind Dix's insistence on Episcopacy and priestly ordination was the theological bedrock of his ecclesiology, the Incarnation. One of his earliest sermons began: "Faith in the Divinity of our Lord Jesus Christ is the beginning of the hope of mankind. On this confession, as on a rock, the Church was founded and built, on this it stands." If Christ was God, how could Paul say God exalted him above all creation after his death? The Creed, Dix explained, provided the answer. Fully God and fully man, Christ's human nature, like our own, was a created thing, attaining perfection by degrees. His mortal nature became immortal, lifted up into the honors of the Deity. It was his human body, a created and material thing, that died and was buried. What went into the tomb was a corpse; what was enthroned on high was that resurrected body made glorious.[15]

Because of the Incarnation, humankind shared in the exaltation of the risen and glorified Christ. Amidst troubled lives, Dix acknowledged, it was hard to grasp the substance of the Easter gospel, that anyone who is in Christ shares his triumph. Yet it was a fundamental teaching of the Catholic faith. Dix pointed to St. Athanasius's use of the word *theopoiesis* in referring to the exaltation of those who die in Christ. The modern praise of humanity as a substitute for the gospel of Christ, Dix asserted, was no match for what the ancient church fathers had said. But there was a profound difference between humanity taken into the glorified Christ and humanity cut off from God by pride, descending into death and decay. "Let us discern between these two Gospels, for our very life's sake; and be our place and portion with Him who deified our nature, and is able to lift us up and make us like God."[16]

Dix's ecclesiology was bound up with the transformative power of the Word made flesh. His Lenten lectures in 1868 and 1869 described the Church's sacramental system as an extension of the Incarnation, a theme he revisited throughout his long ministry and elaborated in the Paddock Lectures in 1892.[17] Christ's body brought the spiritual into the physical world; the church's sacramental ministry sustained his redemptive work.

14. Dix, "On Christian Ministry (3 Advent)."

15. Dix, "Faith in the Divinity of Christ (1 Peter 1:3, 4)."

16. Ibid. cf. Athanasius, *De Decretis* 3.14: "The Word became flesh . . . that we, partaking of his Spirit, might be deified."

17. Dix, "The System of the Church." The Paddock Lectures, 1892: *The Sacramental System Considered as the Extension of the Incarnation* became a text at General Theological Seminary.

This understanding naturally led to a high view of the priesthood. Dix saw Apostolic Succession as a spiritual agency by which an act of God entrusted to a mere man supernatural powers to carry on Christ's priestly work of salvation. "A peculiar order of man is needed; what has been in all ages known as a Priesthood. These men have the keys of another world; these men handle forces to which fire and heat, lightning and gravitation are but child's play."[18]

The rites of the church were not merely ceremonies to encourage faith and promote good behavior. Simple ritual acts carried invisible powers, incorporating people into Christ's mystical body. These rites also taught the doctrines that expressed that supernatural reality: "the Church has from the very beginning employed liturgies which were, substantially, doctrine put into devotional language: for a liturgy, after all, is much the same thing as the Creed thrown into another shape and breathed forth from the heart, in the spirit of devotion, instead of being tersely summed up and spoken by the lips from the thinking brain."[19]

Dix's liturgical theology, like his ecclesiology, focused on the relationship between the natural and supernatural worlds, the link between nature and grace.[20] The sacramental system was anchored in the universe itself, its physicality the medium of spiritual gifts. Rites using physical things have a supernatural foundation, the visible undergirded by the invisible. Christ, summing up in his person the forces of the universe, uses the elements of this world to convey spiritual power. "The application of material agents to spiritual uses . . . is not only a simple idea, it is the sequel to that act of the Eternal Son of God in assuming a mortal body and a human soul. Sacramental religion may accordingly be considered as the purest and simplest of all religions. It follows the line on which our redemption proceeds; on which the release of the creation from vanity is now proceeding."[21]

In developing this theme Dix was influenced early in his ministry by a Roman Catholic theologian, Gioacchino Ventura de Raulica. Devouring Ventura's publications between 1857 and 1860, he recorded in his diary: "I cannot sufficiently admire him as a theological writer. . . . I read him more than any other, and with increasing admiration." Ventura combined an early nineteenth-century post-Enlightenment traditionalist reliance on

18. Dix, "On Christian Ministry (3 Advent)."

19. Dix, "The System of the Church," Lecture III.

20. Dix, "Visible and Invisible Worlds, Lenten Lectures, 1866"; "The Supernatural in Religion and Life (Lenten Lectures, 1872)."

21. Dix, "Lecture I: The Basis of the Sacramental System," 28.

the authority of church and Scripture with a philosophical method that made him a precursor of the neo-scholastic Thomistic revival.[22] Like Ventura, Dix saw nature as a mirror revealing both a benevolent creator and the close relationship human beings have with all creation. No wonder, Dix observed, early church fathers recommended the "lovely study of the visible world and found a basis for their teachings in a rational feeling for the vast grandeur of the external order, 'the sacred economy of the universe,' as St. Gregory [Thaumaturgos] called it."[23] Dix appropriated Ventura's formulation that the Creator of the visible and invisible worlds joined in humankind both spirit and body in a single being. "Matter and body are associated with spirit in man, for the worship of God and for the service of religion."[24] Following Ventura, Dix saw science and theology as different, but not antagonistic, paths to understanding. Science continually expanded knowledge's boundaries of the natural world while theology dealt with truths beyond those boundaries. The marvels of modern science need not threaten the marvels of the resurrected life revealed in Christ and sustained by the church's sacraments and teaching. In this sense, Dix saw the Catholic revival as vital for the defense of religious faith against positivist assaults.

In advocating Catholicism to counter modern disbelief, Dix was concerned with threats from two fronts: Protestantism and Rome's distortions of Catholicism. Preaching on the issue of pulpit exchanges in 1867, he was sympathetic to the motivation of low churchmen seeking alliances with Protestant denominations "as a way of countering the growth of the Church of Rome." But they ignored the weakness of their probable allies. Like other Anglo-Catholics of his generation, Dix held the mistaken belief that Protestantism was in decline. He referred to a *Hartford Current* report on dwindling church attendance in Connecticut's Congregational churches and to an essay by a Yale professor on the growing vitality of Connecticut's Roman Catholic Church. If the Episcopal Church, seeking Protestant alliances, weakened its doctrine and practices, it would vanish along with the Protestants. "Let us take that line, and before this century is closed, Rome will sweep the land, and possess the humble hearts, the pure spirits, but clear minds of this continent, from shore to shore." Dix offered a different future "in which we should yet do a grand and true work on this

22. Dix, "Diary," July 2, 1857; July 13, 1858; July 3, 1860; Perrier, "Forerunners of the Neo-Scholastic Revival."

23. Dix, "Lecture I: The Basis of the Sacramental System," 24–25.

24. Raulica, *La raison philosophique et la raison catholique, conférences.* Cited in Dix, "Lecture I: The Basis of the Sacramental System," 18.

continent. If ever a mission was clearly marked out, ours is that mission: to teach a pure, high, clear Catholicity in this age and land."[25]

When Dix delivered that sermon he was writing a series of eight articles, "Catholic Truth and Roman Error," published anonymously by *Church Monthly* in 1868. With the Vatican Council underway, the time for championing the Catholic cause was both opportune and pressing. Some Episcopalians, disheartened by controversies within their church, were converting to Roman Catholicism. Others, firmly antagonistic to Catholicism, were adopting ultra-Protestant ideas. It was crucial "to see the distinction between what the Church of Rome now offers us and that which was anciently held and believed through the wide compass of the One Holy Catholic and Apostolic Church." Addressing Protestant-leaning Episcopalians, Dix dismissed arguments that Catholicism was idolatrous. It was an unfortunately common Protestant error to confuse what "ignorant Roman Catholics may believe and what the teaching of the Church in fact is." Such arguments could be used against basic Catholic principles to the benefit of skepticism. "Crude Protestantism is a very late and novel development of human thought: like a reed, it pierces the hand of him who leans upon it." Instead, Dix suggested three valid objections to what Rome had done to undermine Catholicism: the claim of the Bishop of Rome to universal supremacy; the elevation of the Blessed Virgin to the mediating role of co-redemptrix; and dogmatic innovations advanced through the claim of infallibility.[26]

The claim to universal supremacy, without justification in history or Scripture, had made Rome "the mother of schisms," contracting and shrinking the church for the sake of a sectarian system that "demanded consolidation by stringent measures and a more exclusive Creed; and thus whole races and nations were crowded out and lost to her forever." The effective use of Scripture and patristic writings by sixteenth-century Anglican reformers had frustrated Roman attempts to show their system was as old as Christianity itself. In consequence, Rome turned to a novel theory of doctrinal development, maintaining faith continued to be revealed in new dogmas, as with the proclamation of the Immaculate Conception in 1856, and Rome was asserting the Pope was infallible and his temporal power essential to his office. It came down to this: "the truth which a man must know for salvation is not a subtle thing but variable." In contrast,

---

25. Dix, "On Church Order (I Thessalonians 2:4)." Another example is Ewer, *Sermons on the Failure of Protestantism, and on Catholicity.*

26. Dix, "Catholic Truth and Roman Error," Part II (February, 1868), 107–8; Part III (March, 1868), 151. The eight articles were published anonymously, draft notes are in Dix Papers, Trinity Parish Archive.

Anglicans believed Catholic truth in its fullness was taught in the first age. "The only developments to be noted in respect to it are in precision of dogmatic statement, in clearness of insight into holy mysteries, and in application to the circumstances of a changing world."[27]

An important motivation for these anonymous articles is seen in Dix's diary entries on counseling people with "Roman Fever." His tone in the series is more stridently polemical. Speculating on why anyone would choose the path to Rome, he suggested certain psychological traits: "a subjective passion, a delirium of self-consciousness and self-will, a pure mania of unreasoning longing and unbridled desire. Alas, in the instances which the writer has known, the elements of sound, intellectual judgment have been wanting." Converts, seemingly compelled by impulses, are susceptible to flattery and pleased by attention. Without a strong constitution, as with typhus, the infected person succumbs when the "Roman Fever" reaches a crisis.[28]

Dix understood some Episcopalians were attracted to Rome by distaste for modern Protestantism and the worry that the Anglican tradition did not hold the pure Catholic faith. But he insisted that converting to Rome because of aversion to Protestantism would be moving from an effect to its own cause, Protestantism being the result of corruptions for which Rome had been mainly responsible. "The remedy for Protestantism is Catholicism, not Romanism. If the Roman Church had not almost destroyed the ancient Catholicism by its bold assumptions and terrible innovations, Protestantism would never have been what it is, a great consolidated, organized and powerful engine." He admitted many Episcopalians were "Protestants at heart" and that some "modern thinkers" had imported "foreign and crude ideas . . . into our system to the great detriment of religion." There was, however, no reason to leave "so long as our formularies are sound and our lineage is pure." When Book of Common Prayer, particularly the Ordinal and the Articles of Religion, was contorted to serve modern sectarianism, the proper course was "to appeal to the sixteenth-century Anglican Reformation to show our model and principles are to be found in the first six centuries, not in the last three. [To vindicate a pure Catholicism] is the work which God hath given us to do."[29]

27. Dix, "Catholic Truth and Roman Error," Part III (March, 1868) 151–55; Part V (May/June, 1868), 316–17; "Address (Ascension Day, 1871)," 65.

28. Dix, "Diary," April 16, 1869; Strong, *Diary*, IV:233–34. Strong, a Trinity vestryman, advocated an "American Catholic Church" to avoid conversions to Rome like that of his god-daughter that year.

29. Dix, "Catholic Truth and Roman Error," Part VII (September, 1868), 119–26.

For Episcopalians upset by differences of opinion in their church, Dix recommended the study of church history. Divisions existed in the earliest Christian communities. Eastern and Western branches of the Catholic church had been divided since 1054. Differences in the Anglican Communion, he argued, paled in historical comparison to the Roman Church with its years of rival popes, feuds between religious orders, and discord between Gallicans and Ultramontanes. Dix noted that *The Dublin Review* had recently savaged the rector of its Catholic University, John Henry Newman, and Newman responded by characterizing popular devotion to the Blessed Virgin as "a bad dream." Instead of concealing conflicts, it was wiser to consider their origin and relationship. Since the Reformation there had been Anglican Protestant and Catholic parties. "Almighty God allows them to exist; it is hard to see how they could but exist; there is a necessary and inevitable antagonism." At this time, when Catholics in the Church of England were advancing, it would be folly to leave. "For hundreds of years there has been no such religious awakening; it is a glorious revival." To loose heart and retreat from the field was to abandon a holy work. "Rather should he trust in God and do his duty, rejoicing that he is able to strive for the holy cause of the Catholic Truth and to advance her sure and final triumph."[30]

Although the storm over ritualism did not weaken Dix's confidence in a Catholic future, it provided a dose of realism. In 1871 he repeated for Episcopalians the guidelines on church unity he had offered other denominations at the Broadway Tabernacle seven years earlier: acceptance of Scriptures, ecumenical councils, and authentic historical traditions were enough that people "though differing very widely indeed in matters of opinion, in taste, in theory, and in ideas of worship and work, may stand, hand in hand . . . mutually securing each other's liberty, in things which are not vital." Three years later he pleaded for tolerance of diversity in liturgical styles in the face of threats to impose restrictive new rubrics, warning against "bishops who would impose their particular views, their theological ideas, or their individual tastes and preferences on their unhappy and, at present, helpless clergy." He characterized both high church and low church partisans as sectarian: "each school took the Church for something narrower than she is." They confused pure Christianity with an unchanging reformed Anglicanism, each seeking "to impale as many as it can upon the sharpened spikes of its little ring-fence." Dix urged a wider

30. Dix, "Catholic Truth and Roman Error," Part VIII (November, 1868), 334–35, 337–40.

vision for the Church, going beyond established traditions from Britain and its colonial offshoots to manifest a larger identity. "She is a branch of the Holy Catholic Church. Her sympathies are with the great body whose organic life she shares. Let her alone and she will assert her lineage. The hand of Almighty God has been with us from the first, through all the work of restoration. For these are not innovations; they are reconstructions. What belongs to us we have been recovering."[31]

After the ritual wars abated following the 1874 General Convention, Dix remained firm in the service of Catholic reconstruction. As rector of Trinity Parish and President of the House of Deputies he steered a steady course, emphasizing theology over ritual, ecclesiological integrity over ecumenism, and sacramental spirituality expressed in social ministry. Trinity's ten parish churches, several ministering to impoverished neighborhoods, offered a judicious range of ritual styles. Its Mission House, a hospital, and various parish schools served the urban poor. Dix worked with William Reed Huntington for the prayer book reform of 1892 but was critical of Huntington's attempt at the 1895 General Convention to use the Lambeth Quadrilateral to forge a less than organic union of "sporadic congregations" of Protestant denominations, fearing a weakening of the Church's Catholic birthright.[32] Indeed, Dix's vision of an American Catholic church, one of many branches of the universal church, remained an idealistic dream. But a longtime member of the Association for Promoting the Unity of Christendom, he never lost heart, using its reliance on prayer and patience and trusting the realization of that vision to God.

31. Dix, "Address (Ascension Day, 1871)," 67; Dix, "A Plea for Toleration (Ascension Sermon, 1874)"; Strong, *Diary*, IV:526.

32. Dix, "Diary," October 16–17, 1895; Dix, *The Birthright of the Church*; "Lambeth Plan Lost"; "Christian Unity."

Bibliography

Chorley, E. Clowes. *Men and Movements in the American Episcopal Church*. The Hale Lectures. New York: Scribner's Sons, 1946.

"Christian Unity." *New York Times*. October 19, 1895.

DeMille, George E. *The Catholic Movement in the American Episcopal Church*. Church Historical Society. Publication No. 12. Philadelphia: Church Historical Society, 1941.

Dix, Morgan. "Address (Ascension Day, 1871)." In *The Church and the City, 1865–1910*, edited by Robert D Cross. The American Heritage Series. Indianapolis, IN: Bobbs-Merrill, 1967.

———. *The Birthright of the Church, Its Nature, and the Risk of Its Loss. A Sermon Preached in Gethsemane Church, Minneapolis, on Sunday, October 20, 1895, During the Session of the General Convention*. Milwaukee, WI: The Young Churchman, 1895.

———. "Catholic Truth and Roman Error." *Church Monthly*, November 1868.

———. "Diary," March 13, 1864. Dix Papers. Trinity Parish Archives.

———. "Faith in the Divinity of Christ (1 Peter 1:3, 4)" Sermon. St. Mark's Church, Philadelphia, April 16, 1854. Dix Papers. Trinity Parish Archives.

———. "Individualism, Sectarianism, Catholicism: A Sermon Preached on the Fourth Sunday after Easter." Sermon presented at the Bishop Seabury Association of Brown University, St. Stephen's Church, Providence, Rhode Island, May 19, 1867. http://anglicanhistory.org/usa/providence/individualism.html.

———. "Lecture I: The Basis of the Sacramental System." In *The Sacramental System Considered as the Extension of the Incarnation*. The Bishop Paddock Lectures 1892. New York: Longmans, Green, 1893.

———. "On Christian Ministry (3 Advent)." Sermon, December 14, 1873. Dix Papers. Trinity Parish Archives.

———. "On Church Order (I Thessalonians 2:4)." Sermon, November 10, 1867. Dix Papers. Trinity Parish Archives.

———. "A Plea for Toleration (Ascension Sermon, 1874)." *Saint Chrysostom's Magazine*, June 1874. http://anglicanhistory.org/usa/mdix/plea1874.html.

———. "Ritualism." *The Galaxy* 4 (December 1867) 285–93.

———. *The Sacramental System Considered as the Extension of the Incarnation*. The Bishop Paddock Lectures 1892. New York: Longmans, Green, 1893.

———. "A Sermon for the Times, Feast of St. Mark" Sermon, April 25, 1867. Trinity Parish Archives.

———. "Sermon Preached for Diocesan Convention (I John 3:23)." Notes. New York, September 26, 1866. Dix Papers. Trinity Parish Archives.

———. "The Supernatural in Religion and Life (Lenten Lectures, 1872)." Notes, 1872. Dix Papers. Trinity Parish Archives.

———. "The System of the Church." Notes, 1868 and 1869. Trinity Parish Archives.

———. *Thoughts on the Lost Unity of the Christian World, and on the Steps Necessary to Secure Its Recovery*. New York: Appleton, 1864. http://anglicanhistory.org/usa/mdix/tabernacle1864.html.

———. "Visible and Invisible Worlds, Lenten Lectures, 1866." Notes, 1866. Dix Papers. Trinity Parish Archives.

Ewer, Ferdinand C. *Sermons on the Failure of Protestantism, and on Catholicity*. New York: Appleton, 1869.

Holifield, E. Brooks. *God's Ambassadors: A History of the Christian Clergy in America*. Grand Rapids: Eerdmans, 2007.

Hopkins, John Henry. *The Law of Ritualism: Examined in Its Relation to the Word of God, to the Primitive Church, to the Church of England, and to the Protestant Episcopal Church in the United States*. New York: Hurd and Houghton, 1867.

"Lambeth Plan Lost." *New York Times*. October 18, 1895.

Nockles, Peter Benedict. *The Oxford Movement in Context: Anglican High Churchmanship, 1760–1857*. Cambridge: Cambridge University Press, 1994.

Perrier, Joseph Louis. "Forerunners of the Neo-Scholastic Revival." In *The Revival of Scholastic Philosophy in the Nineteenth Century*, 153–57. New York: Columbia University Press, 1909.

Raulica, Gioacchino Ventura de. *La raison philosophique et la raison catholique, conférences*. Paris: Gaume Frères, 1852.

Reed, John Shelton. *Glorious Battle: The Cultural Politics of Victorian Anglo-Catholicism*. Nashville, TN: Vanderbilt University Press, 1996.

"Review of Morgan Dix, 'Sermon Preached for Diocesan Convention.'" *New York Times*. September 26, 1866.

"Review of Morgan Dix, 'Thoughts.'" *The Congregationalist*. Boston, March 18, 1864.

Strong, George Templeton. *The Diary of George Templeton Strong*, Vol. IV. Edited by Allan Nevins and Milton Halsey Thomas. New York: Macmillan, 1952.

9

The Gorham Controversy and Infant Baptism as an Ecumenical Problem

John F. Baldovin, SJ

In 1847, George Gorham, a priest of the Church of England, was recommended as vicar of Brampford Speke in the Diocese of Exeter. Upon examining him, the Bishop, Henry Phillpotts, judged that was doctrinally deficient in that he did not hold what the Thirty-Nine Articles taught about baptismal regeneration. Gorham appealed to the ecclesiastical Court of Arches, which held for the Bishop. He appealed further to the (civil) Judicial Committee of Privy Council, which overturned the Court of Arches' judgment in 1850.

The case became famous mainly because of the controversy it ignited over the role that the government should play in the life of the state church, an issue which had helped to spur the Tractarian Movement in 1833. The Gorham Case was the final straw for both Henry Edward Manning and Robert Isaac Wilberforce. They both abandoned the Church of England; Manning was later to become Roman Catholic Archbishop of Westminster and a cardinal, and Wilberforce went on to become a relatively well-known Roman Catholic theologian.

Though this controversy achieved its notoriety over church-state relations, it also brought to a head a robust debate about the nature of Baptism, a debate which had been going on since the beginning of the nineteenth century.[1] The main question is still relevant today: Does bap-

---

1. See Nias, *Gorham*, 8. Wilberforce himself had written in defense of baptismal regeneration against the Rev. William Goode in 1849, *The Doctrine of Holy Baptism: With Remarks on the Rev. W. Goode's "Effects of Infant Baptism."*

tizing infants actually *do* anything? Or as I once heard a fellow Roman Catholic sacramental theologian say, is it that "the only thing that really happens to the baby is that it gets wet"?

This essay, while not pretending to provide a definitive answer to the question of baptismal regeneration, at least hopes to shed some light on the subject and spur further reflection. We shall begin with a review of the reactions to the Gorham Case among nineteenth-century English theologians. Then we shall turn to the landmark Lima Statement, *Baptism, Eucharist, and Ministry* of the Faith and Order Commission of the World Council of Churches (1982) and several official ecclesial reactions to its treatment of infant Baptism. Finally we shall attempt to articulate a coherent approach to the issue of the objectivity of infant Baptism via the sacramental theology of Louis-Marie Chauvet.

Theological Reactions to the Gorham Case

J. C. S. Nias, the chronicler of the Gorham case, divides the parties in the dispute into four categories: the first consists of Bishop Phillpotts himself as well as his chaplain, William Maskell, and people like Manning and Wilberforce who went over to Rome. This group held for an *ex opere operato* understanding of Baptism in which justification coincides with the reception of the sacrament. The second group consists of traditional Tractarians, such as Edward Pusey and John Keble, who "regarded the Judgment as wrong, but did not consider that it irreparably compromised the English Church."[2] This group apparently felt that Evangelicals like Gorham had confused sanctification with justification and had therefore missed the point of baptismal regeneration. A third group took a middle position which denied *ex opere operato*, but thought that children of believing parents were justified at the time of Baptism. The fourth group consists of Gorham himself as well as other evangelicals who represent a rejection of baptismal regeneration—at least with regard to every infant who is baptized.[3]

The crux of the matter has to do with the interpretation of Article 27 of the Thirty-Nine Articles:

> XXVII: Of Baptism.
> Baptism is not only a sign of profession, and mark of difference, whereby Christian men are discerned from others that be not christened, but it is also a sign of Regeneration or

2. Nias, *Gorham*, 142.
3. On this see, Nias, *Gorham*, 172–74.

New-Birth, whereby, as by an instrument, they that receive Baptism rightly are grafted into the Church; the promises of the forgiveness of sin, and of our adoption to be the sons of God by the Holy Ghost, are visibly signed and sealed, Faith is confirmed, and Grace increased by virtue of prayer unto God. The Baptism of young Children is in any wise to be retained in the Church, as most agreeable with the institution of Christ.

And with the Catechism in the Book of Common Prayer (1662):

Question. What is the outward visible sign or form in Baptism?

Answer. Water: wherein the person is baptized In the Name of the Father, and of the Son, and of the Holy Ghost.

Question. What is the inward and spiritual grace?

Answer. A death unto sin, and a new birth unto righteousness: for being by nature born in sin, and the children of wrath, we are hereby made the children of grace.

Question. What is required of persons to be baptized?

Answer. Repentance, whereby they forsake sin: and Faith, whereby they stedfastly believe the promises of God made to them in that Sacrament.

Question. Why then are Infants baptized, when by reason of their tender age they cannot perform them?

Answer. Because they promise them both by their Sureties: which promise, when they come to age, themselves are bound to perform.

And finally, two of the formulas that follow the baptismal bath and consignation are relevant to the theme:

Seeing now, dearly beloved brethren, that *this Child is* regenerate, and grafted into the body of Christ's Church, let us give thanks unto Almighty God for these benefits; and with one accord make our prayers unto him, that *this Child* may lead the rest of *his* life according to this beginning. [The Lord's Prayer follows, then:]
We yield thee hearty thanks, most merciful Father, that it hath pleased thee to regenerate *this Infant* with thy Holy Spirit, to receive *him* for thine own *Child* by adoption, and to incorporate *him* into thy holy Church. And humbly we beseech thee to grant, that *he*, being dead unto sin, and living unto righteousness, and being buried with Christ in his death, may crucify the old man, and utterly abolish the whole body of sin; and that,

as *he is* made partaker of the death of thy Son, *he* may also be partaker of his resurrection; so that finally, with the residue of thy holy Church, *he* may be an inheritor of thine everlasting kingdom; through Christ our Lord. *Amen.*

The official documents of the Church of England clearly support an objective view of Baptism, namely baptismal regeneration. For example, as Manning wrote to Wilberforce in 1850:

Is not this the true statement of baptism?

- That it unites the baptized to the Holy Trinity, to the Father by adoption, to the Son by remission, to the Holy Ghost by indwelling.

- That the agent is the Holy Ghost.

- That the infusion of grace is the *one* principle which brings also Adoption and Redemption.

- That Regeneration comprehends *the whole threefold idea.*[4]

But perhaps the discussion cannot end here, with the affirmation of what amounts to the Roman Catholic doctrine of the *ex opere operato* effect of the sacrament. The reason for this is the necessity for theology to adapt to a new social and cultural situation—one in which it cannot be presumed that infants who are baptized *will* be raised to be Christians. The Book of Common Prayer (1662) catechism quite clearly defends the practice of infant Baptism on the basis that the child will be raised a Christian, as does the exhortation given to the godparents at the end of the prayer book Liturgy of Public Baptism:

Forasmuch as *this Child hath* promised by you *his* sureties to renounce the devil and all his works, to believe in God, and to serve him: ye must remember, that it is your parts and duties to see that *this Infant* be taught, so soon as *he* shall be able to learn, what a solemn vow, promise, and profession, *he hath* here made by you. And that *he* may know these things the better, ye shall call upon him to hear Sermons; and chiefly ye shall provide, that *he* may learn the Creed, the Lord's Prayer, and the Ten Commandments, in the vulgar tongue, and all other things which a Christian ought to know and believe to his soul's health; and that *this Child* may be virtuously brought up to lead a godly and a Christian life; remembering always, that Baptism doth represent unto us our profession; which is, to follow the example of our Saviour Christ, and to be made like unto him; that, as he

4. Cited in Nias, *Gorham*, 125.

> died, and rose again for us, so should we, who are baptized, die from sin, and rise again unto righteousness; continually mortifying all our evil and corrupt affections and daily proceeding in all virtue and godliness of living.

How can one maintain the traditional belief in the objective nature of sacramental acts (at least as old as Augustine's debate with the Donatists[5]) with a new cultural situation that could not assume that baptized infants would really be brought up in the faith? That this kind of question was alive in the Roman Catholic Church, as well, in the nineteenth century is illustrated by the (in)famous case of Edgardo Mortara. Mortara was born to Jewish parents in Bologna (still part of the Papal States) in 1852. In 1858 the police took him from his parents and brought him to Rome where he was eventually adopted by Pope Pius IX and became a priest. The reason for his removal (abduction) from the Mortara home was that a maidservant, who had been fourteen at the time, revealed that she had baptized Edgardo secretly as an infant when he was mortally ill because she feared for his salvation.[6] This event stirred a controversy at the time. The Catholic Church teaches, of course, that a sacrament performed with the correct "matter" and the correct "form" (verbal formula) by a valid minister who intends what the Church intends is valid.[7] Now the crux of this question is how exactly to interpret "intending what the Church intends." A somewhat odd parallel to the Mortara case might be helpful in spelling this question out. An Anglican priest friend once told me that his wife overheard their four year old daughter "baptizing" her (unbaptized) playmate with water and the proper formula. Clearly on some level the daughter "intended" the salvation of her playmate, but the action was performed with no inkling whatsoever of the parents' desire for their child to be baptized. It seems to me that to say someone in this situation is baptized into the faith of the church (since all sacraments are clearly "sacraments of faith"[8]) is stretching the point unreasonably. *Someone's* mature faith must be involved. The alternative is quite frankly magic.

Part of the difficulty, of course, comes with the traditional understanding of original sin, which has rested on St. Augustine's misreading of Romans 5:12. Relying on the Latin mistranslation of this verse, which

---

5. See, for example, Augustine, *On Baptism: Against the Donatists*, Book 1, in Finn, *Early Christian Baptism*, 164–71.

6. See Kertzer, *The Kidnapping of Edgardo Mortara*.

7. See, e.g., *CCC*, #1127–1129; *CIC*, #847, 861:2.

8. See *CCC*, #1123.

should read: "Therefore, just as sin came into the world through one man, and death came through sin, and so death spread to all because all have sinned," Augustine read "in whom (*in* quo) all have sinned instead of "because (ἐφ' ᾧ) all have sinned." As Maxwell Johnson has commented:

> The theological problem, then, was the apparent presence of all people *in* Adam himself. Had he [Augustine] known his Greek better, or, at least used a Greek version of Romans 5, his theology of "original sin" undoubtedly would have been different.[9]

We have seen in this section that the Gorham Case is not merely about the Erastian nature of the Church of England, but the Case also raises serious questions about how to understand the objectivity of baptismal grace. To gain a more secure foothold, we shall turn next to the 1982 ecumenical consensus statement, *Baptism, Eucharist and Ministry*.

Baptismal Grace in the Lima Document

In 1982 the Faith and Order Commission of the World Council of Churches issued a landmark convergence document entitled *Baptism, Eucharist and Ministry*, or BEM.[10] After expounding the richness of the meaning of Baptism under five themes (Participation in Christ's Death and Resurrection, Conversion, Pardoning and Cleansing, The Gift of the Spirit, Incorporation into the Body of Christ, and The Sign of the Kingdom) the Baptism document turns to the question of faith and Baptism. BEM treads a fine line between a simple *ex opere operato* approach and an approach that would deny objective sacramental efficacy:

> 8. Baptism is both God's gift and our human response to that gift. It looks towards a growth into the measure of the stature of the fullness of Christ (Eph. 4:13). The necessity of faith for the reception of the salvation embodied and set forth in baptism is acknowledged by all churches. Personal commitment is necessary for responsible membership in the body of Christ.

> 9. Baptism is related not only to momentary experience, but to life-long growth into Christ. Those baptized are called upon to reflect the glory of the Lord as they are transformed by the

9. Johnson, *The Rites of Christian Initiation*, 195.
10. World Council of Churches, *Baptism, Eucharist and Ministry*.

power of the Holy Spirit, into his likeness, with ever increasing splendour (II Cor. 3:18).

I find the "both/and" and the relation to "life-long growth into Christ" a very appealing way forward in dealing with the question of objective sacramental efficacy. Without settling on an either/or answer the document proceeds to treat specifically of infant Baptism and believer Baptism:

> 12. Both the baptism of believers and the baptism of infants take place in the Church as the community of faith. When one who can answer for himself or herself is baptized, a personal confession of faith will be an integral part of the baptismal service. When an infant is baptized, the personal response will be offered at a later moment in life. In both cases, the baptized person will have to grow in the understanding of faith. For those baptized upon their own confession of faith, there is always the constant requirement of a continuing growth of personal response in faith. In the case of infants, personal confession is expected later, and Christian nurture is directed to the eliciting of this confession. All baptism is rooted in and declares Christ's faithfulness unto death. It has its setting within the life and faith of the Church and, through the witness of the whole Church, points to the faithfulness of God, the ground of all life in faith.

The commentary on #12 goes on to emphasize the fact that the practice infant Baptism relies on the corporate faith of the church while at the same time insisting that the personal faith of the recipient of Baptism and faithful participation in the life of the church are essential for the full fruit of Baptism.

The official ecclesial responses to BEM reveal the particular concerns of the various churches. For example, the Roman Catholic response affirms the objectivity of the removal of original sin while at the same time emphasizing the importance of the preparation of parents of infant candidates as well as the ongoing nurture of those baptized in infancy. The Roman Catholic response goes further in expressing some disquiet with the document's contrast between "infants" and "believers" instead of "infants" and "adults" since infants are considered members of the "believing community."[11] Besides further concerns over the definition of "sacrament" and "sacramentality" in the document as a whole, the Roman Catholic response focuses on the relation between original sin and infant Baptism.[12]

---

11. Thurian, *Churches Respond to BEM*, vol VI, 14.

12. Ibid., 12.

But this is of course precisely the question at issue: how can one say that an infant has somehow been delivered from original sin when it has had no opportunity to grow in the faith? On a practical level the virtual disappearance of the idea of a "Limbo" of the innocents who have not been baptized underlines this difficulty.

Two responses from churches in the Anglican tradition can help fill out the picture with regard to BEM on Baptism. The Episcopal Church quite clearly affirms the objectivity of baptismal grace by saying: "Baptism is given by God and is not dependent on our response in the same way, as the document's phrasing seems to suggest."[13] The Church of England, on the other hand, appreciates the balance represented by the Lima text's insistence on both gift and response. The Church of England response also highlights Baptism as the beginning of a process.[14]

It seems to me that BEM does signal an advance in answering the quandary that pastors like George Gorham were facing in the mid-nineteenth century and has only been exacerbated today. The final section of this essay will try to articulate a theological response to our quandary that also respects the church's continuous tradition.

Infant Baptism as a Gift of God

How then might it be possible to square the contemporary reality of large numbers of infants who are baptized but whose faith never becomes "operative" with the traditional Christian affirmation of the objective working of the sacraments (when no obstacle is put in their way)?[15] I propose that a way forward may be found in the sacramental theology of Louis-Marie Chauvet, a long time professor at the Institut Catholique of Paris who has written several significant books on sacraments. I will focus on two of them: *Symbol and Sacrament* (1987) and *The Sacraments* (1997).[16] A main objective of Chauvet's project is to speak of sacramental efficacy without recourse to the traditional metaphysical productionist mode, which is characteristic of much of medieval theology and especially Neo-Scholasticism. The problem with that mode of discourse was that it was

13. Thurian, *Churches Respond to BEM*, vol II, 59.

14. Thurian, *Churches Respond to BEM*, vol III, 34–35.

15. Council of Trent, *Decree on the Sacraments*, 1547, in Denzinger and Schönmetzer, *Enchiridion Symbolorum*, sec. 1606.

16. *Symbol and Sacrament*; *Sacraments*. His other major work has not been translated: *Du symbolique au symbole*.

encouraged by a Western philosophical tendency toward objectifying spiritual realities, thereby missing or at least undervaluing the dynamic nature of sacramental activity. As has been said many times, sacraments are better understood as verbs than as nouns. And so, Chauvet employs contemporary philosophy (Heidegger), linguistic theory (Benveniste, Ortigues), and psychoanalytic theory (Lacan) to try to find a useful way of speaking of sacramental efficacy. In the process Chauvet emphasizes the gift character of the sacraments by describing what he calls "the process of symbolic exchange."[17] For Chauvet the gift (God's self-communication) demands a return-gift which must be verified in day-to-day life. The response to God's self-gift in the Eucharist, for example, is symbolically represented by thanks and praise, but that thanks and praise needs to be activated in a person's life, for "Every gift received obligates."[18]

Chauvet goes on to offer the "middle way of Vatican II" as an alternative to the impasse created by an overly objective (productionist) approach to sacramental theology and one that overemphasizes the subjective dimension (as for example in Karl Barth). So, he insists that sacraments are both revealers and operators. They reveal a grace already present in the world and at the same time create the occasion of working out the response to that grace. In this way he explains the categories of "summit" and "source" that Vatican II's *Constitution on the Church* (#11) applies directly to the Eucharist. Chauvet spells out the implications of this approach:

> Christ cannot be alive if none claim to belong to him: his resurrection is inseparable from the witness people—first those who form the Church—give of him. Of course, it is not faith which makes God father or Jesus Lord. But the identity of God as Father or of Jesus as Christ and Lord would be reduced to nothing if none named it by confessing it and thus acknowledging themselves *at the same time* as children of God and disciples of Jesus. The language of faith reveals the identity of God as Father and our own identity as sons and daughters, brothers and sisters; and by revealing this identity makes effective the paternity of God, as well as our own filiation and condition as brothers and sisters.[19]

Chauvet is trying to show how faith is necessary for the operation of the sacraments in a way that acknowledges them as both preceding us

---

17. Chauvet, *Symbol and Sacrament*, 266ff. The question of the possibility of a real gift at all is a lively question in current philosophy and theology. See, e.g., Caputo and Scanlon, *God, the Gift, and Postmodernism*; Milbank, "Grace: The Midwinter Sacrifice."

18. Chauvet, *Symbol and Sacrament*, 267.

19. Ibid., 428. Emphasis in original.

and being engaged by us. He goes on to apply his principles to Baptism in particular; because Baptism is eschatological, it has to be realized in ethical practice.[20] Key here is his radical notion of grace:

> It seems to us that grace (baptismal grace in this case) is not a "something" to be received (even as a "seed"), but a *self-reception*: a receiving of oneself from God as son or daughter, and from others as brother or sister, the two aspects being symbolically distinct but indissolubly linked.[21]

Thus, for Chauvet, grace is inherently relational. I would suggest the analogy of a check. A check is a check—for whatever amount of money. It is certainly real, but it needs to be cashed if it is to be put to use. This solution is similar to Thomas Aquinas treatment of the medieval *topos* of the mouse who consumes the consecrated host. For Thomas, the host is clearly the body of Christ, but the mouse cannot eat sacramentally because it lacks faith. Thus the priority of the *res* (grace or point of the sacrament which is unity in and with Christ) is affirmed over the *res et sacramentum* which is the objective real presence of Christ in the consecrated species.[22]

Employing a complex social analysis of the post-modern situation (especially in France), Chauvet comes to the conclusion that there is often a disconnect between what the ministers of the church understand is happening in an act like Baptism and the preconceptions of those asking for the sacrament for their child. He opts for a gentle yet pastorally responsible way of helping those who come to request Baptism with "tribal" preconceptions to be invited to authentic Christian faith.[23] It seems to me that Chauvet's thinking represents a way forward through the impasse of merely understanding Baptism as regeneration objectively understood, one that takes into account the necessity of faith for Baptism.

Conclusion

The honoree of this volume, Louis Weil, comes to a conclusion that is similar to that of Chauvet while commenting on John Henry Newman and the integrity of (infant) Baptism:

---

20. Ibid., 440.
21. Ibid., 442. Emphasis in original.
22. See Thomas Aquinas, *Summa Theologiae* III.Q80.a1.
23. Chauvet, *Sacraments*, 190–99.

> Indiscriminate Baptism of infants continues in our own day to raise this question because it is either an empty form, or else, if it is the instrument of grace of regeneration, it is a gift of grace conferred upon conditions which should affect the life-style of the whole family in living their baptismal promises.[24]

Weil goes on to say compellingly:

> Mature membership in the Body of Christ requires a true personal commitment. The rite of Baptism must not be isolated from the implications of such mature participation in the Church's life. It is not a brief ritual experience but rather an ongoing growth into Christ. The work of the Holy Spirit is not focused in a magic moment but is rather the gradual and progressive work of transformation.[25]

For his contemporaries, George Gorham represented a denial of traditional sacramental theology and a significant challenge to the notion of baptismal regeneration. But the basic issues his case raised, both in terms of the relation between church and state, and in terms of baptizing infants in an increasingly de-Christianized world, are matters in which churches across the Christian spectrum do well to heed.

24. Weil, *Sacraments and Liturgy*, 46–47.
25. Ibid., 69–70.

Bibliography

Canon Law Society of America. *Code of Canon Law: New English Translation (=CIC).* Latin-English ed. Washington, DC: Canon Law Society of America, 1999.

Caputo, John D., and Michael J. Scanlon, editors. *God, the Gift, and Postmodernism.* Bloomington, IN: Indiana University Press, 1999.

Chauvet, Louis-Marie. *The Sacraments: The Word of God at the Mercy of the Body.* Collegeville, MN: Liturgical, 2001.

————. *Du symbolique au symbole: Essai sur les sacrements.* Paris: Du Cerf, 1979.

————. *Symbol and Sacrament: A Sacramental Reinterpretation of Christian Existence.* Collegeville, MN: Liturgical, 1993.

Denzinger, Heinrich, and Adolf Schönmetzer, editors. *Enchiridion Symbolorum: Definitionum et declarationum de rebus fidei et morum.* New York: Herder, 1965.

Finn, T. M. *Early Christian Baptism and the Catechumenate: Italy, North Africa, and Egypt.* Message of the Fathers 6. Collegeville, MN: Liturgical, 1992.

Johnson, Maxwell E. *The Rites of Christian Initiation: Their Evolution and Interpretation.* Collegeville, MN: Liturgical, 2007.

Kertzer, David. *The Kidnapping of Edgardo Mortara.* New York: Knopf, 1997.

Milbank, John. "Grace: The Midwinter Sacrifice." In *Being Reconciled: Ontology and Pardon,* 138–61. London: Routledge, 2003.

Nias, J. C. S. *Gorham and the Bishop of Exeter.* London: SPCK, 1951.

Thurian, Max, editor. *Churches Respond to BEM.* 6 vols. Faith and Order Paper. Geneva: World Council of Churches, 1986.

United States Catholic Conference. *Catechism of the Catholic Church (=CCC).* Washington, DC: United States Catholic Conference of Catholic Bishops, 1994.

Weil, Louis. *Sacraments and Liturgy: The Outward Signs: A Study in Liturgical Mentality.* Oxford: Blackwell, 1983.

Wilberforce, Robert Isaac. *The Doctrine of Holy Baptism: With Remarks on the Rev. W. Goode's "Effects of Infant Baptism."* London: Murray, 1849.

World Council of Churches. *Baptism, Eucharist and Ministry.* Faith and Order Paper 111. Geneva,: World Council of Churches, 1982.

10

A Primatial Grace for a Baptismal Church

Jeffrey Gros, FSC

Louis Weil notes that: "The issue of authority and the various ways in which it is exercised in the diverse Christian traditions is at the heart of some of the most difficult ecumenical questions," adding his own tradition's unique gift in contributing to this thorny question:

> The stance of the Anglican Communion with regard to the papacy is distinct from other non-Roman churches of the West—the so-called "Churches of the Reformation"—because of the particular character of the English Reformation. The Church of England maintained the episcopal polity of Western Catholicism, and so it is not surprising to find that Anglican writers from the 16th century onward did not call for the abolition of the papacy but rather for its reform. In particular, for those formed within the Anglo-Catholic tradition of Anglicanism, the hope for eventual reunion with Rome remained even while alienation among the various Christian traditions dominated the religious atmosphere.[1]

The heritage of authority and church order discussions in the ecumenical tradition has been a particular contribution of the Anglican Communion since the 1888 Chicago-Lambeth Quadrilateral.[2] Weil has given special attention to this theme, especially since the invitation of John Paul II for a "patient and fraternal dialogue" on the papacy and its exercise in the 1995

---

1. Weil, "Pilgrimage of Hope," 399. See also his "Rome and Canterbury—Steps Toward Reconciliation through the Sharing of Gifts."

2. See Gros, "The Chicago-Lambeth Quadrilateral and the USA Faith and Order Movement."

encyclical *Ut unum sint*.[3] The many ironies in the 2005 funeral of Pope John Paul II and inauguration of his successor, Joseph Ratzinger, Pope Benedict XVI, are not lost on the attentive ecumenist. Indeed, such an ecumenical openness on the part of the Vatican and outpouring on the part of fellow Christians would have been unimaginable a short quarter century before at the last papal transition, much less when Louis Weil entered seminary in 1958. The presumptive successor to Henry VIII had to postpone a wedding to attend the papal funeral. The new pope spent his first day in office in conversation with his ecumenical guests, including Orthodox Metropolitan John Zizioulas of Pergamum, longtime colleague and the voice who had introduced the theme of universal ministry into the World Council discussions in 1993,[4] and Archbishop Rowan Williams, possibly the scholar most knowledgeable of the Ratzinger corpus among the illustrious guests.

This is a new day none of us who were alive even a few decades ago could imagine in the reception of relations among all baptized Christians, the Bishop of Rome among us. "The atmosphere and climate in which the issue is discussed have been transformed," as Cardinal Walter Kasper notes.[5] These gifts of new relations have been backed up by a depth of pastoral and theological research, personal interchange, and indeed changes in church order, unimaginable before the modern ecumenical movement.

As we look toward the horizon of full communion among all the baptized, the role of the episcopacy and primacy is not at the center of the hierarchy of truths that need to be resolved, but they must be addressed. We are grateful to Louis Weil, other scholars, and the formal dialogues that help us address these challenges responsibly:

> For centuries the papal ministry has not ceased to cause uneasiness and even bewilderment among Christians. As much as it is by its very nature a ministry of unity, it has in fact equally been a stumbling block and a reason for several divisions and insurmountable tension between churches and confessions—even within the ranks of the Roman Catholic Church.[6]

---

3. John Paul II, "Ut unum sint," 96. For an early review of the responses see Pontifical Council for Promoting Christian Unity, "Petrine Ministry."

4. Zizioulas, "The Church as Communion," 103–11. For his more developed positions see "Recent Discussions on Primacy in Orthodox Theology," and "Future Exercise of Papal Ministry."

5. Kasper, "Petrine Ministry," 213.

6. Nørgaard-Højen, "Introduction," 1.

We have much for which to be grateful, already, in these discussions. This essay will survey three themes related to this issue: the papacy in the formal dialogues; the contribution of particular scholars on some of these themes; and some reflections on a way forward.

The question of authority and the role of the papacy carry a particular fascination in Christian piety and the imagination of the human community. There is a history of the stories around this particular office in the Western churches that continue to evolve, as much influenced by ecclesial location, personality and, in our present age, media images, as any theological claims. Once, the majority of Christians undoubtedly did not know who the current bishop in Rome (or even their own local bishop) was, but we are in a time when a great portion of the human family knows the image, if not the name of the pope. Many have come to know their own church leaders in the context of ecumenical events involving this global visitor.

The original invitation in Pope John Paul II's 1995 encyclical notes two areas for discussion of the papacy: its exercise to better serve the unity of the church, without prejudice to Catholic claims and prior to resolution of the theological issues of authority,[7] and "the Magisterium of the Church, entrusted to the Pope and the Bishops in communion with him, understood as a responsibility and an authority exercised in the name of Christ for teaching and safeguarding the faith."[8] The invitation suggests two corresponding but distinct agendas: ecumenical reform of present papal structures, and theological resolution of authority issues.

Contribution of the Dialogues

A number of dialogues have treated the theology and exercise of authority in episcopacy and particularly in the papal office.[9] We will review Anglican, Lutheran, and Orthodox contributions.

Anglican

In both practice and theology, the Anglican–Roman Catholic International Commission (ARCIC) has made substantive contributions and Weil has

7. John Paul II, "Ut unum sint," 94–97.

8. Ibid., 79:4.

9. See Le Bruyns, "The Papacy as Ecumenical Challenge"; Kasper, *Harvesting the Fruits*, 125–58; Roberson, "The Papacy in Ecumenical Discussion Today."

suggested even more mutual learnings, as we begin to live together more closely as worldwide communions. Weil writes:

> One particular fruit of the Anglican-Roman Catholic dialogue has been a growing awareness of what we might call "a reciprocity" between the two traditions with regard to the ways in which authority is exercised.

The two models are quite different: in the Roman Catholic Church, there is a high level of centralized authority in the papal office and thus in the governance of the Church by an extensive range of Vatican officials whose ministry it is to regulate all aspects of the Church's life. It is important to note, however, that this high level of centralization has not been constant. To a great extent, the current level of centralization begins from the pontificate of Pope Pius IX, who to a great degree was reacting to the intense political and social instability of the mid-nineteenth century in Europe. The Church and the office of the pope became a bulwark against the sometimes chaotic developments in social structures at that time. The pope came to represent in the minds of many people a focus of stability when traditional structures, such as monarchy, for example, were collapsing.

> Within the Anglican Communion, on the other hand, there developed what we might call a "diffused model of authority." Synodical government is characteristic of the Anglican tradition at all levels of the Church's life, the deanery, the diocese, the province, and the national Church. At the international level, the Anglican Communion is a fellowship of self-governing national provinces, a commonwealth of churches without a central constitution, but which share a common faith and order. Each province is autonomous in the ordering of its own life. On the whole this model served the Communion well since the time when the first Lambeth Conference was summoned in 1888.[10]

Both the exercise of papal leadership, and the theological understanding of its role in the magisterium, are evolving in Catholicism; the challenges of a diffused authority and weakened bonds of communion among Anglicans and other churches are becoming clearer in a globalized, interdependent world.

Thus, as Weil points out, Anglicans have been most disposed to include the "great Latin Church of the West" in dialogue in search of "fulfillment of the Divine purpose in any scheme of reunion," since the 1908

---

10. Weil, "Pilgrimage of Hope," 400–401.

Lambeth Conference.[11] The three texts of ARCIC I and II, culminating in *The Gift of Authority*, clear away misunderstandings and make concrete proposals for both theological agreement and internal renewal in both communions that will accelerate common witness, deepening bonds of communion and move forward the process toward full ecclesial communion.[12] These texts are especially important in providing consensus on baptismal ministry, in which ordained ministry and authority are situated, balancing primacy with synodality in the church's teaching and governing roles, and developing specific recommendations and strategies for change along the pilgrim road toward full communion.

While not under consideration here, it should be noted that *Mary: Grace and Hope in Christ*[13] is a further expansion of the authority discussion as it touches on the Marian dogmas, and that *Life in Christ: Morals, Communion and the Church*[14] provides significant background for current authority discussions as they touch on human sexuality.

Lutheran

Lutherans have proved to be a robust conversation partner with Roman Catholics for several reasons: they have similar theological methodologies and interests, a corpus of more direct confrontational literature from the sixteenth century exists, for "underneath [Luther's] polemic something like a fundamental openness for papal ministry" persisted,[15] and outside of Scandinavia, Lutherans gave up the historic episcopate and a sense of primacy. The United States Lutheran–Roman Catholic dialogue has done pioneering work in taking up the theme of Petrine ministry, and providing contributions on which other dialogues have been able to build. The

11. Quoting Davidson, *The Six Lambeth Conferences, 1867–1920*, 422.

12. Anglican/Roman Catholic International Commission, "Authority in the Church I"; "Elucidation (1981) [On Authority in the Church I]"; "Authority in the Church II"; "The Gift of Authority (Authority in the Church III)."

13. Anglican/Roman Catholic International Commission, "Mary: Grace and Hope in Christ," and supporting essays Butler, "The Immaculate Conception: Why Was It Defined as a Dogma?"; Morerod, "The Question of the Authority of the Recent Marian Dogmas."

14. Anglican/Roman Catholic International Commission, "Life in Christ: Morals, Communion and the Church."

15. Meyer, "How Can the Petrine Ministry Be a Service to the Unity of the Universal Church?," 229.

1973 text on papal primacy[16] was followed by a 1978 proposal on *Teaching Authority and Infallibility*.[17] Its background biblical work, *Peter in the New Testament*, has been a resource for many subsequent dialogues on the theme.[18] Casting the questions of doctrinal teaching, so important after Vatican I's formulations on infallibility and jurisdiction, into categories of hope rather than certitude is particularly promising.

After the 1999 Lutheran World Federation and Catholic Church *Joint Declaration on the Doctrine of Justification*[19] the question of primacy and a pastoral ministry for the universal church had to be taken up again, this time in the context of dialogue on the congregations and dioceses/synods and the structures and ministry which serve them.[20] As modest as the treatment of the Petrine Ministry is in this extensive text, the background essays are essential for understanding Lutheran approaches to the theology and future exercise of the papal service.[21]

Orthodox

Orthodox–Roman Catholic conversations on this subject are complicated by a millennium of common history of full communion with different interpretations of the Roman Patriarchate, alien forms of theological reflection and ecclesial practice not shared by churches of East and West, and the dislocations and remerging conflicts in Eastern Europe following the 1989 fall of Marxism. Since then, the international dialogue has had a difficult time functioning, and has had to address the challenge of Eastern

---

16. U.S. Lutheran-Catholic Dialogue, "Differing Attitudes Toward Papal Primacy," see also Bilateral Working Group of the German National Bishops' Conference and Church Leadership of the United Evangelical Lutheran Church of Germany, *Communio Sanctorum: The Church as the Communion of Saints*, 153–200.

17. Empie, Murphy, and Burgess, *Teaching Authority & Infallibility in the Church*.

18. Brown, Donfried, and Reumann, *Peter in the New Testament*.

19. Lutheran World Federation and Roman Catholic Church, "Joint Declaration on the Doctrine of Justification."

20. U.S. Lutheran-Catholic Dialogue, "The Church as Koinonia of Salvation: Its Structures and Ministries." For a discussion of the importance of the *Joint Declaration* to this theme see Birmelé, "Does the Joint Declaration on the Doctrine of Justification Have Any Relevance to the Discussion of Papal Ministry?" 251ff.

21. Lee and Gros, *The Church as Koinonia of Salvation*, 114–25, and supporting essays Ickert, "Recent Lutheran Reflections on Universal Ministry"; Granfield, "The Universality and Particularity of the Catholic Church." For other Lutheran essays touching this theme see those in Puglisi, *How Can the Petrine Ministry Be a Service to Unity?*

churches in communion with Rome.[22] It produced a text touching on this issue that made some of the Orthodox churches unable to participate.[23]

Because of the international tensions among the Orthodox, and between the Orthodox and their ecumenical partners, it has been important to find alternate ways to address the question raised by Pope John Paul in his call for dialogue on papal reform. In order to do this, Cardinal Walter Kasper invited representative Orthodox scholars to meet informally, but with sanction of their bishops, to review the issue.

While the dialogue in the United States has been more tranquil, it defers to the international dialogue.[24] Nonetheless, it produced some encouraging texts and has developed an important rapport. Responses to the international statements on ecclesiology touching on primacy and uniatism make important contributions.[25] It has also made its own contribution on the issue of *Conciliarity and Primacy in the Church*.[26]

This conversation is important for all of the churches, because it begins the process of review and rereception of the unilateral developments in Roman Catholic understandings and practice of the papal primacy in the period after the schism of 1054.[27] The product of this conversation, while carrying no official status, will be a resource for all the churches as they gradually rebuild communion, including communion with the bishop of Rome, in that process.

---

22. Joint International Commission for the Theological Dialogue between the Roman Catholic Church and the Orthodox Church, "Uniatism,"

23. Joint International Commission for the Theological Dialogue between the Roman Catholic Church and the Orthodox Church, "Ecclesiological and Canonical Consequences of the Sacramental Nature of the Church."

24. North American Orthodox-Catholic Theological Consultation, "Steps Towards a Reunited Church: A Sketch of an Orthodox-Catholic Vision for the Future."

25. North American Orthodox-Catholic Theological Consultation, "A Common Response to the Joint International Commission for the Theological Dialogue between the Roman Catholic Church and the Orthodox Church Regarding the Ravenna Document: 'Ecclesiological and Canonical Consequences of the Sacramental Nature of the Church: Ecclesial Communion, Conciliarity and Authority'"; North American Orthodox-Catholic Theological Consultation, "A Response of the Orthodox/Roman Catholic Consultation in the United States to the Joint International Commission for Theological Dialogue between the Orthodox Church and the Roman Catholic Church Regarding the Balamand Document (Dated June 23, 1993) 'Uniatism, Method of Union of the Past, and the Present Search for Full Communion.'"

26. North American Orthodox-Catholic Theological Consultation, "An Agreed Statement on Conciliarity and Primacy in the Church."

27. Kasper, *The Petrine Ministry.*

These dialogues, additional official responses to the encyclical, and the introduction of a discussion of the universal ministry in the ecclesiology work of the Faith and Order movement of the World Council of Churches,[28] have created the foundation of a whole new phase of ecumenical development.

Contribution of Scholars

It is important to move beyond the official dialogues and the formal responses of the churches because deeper and more creative proposals can be made by scholars from traditions that would not otherwise participate. These conversations can contribute to the dialogue because changing issues, ethos, and debates within our churches are more easily addressed by scholarly flexibility than within official dialogues, as Weil notes.

We will look at two approaches to our theme: an evangelical study of the authority and epistemological issue, and the development of the theme of dialogue in Roman Catholic practice. Among a variety of informal conversations[29] there are two volumes of essays, *Petrine Ministry and the Unity of the Church* and *How Can the Petrine Ministry be a Service to the Unity of the Universal Church?*, that bring together important reflections from conferences on the theme held in Rome.[30]

Evangelical Conversations

Many of the evangelical, pentecostal, or holiness churches have not responded because of their lack of participation in the ecumenical movement and ecclesial aversion to ecclesiastical hierarchy, even when they may have good collaborative relationships with the Catholic Church. The Faith and Order Commission of the National Council of Churches in the USA provided a context where these churches were able to give a response

---

28. World Council of Churches, *The Nature and Mission of the Church.*

29. Braaten and Jenson, *Church Unity and the Papal Office*; Quinn, *The Reform of the Papacy*; Groupe des Dombes, "One Teacher"; Clifford, *For the Communion of the Churches*, 95–148; Dionne, *The Papacy and the Church*; Garuti, *The Primacy of the Bishop of Rome and Ecumenical Dialogue*; Tillard, *The Bishop of Rome.*

30. Puglisi, *Petrine Ministry and the Unity of the Church*; *How Can the Petrine Ministry Be a Service to Unity?*

to the 1995 encyclical, including representatives who would not otherwise participate in this dialogue on the papacy.[31]

Mark Powell, a scholar from the Churches of Christ, a conservative branch of the Stone/Campbell movement, has an important discussion of infallibility. The questions of certainty are central to the ecumenical discussion of authority, to common developments in nineteenth-century Catholicism in the formulations of Vatican I and in American evangelicalism and fundamentalism, and they are widely discussed today in theoretical considerations of religious epistemology in a post-modern philosophical and theological context.[32]

Powell's thesis is that, like overly narrow versions of biblical infallibility and literalism, epistemological approaches to papal primacy have to be revisited using more historically conditioned, community connected understandings of symbolic language, similar to those developed by Avery Dulles and William Abraham, to articulate the basis of Christian knowledge and authority in the modern world. In his study, papal infallibility and four interpretations of it are analyzed. This study, by a scholar with no commitments to episcopacy, primacy, or conciliar magisterium and from a church with a radical congregational ecclesiology and an aversion to critical scholarship is a promising sign of how a common epistemological problem can provide a unitive agenda in ecumenical scholarship.

The Theme of Dialogue

Weil's characterization, above, of Roman Catholicism on the eve of the First Vatican Council as monarchial and centralized will be recognized by any Catholic as accurate and even generous. Unfortunately, many would say that this style has not wholly disappeared, though there have been dramatic developments in theology, practice and in the ability to learn from history and from ecumenical partners.

Pope Paul VI began his papacy with a call for dialogue in his encyclical *Ecclesiam suam*, a vision which has energized Catholics ever since.[33] Bradford Hinze has done an extensive, if selective study of the development of dialogue since the Council.[34] It is important for Catholic and

31. Faith and Order Commission of the National Council of Churches in the USA, "Response to 'Petrine Ministry: A Working Paper.'"

32. Powell, *Papal Infallibility*.

33. Paul VI, "Ecclesiam suam"

34. Hinze, *Practices of Dialogue in the Roman Catholic Church.*

ecumenical partners to keep these developments in mind as they face the question of the future exercise of the papal office, ecumenically and within the Catholic communion.

Some Suggestions for the Ecumenical Imagination

From the standpoint of this author as a Roman Catholic, we can be grateful for Weil's contribution and the dialogues and authors reviewed here. The personal leadership of those primates like Frank Griswold, John Paul II, and a line of twentieth- and twenty-first-century archbishops of Canterbury provide initiatives, proposals, and experiences that are gifts on our reconciling journey. An aesthetic view that envisions the whole network of relations, embedded in our baptismal identification with Christ and his church, on the one hand; and with the global calling to be a Christian mission for the whole world, can help us keep the appropriate faith horizon that enables us to imagine new ways of seeing a worldwide communion in service of mission. I do not feel that we could do better than receive these initiatives into the lives of our churches.

What Weil says of Baptism can equally be said of the witness of primacy in service of communion:

> I believe that when our sacramental acts are ritually minimized, eventually this diminished ritual undermines the church's understanding of the sacramental act itself. This is true, I believe, whatever may be the initial causes that led to the erosion of the original ritual model. What results is not only ritual change, but eventually a subversion of meaning.[35]

Episcopacy, and primacy within it, must demonstrate its gift to the whole by its transparency to Christ's sacramental service to the unity of the churches for the transformation of the world. If universal Petrine ministry is minimized by too much reliance on control and juridical models, which has too long been characteristic of the exercise of the Roman primacy in the second millennium, it not only erodes the transparence of its ritual and sacramental witness, but it also subverts its credible service in a postmodern culture of choice.

In line with Weil's invitation to see these "gift exchanges" together, I will make three reflections that may contribute to our journey, 1) the need for global signification of our catholicity, 2) structural gifts that can be

---

35. Weil, "Baptism as the Model for a Sacramental Aesthetic," 266.

shared on the road to full communion, and 3) strategies for reception of the monumental contributions reviewed here.

Global Signification of Catholicity

As for any element in our church life, from Baptism to papacy, "The issue here is not validity; it is signification."[36] If the papacy is to be reformed, the churches need first to be reformed to be open to a signification of the universal, interdependence of the global community, rooted in Baptism, the global mission flowing from our eschatological calling. As the Lutheran dialogue acknowledges: the "need for symbols and centers of unity," able "to give concrete expression to our concern for the unity of the whole empirical church."[37]

It is only when we all can see our global calling and solidarity that we can understand the role of a pastor, above the level of our congregation signifying oversight and interdependence. Only when we reimage the significance of the bishop in the local church, will primacy among local churches, and a primacy for a global church touch our imaginations. The funeral of Pope John Paul II, the installation of Pope Benedict XVI, the 1986 and 2002 Assisi gatherings of global religious leaders around the call to prayer for peace can help the Christian and religious imagination move beyond juridical, validity models of primacy to a personal, global ministry that signifies that solidarity which the world demands.

Christian faith needs to begin to look to the possibilities that all of God's people can bring to the role of a personal, primatial ministry of service to the world. It is within this vision of baptismal service and the solidarity of the human family that we can see the mission of all Christians. We can begin to take these building blocks—with all of the accretions they have accumulated over the centuries—and reshape them into that church of service for which Christ prayed. It is within this vision of the needs of the world, and all Christians within it, that the papacy can be rereceived, reconceptualized and reformed.

---

36. Ibid., 269.

37. U.S. Lutheran-Catholic Dialogue, "Differing Attitudes toward Papal Primacy," 32. See also Wainwright, "Petrine Ministry."

Structural Gifts

We have to be free enough to use our imagination in revisioning a common future drawing on all of the riches we have developed in our centuries of separation. In a recent Methodist–Roman Catholic dialogue, it was suggested we can learn together from the primacy and global vision of John Wesley. We might also learn from the episcopal itineracy of early American Methodism and today's polity, in which bishops are evaluated and redeployed every four to eight years to places where they can best serve the oversight of the churches. If Roman Catholics were to consider this model, including itinerating the person holding the office at Rome, it might enhance the mission and accountability of the church and undercut the careerism that sometimes taints the pastoral focus of episcopal ministry. Although neither of these suggestions emerged in the final text,[38] the Wesley model has been spelled out elsewhere.[39] Indeed, small steps like those proposed in *Gift of Authority*—the ecumenical encounters in papal trips and visits of delegations of Christians from a variety of churches to Rome to understand the inner workings of Catholic leadership as well as to visit the person of the current pope—can enable us to envisage together a common, transformed future.[40]

Offices and committees of the Roman Curia, and those of the governing entities of all of our churches, can invite one another to participate as advisors, prayer support and communicators in the process that make decisions and drafts teaching documents in our churches.[41] The texts of the popes and of the Roman Curia would be immeasurably enhanced, both in their quality and reception, by input from ecumenical colleagues who share the same goal of full communion, and understand how texts might be misinterpreted outside of the curial culture.

The personal styles of both Popes John XXIII and John Paul II, although at times internally polarizing, have witnessed to ecumenical partners the potential for Catholicism to develop, to find a new role in the world, and to change an office with a venerable and polemical history.

---

38. United Methodist-Catholic Dialogue (United States), "Through Divine Love: The Church in Each Place and All Places (Report of Round VI)."

39. Wainwright, "Petrine Ministry," 296.

40. See, for example, Gros, "Episcopal–Roman Catholic Bishops Pilgrimage Witnesses Commitment and Realism," 9–11.

41. The Roman Synods and some episcopal conferences have ecumenical participant/observers, for example, Sepúlveda, "The Fifth General Conference of the Bishops of Latin America and the Caribbean," 9–11.

Pope John Paul II demonstrated a "peripatetic primacy," with consequences in both ecumenical and conservative evangelical perceptions alike.[42]

Strategies for Reception

A key element in the reformulation of the papacy, and all of the churches grounded in the baptismal unity given in Christ, is reception. One Lutheran formulates the issue as it worked itself out in the sixteenth century:

> Reception describes the extent and manner of later generations' use and interpretation of the thought or writing of a figure of influence [and in this case of an institution]. When scholars stake out the parameters for studying the influence of an author and his or her work, they enter into a conversation, a conversation that goes back centuries . . .[43]

Of course, the rereception of the papacy for a united church entails first receiving the ecumenical imperative as central to the gospel.[44] This implies the reception of the Roman Catholic Church as a legitimate ecumenical partner on its own terms,[45] reception of the visible unity of the church and the goal of full communion as the biblical and eschatological foundation for our work,[46] and a fundamental openness of the Roman Catholic Church itself to dialogue and transformation as central to its identity in Christ.[47] Michael Root has suggested that the rereception of papacy will need to involve a common narrative including the "specific experience" of Anglican, Lutheran and other Christians with the papacy since separation.[48]

Reception is a gift of the Holy Spirit. If the seeds of unity are planted in Baptism, and the longing for full visible unity in a global communion of faith, sacramental life and witness are integral to Christian nurture; then the pioneering efforts of Louis Weil to enliven our baptismal consciousness, nurture our zeal for unity, and propose how to find an appropriate primacy to serve our unity and mission, are indeed a great blessing for the church on its pilgrim way, for which we can all be grateful.

42. Wainwright, "Petrine Ministry," 307.

43. Kolb, *Bound Choice, Election, and Wittenberg Theological Method*, 272.

44. Rusch, *Ecumenical Reception*.

45. Gros, "Reception and Roman Catholicism for the 1990s."

46. Gros, "The Requirements and Challenges of Full Communion: A Multilateral Evaluation?"

47. Hinze, *Practices of Dialogue in the Roman Catholic Church*.

48. Root, "Vatican I and the Development of Doctrine," 139.

Bibliography

Anglican/Roman Catholic International Commission. "Authority in the Church I," January 19, 1977. http://www.prounione.urbe.it/dia-int/arcic/doc/e_arcic_authority1.html.

———. "Authority in the Church II," 1981. http://www.prounione.urbe.it/dia-int/arcic/doc/e_arcic_authority2.html.

———. "Elucidation (1981) [On Authority in the Church I]," 1981. http://www.prounione.urbe.it/dia-int/arcic/doc/e_arcic_elucid_auth.html.

———. "The Gift of Authority (Authority in the Church III)," September 3, 1998. http://www.prounione.urbe.it/dia-int/arcic/doc/e_arcicII_05.html.

———. "Life in Christ: Morals, Communion and the Church," 1994. http://www.prounione.urbe.it/dia-int/arcic/doc/e_arcicII_morals.html.

———. "Mary: Grace and Hope in Christ," 2004. http://www.prounione.urbe.it/dia-int/arcic/doc/e_arcic_mary.html.

Bilateral Working Group of the German National Bishops' Conference, and Church Leadership of the United Evangelical Lutheran Church of Germany. *Communio Sanctorum: The Church as the Communion of Saints*. Collegeville, MN: Liturgical, 2004.

Birmelé, André. "Does the Joint Declaration on the Doctrine of Justification Have Any Relevance to the Discussion of Papal Ministry?" In *How Can the Petrine Ministry Be a Service to the Unity of the Universal Church?*, edited by James F. Puglisi, 169–78. Grand Rapids: Eerdmans, 2010.

Braaten, Carl E, and Robert W Jenson, editors. *Church Unity and the Papal Office: An Ecumenical Dialogue on John Paul II's Encyclical Ut Unum Sint (That All May Be One)*. Grand Rapids: Eerdmans, 2001.

Brodd, Sven-Erik. "Papal Ministry in a Communication Ecclesiology: A Search for Some Possible Themes." In *How Can the Petrine Ministry Be a Service to the Unity of the Universal Church?*, edited by James F. Puglisi, 155–68. Grand Rapids: Eerdmans, 2010.

Brown, Raymond E., Karl P. Donfried, and John Reumann, editors. *Peter in the New Testament*. Minneapolis, MN: Augsburg, 1973.

Le Bruyns, Clint Charles. "The Papacy as Ecumenical Challenge: Contemporary Anglican and Protestant Perspectives on the Petrine Ministry." DTh thesis, Stellenbosch University, 2004. https://scholar.sun.ac.za/handle/10019.1/1374.

Butler, Sara. "The Immaculate Conception: Why Was It Defined as a Dogma?" In *Studying Mary: Reflections on the Virgin Mary in Anglican and Roman Catholic Theology and Devotion*, edited by Nicholas Sagovsky and Adelbert Denaux, 147–63. London: T. & T. Clark, 2007.

Chadwick, Owen. *A History of the Popes, 1830–1914*. The Oxford History of the Christian Church. Oxford: Oxford: Oxford University Press, 1998.

Clifford, Catherine E., editor. *For the Communion of the Churches: The Contribution of the Groupe Des Dombes*. Grand Rapids: Eerdmans, 2010.

Costigan, Richard F. *The Consensus of the Church and Papal Infallibility: A Study in the Background of Vatican I*. Washington, DC: Catholic University of America Press, 2005.

Davidson, Randall Thomas. *The Six Lambeth Conferences, 1867–1920*. London: SPCK, 1929.

Dionne, J. Robert. *The Papacy and the Church: A Study of Praxis and Reception in Ecumenical Perspective.* New York: Philosophical Library, 1987.

Empie, Paul C., T. Austin Murphy, and Joseph A Burgess, editors. *Teaching Authority & Infallibility in the Church.* Lutherans and Catholics in Dialogue 6. Minneapolis, MN: Augsburg, 1980.

Faith and Order Commission of the National Council of Churches in the USA. "Response to 'Petrine Ministry: A Working Paper," May 23, 2003. http://www.ncccusa.org/news/petrineresponse.html.

Garuti, Adriano. *The Primacy of the Bishop of Rome and Ecumenical Dialogue.* San Francisco: Ignatius, 2004.

Gassmann, Günther. "Protestant Reaction to the Post-Reformation Development of Papal Authority." In *How Can the Petrine Ministry Be a Service to the Unity of the Universal Church?*, edited by James F. Puglisi, 81–97. Grand Rapids: Eerdmans, 2010.

Granfield, Patrick. "The Universality and Particularity of the Catholic Church." In *The Church as Koinonia of Salvation: Its Structures and Ministries*, edited by Randall R. Lee and Jeffrey Gros, 267–86. Lutherans and Catholics in Dialogue 10. Washington, DC: United States Conference of Catholic Bishops, 2005.

Gros, Jeffrey. "The Chicago-Lambeth Quadrilateral and the USA Faith and Order Movement." *Anglican Theological Review* 10 (1988) 195–212.

———. "Episcopal–Roman Catholic Bishops Pilgrimage Witnesses Commitment and Realism." *Ecumenical Trends* 24.1 (January 1995) 1, 3–14.

———. "Reception and Roman Catholicism for the 1990's." *One in Christ* 31.4 (1995) 295–328.

———. "The Requirements and Challenges of Full Communion: A Multilateral Evaluation?" *Journal of Ecumenical Studies* 42 (2007) 217–42.

Groupe des Dombes. *"One Teacher": Doctrinal Authority in the Church.* Grand Rapids: Eerdmans, 2010.

Hinze, Bradford E. *Practices of Dialogue in the Roman Catholic Church: Aims and Obstacles, Lessons and Laments.* New York: Continuum, 2006.

Houvinen, Eero. "A Ministry of Unity in the Context of Conciliarity and Synodality." In *How Can the Petrine Ministry Be a Service to the Unity of the Universal Church?*, edited by James F. Puglisi, 269–83. Grand Rapids: Eerdmans, 2010.

Ickert, Scott. "Recent Lutheran Reflections on Universal Ministry." In *The Church as Koinonia of Salvation: Its Structures and Ministries*, edited by Randall R Lee and Jeffrey Gros, 247–66. Lutherans and Catholics in Dialogue 10. Washington, DC: United States Conference of Catholic Bishops, 2005.

John Paul II. "Ut unum sint," May 25, 1995. http://www.vatican.va/holy_father/john_paul_ii/encyclicals/documents/hf_jp-ii_enc_25051995_ut-unum-sint_en.html.

Joint International Commission for the Theological Dialogue between the Roman Catholic Church and the Orthodox Church. "Ecclesiological and Canonical Consequences of the Sacramental Nature of the Church," October 15, 2007. http://www.prounione.urbe.it/dia-int/o-rc/doc/e_o-rc_ravenna.html.

———. "Uniatism, Method of Union of the Past, and the Present Search for Full Communion," June 23, 1993. http://www.prounione.urbe.it/dia-int/o-rc/doc/e_o-rc_07_balamand_eng.html.

Kasper, Walter. *Harvesting the Fruits: Aspects of Christian Faith in Ecumenical Dialogue.* London: Continuum, 2009.

———. "Introductory Considerations in the Ecumenical Dialogue on the Petrine Ministry from a Catholic Viewpoint." In *How Can the Petrine Ministry Be a Service to the Unity of the Universal Church?*, edited by James F. Puglisi, 169–78. Grand Rapids: Eerdmans, 2010.

———, editor. *The Petrine Ministry: Catholics and Orthodox in Dialogue*. New York: Newman, 2005.

Kolb, Robert. *Bound Choice, Election, and Wittenberg Theological Method: From Martin Luther to the Formula of Concord*. Grand Rapids: Eerdmans, 2005.

Lee, Randall R, and Jeffrey Gros, editors. *The Church as Koinonia of Salvation: Its Structures and Ministries*. Lutherans and Catholics in Dialogue 10. Washington, DC: United States Conference of Catholic Bishops, 2005.

Löning, Peter. "Universal *Episkopē* and Papal Ministry: A Critical Overview of Responses to *Ut Unum Sint*." In *How Can the Petrine Ministry Be a Service to the Unity of the Universal Church?*, edited by James F. Puglisi, 237–50. Grand Rapids: Eerdmans, 2010.

Lutheran World Federation, and Roman Catholic Church. "Joint Declaration on the Doctrine of Justification," October 31, 1999. http://www.vatican.va/roman_curia/pontifical_councils/chrstuni/documents/rc_pc_chrstuni_doc_31101999_cath-luth-joint-declaration_en.html.

Meyer, Harding. "Papal Primacy—A Possible Subject of Lutheran Theology?" In *How Can the Petrine Ministry Be a Service to the Unity of the Universal Church?*, edited by James F. Puglisi. Grand Rapids: Eerdmans, 2010.

———. "Towards a Common Lutheran/Roman Catholic Understanding of Papal Ministry." In *How Can the Petrine Ministry Be a Service to the Unity of the Universal Church?*, edited by James F. Puglisi, 335–54. Grand Rapids: Eerdmans, 2010.

Morerod, Charles. "The Question of the Authority of the Recent Marian Dogmas." In *Studying Mary: Reflections on the Virgin Mary in Anglican and Roman Catholic Theology and Devotion*, edited by Nicholas Sagovsky and Adelbert Denaux, 202–15. London: T. & T. Clark, 2007.

Nørgaard-Højen, Peder, "Introduction" In *How Can the Petrine Ministry Be a Service to the Unity of the Universal Church?* edited by James F. Puglisi, 1–10. Grand Rapids: Eerdmans, 2010.

———. "Is Papal Infallibility Compatible with Ecclesial Indefectibility?" In *How Can the Petrine Ministry Be a Service to the Unity of the Universal Church?*, edited by James F. Puglisi, 194–211. Grand Rapids: Eerdmans, 2010.

North American Orthodox-Catholic Theological Consultation. "An Agreed Statement on Conciliarity and Primacy in the Church." United States Conference of Catholic Bishops, October 1989. http://old.usccb.org/seia/conprim.shtml.

———. "A Common Response to the Joint International Commission for the Theological Dialogue between the Roman Catholic Church and the Orthodox Church Regarding the Ravenna Document: 'Ecclesiological and Canonical Consequences of the Sacramental Nature of the Church: Ecclesial Communion, Conciliarity and Authority.'" United States Conference of Catholic Bishops, October 24, 2009. http://old.usccb.org/seia/RavennaResponse.pdf.

———. "A Response of the Orthodox/Roman Catholic Consultation in the United States to the Joint International Commission for Theological Dialogue Between the Orthodox Church and the Roman Catholic Church Regarding the Balamand Document (Dated June 23, 1993) 'Uniatism, Method of Union of the Past, and the Present Search for Full Communion." United States Conference of Catholic Bishops, October 15, 1994. http://old.usccb.org/seia/balamand.shtml.

———. "Steps towards a Reunited Church: A Sketch of an Orthodox-Catholic Vision for the Future." United States Conference of Catholic Bishops, October 2, 2010. http://old.usccb.org/seia/steps-towards-reunited-church.shtml.

Paul VI. "Ecclesiam suam," August 6, 1964. http://www.vatican.va/holy_father/paul_vi/encyclicals/documents/hf_p-vi_enc_06081964_ecclesiam_en.html.

Pontifical Council for Promoting Christian Unity. "Petrine Ministry." *Information Service* 109.I–II (2002) 29–42.

Pottmeyer, Hermann J. *Towards a Papacy in Communion: Perspectives from Vatican Councils I & II*. New York: Crossroad, 1998.

Powell, Mark E. *Papal Infallibility: A Protestant Evaluation of an Ecumenical Issue*. Grand Rapids: Eerdmans, 2009.

Puglisi, James F., editor. *How Can the Petrine Ministry Be a Service to the Unity of the Universal Church?* Grand Rapids: Eerdmans, 2010.

———. *Petrine Ministry and the Unity of the Church*. Collegeville, MN: Liturgical, 1999.

Quinn, John R. *The Reform of the Papacy: The Costly Call to Christian Unity*. New York: Crossroad, 1999.

Reumann, John. "The Petrine Ministry in the New Testament and in Early Patristic Tradition." In *How Can the Petrine Ministry Be a Service to the Unity of the Universal Church?*, edited by James F. Puglisi, 49–80. Grand Rapids: Eerdmans, 2010.

Roberson, Ronald. "The Papacy in Ecumenical Discussion Today." *Origins* 39.10 (2009) 171–75.

Root, Michael. "Vatican I and the Development of Doctrine: A Lutheran Perspective." In *How Can the Petrine Ministry Be a Service to the Unity of the Universal Church?*, edited by James F. Puglisi, 124–43. Grand Rapids: Eerdmans, 2010.

Rusch, William G. "A Contemporary Lutheran View of the Papacy." *Centro Pro Unione Bulletin* 70 (2006) 19–24.

———. *Ecumenical Reception: Its Challenge and Opportunity*. Grand Rapids: Eerdmans, 2007.

Sepúlveda, Juan. "The Fifth General Conference of the Bishops of Latin America and the Caribbean." *Ecumenical Trends* 37.4 (2008) 9–11.

Tillard, Jean-Marie-Roger. *The Bishop of Rome*. London: SPCK, 1983.

U.S. Lutheran-Catholic Dialogue. "The Church as Koinonia of Salvation: Its Structures and Ministries." US Conference of Catholic Bishops, 1973. http://old.usccb.org/seia/koinonia.shtml.

———. "Differing Attitudes toward Papal Primacy." US Conference of Catholic Bishops, 1973. http://old.usccb.org/seia/differingattutidues.pdf.

United Methodist-Catholic Dialogue (United States). "Through Divine Love: The Church in Each Place and All Places (Report of Round VI)." United States Conference of Catholic Bishops, May 1, 2005. http://old.usccb.org/seia/finalUMC-RC5-13masterintro.pdf.

Wainwright, Geoffrey. "A Primatial Ministry of Unity in a Conciliar and Synodical Context." In *How Can the Petrine Ministry Be a Service to the Unity of the Universal Church?*, edited by James F. Puglisi, 284–309. Grand Rapids: Eerdmans, 2010.

Weil, Louis. "Baptism as the Model for a Sacramental Aesthetic." *Anglican Theological Review* 92 (2010) 259–70.

———. "A Pilgrimage of Hope: Our Ecumenical Situation: A Response." *Emmanuel* 116.5 (2010) 398–402.

———. "Rome and Canterbury—Steps toward Reconciliation through the Sharing of Gifts." *Centro Pro Unione Bulletin* 67 (Spring 2005) 16–20.

World Council of Churches. *The Nature and Mission of the Church: A Stage on the Way to a Common Statement.* Faith and Order Paper 198. Geneva: World Council of Churches, 2005. http://www.oikoumene.org/en/resources/documents/wcc-commissions/faith-and-order-commission/i-unity-the-church-and-its-mission/the-nature-and-mission-of-the-church-a-stage-on-the-way-to-a-common-statement.html.

Zizioulas, John. "The Church as Communion." In *On the Way to Fuller Koinonia: Official Report of the Fifth World Conference on Faith and Order,* edited by Thomas F. Best and Günther Gassmann, 103–11. Faith and Order Paper 166. Geneva: World Council of Churches, 1994.

———. "The Future Exercise of Papal Ministry in the Light of Ecclesiology: An Orthodox Approach." In *How Can the Petrine Ministry Be a Service to the Unity of the Universal Church?*, edited by James F. Puglisi, 169–78. Grand Rapids: Eerdmans, 2010.

———. "Recent Discussions on Primacy in Orthodox Theology." In *The Petrine Ministry: Catholics and Orthodox in Dialogue: Academic Symposium Held at the Pontifical Council for Promoting Christian Unity,* edited by Walter Kasper, 231–48. New York: Newman, 2005.

11

Charism, Patrimony, or Ethos?

How Anglicans and Roman Catholics Talk about Spiritual Traditions

Arthur Holder

As several generations of his students can attest, my friend and colleague Louis Weil has a gift for telling autobiographical stories that illustrate profound theological truth. One such memorable story recalls an occasion in the 1970s when he was speaking at a joint meeting of Roman Catholic and Episcopal clergy. It seems that one of the former group asked Louis why he always referred to them as *Roman* Catholics although no one ever refers to Episcopalians as Canterburians. (They are, however, frequently called Anglicans, with reference to their church's English origins.) Returning a serious answer to a jocular question, Louis explained that in his understanding Christian communities are always grounded in time and place:

> To say that I am a Roman Catholic or a Lutheran or an Episcopalian indicates more than merely the name of the particular tradition in which I worship. Inherent to these names is a geographical association that, at least historically, has had a formative impact. In other words, the dominant characteristics of our traditions were shaped within specific cultural contexts. The geographical association of Rome or Augsburg or Canterbury within these three traditions carries the wider implication of how people living within a particular historical and cultural

context have had their experience and understanding of Christian faith shaped by it.[1]

Professor Weil's recognition of the inherent connections between history, culture, and ecclesial tradition is a profound insight, with critical significance for ecumenical relations today. In what follows I want to explore some implications of the language we use to talk about diverse spiritual traditions in Christianity, with a particular focus on past and present relations between Roman Catholics and Anglicans in ecumenical dialogue and debate. But first I need to explain what I mean by the terms "spirituality" or "spiritual tradition." Here I want to borrow a definition of spirituality from Oliver Davies, a historical theologian who has written extensively about Christianity in early medieval Wales. He says that spirituality is "a complex of theological ideas, sacramental experience, religious forms of life and interior piety that construct Christian existence at a particular time and place."[2] According to this definition there are as many Christian spiritualities as there are identifiable groups of Christians. It is worth noting that Davies, like Louis Weil, thinks of Christian spiritualities as grounded in the particularities of time and place.

But how should we think theologically about the relationships among spiritual traditions? And what language should we use to talk about them? In the period of the Reformations (both Protestant and Catholic) and for some time afterward, spiritualities that were very different from one's own were commonly identified as heretical and defective, or at least as unwelcome competitors for ecclesiastical market share. By the early twentieth century, historians of spirituality had often come to consider different spiritual traditions—insofar as they were acknowledged as Christian—as more or less incidental variations on a common theme derived from dogmatic theology.[3] Since the early days of the ecumenical movement, and particularly with the active participation of the Roman Catholic Church that began with Vatican II, the diversity of spiritual traditions has frequently been talked about in terms of "charism," "patrimony," or "ethos." In the context of ecumenical dialogue, each of these terms has both promise and peril, as will be evident from a brief genealogical foray into their respective histories and current usage.

---

1. Weil, *A Theology of Worship*, 53–54.

2. Davies, *Celtic Christianity in Early Medieval Wales*, 2.

3. Sheldrake, *Explorations in Spirituality*, 33.

Charism

To speak of diverse spiritualities as "charisms" (from the Greek for "gifts") is to imply both that they are God-given and that each one has a beneficial contribution to make to the Christian community as a whole. Since Vatican II called for each Roman Catholic religious order to return to the spirit of its founder in order to recover its own distinctive charism, both scholars and participants in ecumenical dialogue have often understood the witness of different spiritual traditions in similar fashion, with reference to the Pauline notion of a diversity of gifts bestowed by the Holy Spirit for the building up of the entire body of the church.

Interestingly enough, the Roman Catholic magisterium has sometimes seemed to apply this notion of diverse spiritualities as charisms to Protestant communities (famously referred to in the documents of Vatican II as the "separated brethren"). Thus in the Council's *Decree on Ecumenism* we find the following remarkable statement:

> Catholics must gladly acknowledge and esteem the truly Christian endowments from our common heritage [*patrimonio*] which are to be found among our separated brethren. It is right and salutary to recognize the riches of Christ and virtuous works in the lives of others who are bearing witness to Christ, sometimes even to the shedding of their blood. For God is always wonderful in His works and worthy of all praise.
>
> Nor should we forget that anything wrought by the grace of the Holy Spirit in the hearts of our separated brethren can be a help to our own edification. Whatever is truly Christian is never contrary to what genuinely belongs to the faith; indeed, it can always bring a deeper realization of the mystery of Christ and the Church.[4]

What we might call the "charismatic" interpretation of Christian denominationalism actually has a long and venerable history in ecumenical circles. As long ago as 1885, the great German Reformed church historian Philip Schaff wrote:

> Every Christian church or denomination has its special charisma and mission, and there is abundant room and abundant

---

4. Vatican II, "Unitatis Redintegratio," I.4. Note that in the original Latin text the words translated as "common heritage" are *communi patrimonio.* Here "patrimony" is what Christians have in common, while the admirable elements distinctive to non-Catholic traditions are described as things "wrought by the grace of the Holy Spirit in the hearts of our separated brethren."

labor for all in this great and wicked world. The Roman Church can not do the work of the Greek, nor the Protestant that of the Roman, nor the Lutheran that of the Reformed, nor the Anglican that of the Independent or Wesleyan. We do not wish the Episcopalian to become a Presbyterian or Congregationalist; nor the Lutheran to become a Calvinist; nor the Calvinist to become an Arminian, or *vice versa*. The cause of Christ would be marred and weakened if any one of the historic churches should be extinguished, or be absorbed into another. Every denomination ought to be loyal to its own standards, and walk in the paths of its ancestry, provided only its *esprit de corps* do[es] not degenerate into spiritual pride and sectarian bigotry.[5]

There is much to appreciate in this language of charism as applied to denominational traditions, whether it appears in strong form (as in Schaff's explicit affirmation of a continuation of separate institutional loyalties) or in the weaker form of Vatican II's assessment of Protestant spiritualities primarily in terms of how closely they approximate the doctrines and practices of the Roman Catholic Church. In both cases there is a clear acknowledgement that the Holy Spirit is at work in diverse spiritual traditions. To consider denominational charisms as in some sense gifts to Christians of other traditions is implicitly to recognize that all Christians share not only a common heritage from the past, but a common present and future as well.

However, while such irenic understandings of denominations as bearers of diverse charisms is certainly to be preferred to blanket condemnations of heresy, a simplistic application of this concept may distort the historical realities and impede real ecumenical advance. To the extent that we think of distinctive spiritual traditions as possessing distinct charisms, we typically consider those traditions as precious and unchanging treasures to be preserved and maintained in pure condition. So naturally we want to trace the stream back to its source before it commingled with other streams. We assume that earlier is better, change is vandalism, and hybridity is a form of treason. But this is to forget that in Christian theology charisms are gifts of that same Holy Spirit of which Jesus declared that it "blows where it chooses" (John 3:8).

Most histories of Christian spirituality devote a chapter or a book each to the spiritualities of various religious orders, "schools," or denominations. Of course there are other ways of categorizing spiritualities, for example by gender, race, language group, or country of origin, or by using

5. Schaff, *Christ and Christianity*, 299–300.

typologies such as cataphatic vs. apophatic, contemplative vs. active, or culturally accommodated vs. counter-cultural. But the "spiritual traditions" approach has been dominant.[6] At first glance this method of categorization may seem obvious, but perhaps it is not so obvious when we stop to think about it. Most of the founders of these various Christian movements did not set out to start a distinct "school." None of the traditions has ever existed in isolation. Many were intentional blendings of two or more other traditions. For instance, early Methodist spirituality brought together elements taken from Anglican, Puritan, Lutheran, Moravian, and French Catholic sources. Often what is most interesting and inspiring about the various spiritual traditions is not how they have kept themselves separate from each other but how they have interacted from their very beginnings right up to the present day. As Philip Sheldrake has observed, "In fact, spiritual traditions have never been pure in the sense of entirely original, self-contained and free from a process of borrowing ideas and practices from beyond their own boundaries."[7] An uncritical focus on the distinctive charism of a movement or denomination may blind us to the complex hybridity of every spiritual tradition, including our own. It may also lead us to forget that the grace of the Holy Spirit is a gift that is ever being renewed and refreshed in the churches, not just something given once a long time ago.

Patrimony

The second term under consideration here has in recent times been frequently invoked with specific reference to what can be carried from one spiritual tradition into another, especially by converts. Thus in the 2009 Apostolic Constitution known from its opening words as *Anglicanorum Coetibus* ("Groups of Anglicans"), Pope Benedict XVI spoke of the "Anglican patrimony" as something worthy of being preserved by any groups of Anglicans who would accept his invitation to enter the new personal ordinariates he was intending to establish within the Roman Catholic Church.[8]

6. Sheldrake, "Types of Spirituality."

7. Sheldrake, "Christian Spiritual Traditions," 38.

8. Benedict XVI, "Anglicanorum Coetibus," VI.5. Section III affirms the desirability of maintaining the "liturgical, spiritual and pastoral traditions of the Anglican Communion within the Catholic Church, as a precious gift nourishing the faith of the members of the Ordinariate and as a treasure to be shared." Section VI.5 calls for seminary programs or houses of formation that can provide candidates for ordination with "formation in Anglican patrimony."

This has prompted numerous attempts by Roman Catholics and recent or prospective Anglican converts to define just exactly what constitutes the Anglican patrimony.[9] Typical is the pronouncement of Fr. Marcus Stock, the General Secretary of the Catholic Bishop' Conference of England and Wales, that "Anglican patrimony is difficult to define but it would include many of the spiritual writings, prayers, hymnody, and pastoral practices distinctive to the Anglican tradition."[10] Some commentators would go further to include specific practices such as married clergy, the English parochial system, synodical government that includes the laity, or the use of English language forms from the age of the Tudors, while others prefer hazier appeals to an Anglican mindset, style, or approach. However they define it, most people who use the term apparently consider it an essential characteristic of a spiritual patrimony that it be sufficiently portable so that it can be transferred from one ecclesial context to another, and then shared with others who have never belonged to the patrimony's tradition of origin.

It seems that Pope Paul VI was the first person to refer to a distinctly Anglican patrimony in an ecumenical context. In his sermon on the occasion of the canonization of the Forty Martyrs of England and Wales in 1970, the pope looked forward to a time when the separation between Anglicans and Roman Catholics would come to an end. He assured those Anglicans present that reunification would mean no offense to English honor and sovereignty.

> There will be no seeking to lessen the legitimate prestige and the worthy patrimony of piety and usage proper to the Anglican Church when the Roman Catholic Church—this humble "Servant of the Servants of God"—is able to embrace her ever beloved Sister in the one authentic communion of the family of Christ: a communion of origin and of faith, a communion of priesthood and of rule, a communion of the Saints in the freedom and love of the Spirit of Jesus.[11]

---

9. For a "thesaurus" of definitions and descriptions of the Anglican patrimony compiled by David Murphy, see "Anglican Patrimony." See also Edwards, Ousley, and LaRue, "What Is the Anglican Patrimony?".

10. "Bishops' Conference Issues Guide to the Ordinariate."

11. Paul VI, "Canonizzazione Di Quaranta Martiri." In his use of the term "patrimony," it is possible that Paul VI was thinking by analogy with Vatican II, "Orientalium Ecclesiarium," 5, which speaks of the "ecclesiastical and spiritual heritage [Latin: patrimonium]" of the Eastern churches.

This was in many ways a quite remarkable declaration. For a pope to speak of the Anglican Church's "legitimate prestige" is no less astonishing than the clear implication that Rome and Canterbury are "ever beloved" sister churches, rather than mother and daughter, or rivals for the soul of a nation. (It was also a nice touch for Pope Paul to evoke the spirit of his predecessor Gregory the Great—that renowned Apostle to the English—by applying Gregory's sobriquet "Servant of the Servants of God" not to himself as pontiff but to the entire Roman Church.) Some would claim that the hopes of Paul VI are being fulfilled in the ordinariates established by Benedict XVI, but we should note a significant difference, which is that the earlier pope envisioned an eventual reunion of entire churches whereas in the changed circumstances following the ordination of women in many provinces of the Anglican Communion, Benedict XVI was appealing only to "groups of Anglicans" who must leave their church in order to join another. In both cases, however, there is the recognition of a patrimony—a valuable inheritance or legacy of spiritual goods.

But an inheritance from whom? And passed on by which channels of transmission? One account of the Anglican patrimony from the Roman Catholic perspective would be that Anglicanism has managed to preserve significant elements of the precious legacy it received from the medieval church: a form of episcopacy, an ordered liturgy, a sacramental life, and so on. It was such an assessment that led the fathers of Vatican II to write in the *Decree on Ecumenism* that among those Reformation communions "in which Catholic traditions and institutions in part continue to exist, the Anglican Communion occupies a special place."[12] But if the Anglican patrimony were simply whatever can be identified as having been passed on from medieval English Catholicism through the Caroline Divines and the Tractarians to Anglo-Catholics today, how could it be distinctively Anglican? Obviously both Paul VI and Benedict XVI meant for the Anglican patrimony to include at least some fruits of the creative development of Anglican spirituality over the past 450 years.

Here is where the concept of patrimony encounters two difficulties in the ecumenical context. One problem is that a good deal of Anglican material has already made its way into Roman Catholic life in the English-speaking world, quite apart from any institutionalized path for corporate conversions. For example, whenever Roman Catholics say the Our Father in English, the translation they use is essentially that of Thomas Cranmer from the 1549 Book of Common Prayer. The four volumes of the English

12. Vatican II, "Unitatis Redintegratio," III.13.

language *Liturgy of the Hours* contain numerous hymns by Anglican authors and translators including Thomas Ken, Charles Wesley, John Mason Neale, William Chatterton Dix, and the twentieth-century American priest F. Bland Tucker, as well as devotional poetry by Anglicans such as John Donne, George Herbert, William Wordsworth, Mary Coleridge, Christina Rossetti, W. H. Auden, and many more. Is all of this still part of the Anglican patrimony even if its origins are unmarked and probably unknown to many contemporary Roman Catholics today? So one difficulty with the concept of a distinctive patrimony is that the inheritance has in many cases already been dispersed.

The other difficulty is the vexed issue of who gets to decide what counts as Anglican patrimony and what does not, and by which criteria. The recently published *Customary of Our Lady of Walsingham* is a case in point. Described by the publisher as "a daily prayer book for the Ordinariate," this volume is said to be "replete with the riches of Anglican patrimony."[13] Along with Morning and Evening Prayer from the Book of Common Prayer, the Litany, and the Coverdale psalter, the *Customary* comprises spiritual readings not only from pre-Reformation English sources and post-Reformation English Catholics, but many (in fact, a preponderance) from Anglican sources among the Caroline Divines, the Tractarians (including Newman prior to his conversion), and more recent Anglo-Catholics. For the most part, the liturgical material is in traditional (that is, Tudor style) English. No one is likely to deny that the contents of this book are predominantly of Anglican origin, or that they have been treasured and beloved by many Anglicans. But the 1662 Book of Common Prayer and the writings of high church authors hardly exhaust the inheritance of Anglican spirituality.

Some former Anglicans in the ordinariates will be disappointed if they are not able to use the *English Missal*, which is a translation of the traditional Latin Mass with some prayer book additions, while others (especially in England) have been accustomed to follow the modern Roman Rite ever since it appeared in 1969. Still other socially conservative Anglicans who might otherwise be attracted to the ordinariates will probably demur if they cannot bring their evangelical patrimony along with them. Moreover, the liturgical services familiar to most Anglicans in many parts of the world are much closer in language, text, ceremonial, and lectionary scheme to the Missal of Paul VI than to any pre-1970 edition of the Book of Common Prayer. If Anglican spirituality is a patrimony capable of

---

13. "Customary of Our Lady of Walsingham by Andrew Burnham."

being transported beyond the churches of its origin, there is bound to be some squabbling over the inheritance among the heirs. Surely something important is lost when the focus is on the thing itself (text, ornament, practice, etc.) rather than on how it is used or on the character and disposition of those who use it.

Ethos

While Roman Catholics and former Anglicans have favored the term "patrimony" when talking about the distinctiveness of Anglican spirituality, Anglicans themselves have tended to prefer the word "ethos," which puts the focus squarely on matters of communal character and disposition. Perhaps because Anglicanism is famous (or in some circles notorious) for possessing no definitive creedal statement, founding figure, or centralized institutional structure, the notion of an Anglican ethos has been very appealing to those who are striving to determine what sets it apart. But what exactly is an ethos? And what is distinctive about the ethos of Anglican spirituality?

Among recent authors who employ the term with reference to Anglicanism, ethos has been rather loosely defined as "the church's fundamental character reflected through its basic institutions, personalities, and movements,"[14] "an attitude, a frame of mind,"[15] and a "typical set of dispositions and attitudes, priorities and worries, enthusiasms and concerns."[16] But the term has had a rich and somewhat more precise connotation in Anglicanism stretching back to the early days of the Oxford Movement. As James Pereiro has shown in an illuminating study, it was John Keble who first developed the characteristic Tractarian notion of ethos as "a concept rich in consequences, involving a complex theory of religious knowledge."[17] According to Pereiro, the primary influences on Keble's concept of ethos were Aristotle's *Nicomachean Ethics* and Bishop Joseph Butler's *Analogy of Religion*, both of which were required reading for Oxford undergraduates in his day. From Aristotle, Keble took the importance of *phronesis* or practical reason; from Butler came the insight that "probability [not certainty] is the very guide of life." From both of these authors, Keble derived support for his conviction that "the search for truth could

14. Quinn, *To Be a Pilgrim*, 3.

15. Peake, "The Anglican Ethos," 17.

16. Yeago, "Theological Renewal in Communion: What Anglicans and Lutherans Can Learn from One Another," 207.

17. Pereiro, *Ethos and the Oxford Movement*, 2.

not be separated from the pursuit of goodness."[18] All of this he attached to Quintilian's concept of ethos as what Keble called "the permanent tenor of a lifetime and a certain stable character"[19] in order to argue that the purpose of education and spiritual formation is not so much to provide intellectual reasons for right belief and good behavior as to attune a person's mind and heart to divine guidance.

It was primarily Keble's Tractarian colleagues who translated the concept of ethos from the level of individual character to the corporate plane of ecclesiology. In Tract 86, Isaac Williams explained how in any test of obedience an Anglican is guided not only by the voice of conscience within but also by "our own Church, which, looking back to the early Church, and bringing down its teaching, is ever heard as a gentle voice behind us." Since this voice constitutes a "peculiar and distinguishing *ethos* in our Church, we may expect to find the same realized in the peculiar temper of her sons, if in churches, as in nations, there prevail certain characteristic qualities, which are shown by a predominant influence of the same in their members."[20] Pusey thought that a difference in ethos explained why the Church of England followed a different trajectory from that of the Lutheran and Calvinist movements: "Our Reformation has had a steady tendency to develop itself into Catholicism; and therefore I think we have a right to infer that there was a difference in their original *ethos*."[21] In his Anglican days, Newman used the concept to explain why some people find Catholic truth while others fall into Protestant heresy: "I think a Churchman is (abstractly speaking) a man of a certain *ethos*—and a Dissenter of another—And in like manner that, abstractedly, the Church has a tendency to produce in individuals a Church *ethos*, and Dissent a Dissenting *ethos*."[22] Later, as a Roman Catholic, he used the same concept to defend the continuity of his adopted communion with the apostolic church:

> I have a clear perception, clearer and clearer as my own experience of existing religions increases, and such as every one will share with me, who carefully examines the matter, that this

18. Ibid., 85–99; the specific quotations are from 86 and 91.

19. Keble, *Keble's Lectures on Poetry, 1832–1841*, vol. 1, 92.

20. Williams, "Indications of a Superintending Providence in the Preservation of the prayer book and in the Changes Which It Has Undergone," Tract no. 86, p. 87.

21. Liddon, *Life of Edward Bouverie Pusey*, vol. 2, 225.

22. John Henry Newman to Francis Newman, November 10, 1840, quoted in Pereiro, *Ethos and the Oxford Movement*, 105.

ethical system (*ethos* we used to call it at Oxford as realised in individuals) is the living principle also of present Catholicism, and not of any form of Protestantism whatever . . . ; even supposing there have been changes in doctrine and polity, still the *ethos* of the Catholic Church is what it was of old time, and whatever and whoever quarrels with Catholicism now, quarrels virtually, and would have quarrelled, if alive, 1800 years ago, with the Christianity of Apostles and Evangelists.[23]

For the Tractarians, ethos was more than a vague sentiment or natural inclination. There was about it a mystical quality, something akin to the classical Roman notion of the *genius* as a guiding spirit or tutelary deity who superintends the course of life for an individual, city, nation, or group. For the Tractarians, as for many who speak of an Anglican ethos today, the term connotes a vital force that is actively prescriptive, not just objectively descriptive, of that church's behavior in the world. To claim an ethos is to acknowledge both a line of past historical development and a direction for the future. Above all, it is to possess a character that has been formed slowly and steadily over time, through sustained association with others who share the same commitments, habits, and lineage.[24] This, I think, is what it meant when the faculty of the Episcopal seminary where I used to teach once declared that prospective faculty members should have been "steeped in the Anglican tradition." We used to laugh about the apparent preference for tea drinkers implied by the word "steeped," but the allusion was apt. We were looking for people who had been repeatedly immersed in Anglican communal practices for a substantial period of time. There is no such thing as "instant ethos," for coming to maturity in any spiritual tradition requires the patient cultivation of what Alexis de Tocqueville called "habits of the heart."

What then is distinctive about the Anglican ethos? For Harvey Guthrie, it is "corporate and liturgical and sacramental."[25] From the perspective of a sympathetic Lutheran, David Yeago, it is a "concrete pneumatology" focusing on "the contingencies and particularities of ecclesial and believing life."[26] For Taylor Stevenson, the Anglican ethos comprises two funda-

23. Newman, "Letter to John Rickards Mozley."

24. There are obvious implications here for the process of Christian initiation. On the reasons for preferring the "substantial, unhurried program" of the catechumenate as "an integrated process of mature formation" over the "encapsulated and trivialized" ceremonies of private Baptism, see Weil, "Worship and Pastoral Care," 120–23.

25. Guthrie, "Anglican Spirituality," 4.

26. Yeago, "Theological Renewal in Communion: What Anglicans and Lutherans

mental aspects: "the assumption that consensus, comprehensiveness, and contract is the normative mode for establishing and maintaining the order of society," and "a certain pragmatism and lack of speculative interest in the approach to human affairs."[27] But perhaps the most familiar description of the ethos of Anglican spirituality is that of Martin Thornton, who identified six characteristics of an "English School" that he traced back to St. Anselm, the fourteenth-century English mystics, and the Caroline Divines: (1) a synthesis of speculative and affective elements, (2) a pastoral insistence on the unity of the church militant, (3) humanism and optimism, (4) the liturgy (both Mass and Office) as foundation of Christian life, (5) formal private prayer as subservient to habitual recollection, and (6) spiritual direction both as pastoral practice and as the source of ascetical theology.[28] What is at once evident in all of these descriptions of the Anglican ethos is that none of them suggests something that could be easily detached from its historical, cultural, and ecclesial moorings so that it might be transferred into another Christian communion. This is the difference between ethos and patrimony, which accounts in large measure for the Anglican preference for the first term and the Roman Catholic (and former Anglican) preference for the second.

The main problem with the concept of spirituality as ethos is that it is all too readily merged with notions of ethnicity or cultural temperament. Thornton nearly admits as much but does not shy away from the implications of finding the roots of Anglican spirituality in the English national temperament.[29] The compilers of the anthology *Love's Redeeming Work: The Anglican Quest for Holiness* strike an appropriate note of caution:

> It is not a matter of national style or national genius—as if Anglicanism's gift to the Christian world were indistinguishable from a purely cultural and local way of talking and doing things. As has been said, there are reasons in the history and culture of Britain that produced this kind of style at a particular moment, at the Reformation period; but it would be dangerous to ally it with any sort of national peculiarity—English talent for compromise, English reticence or whatever. No one is claiming or should claim that the strengths of the classical Anglican idiom for exploring and recognizing holiness are unique to Anglicanism; only that Anglicanism's evolution and position have

---

Can Learn from One Another," 208.

27. Stevenson, "Lex Orandi—Lex Credendi," 190–91.

28. Thornton, *English Spirituality*, 48–52.

29. Ibid., 55–57.

allowed it to develop and to nurture these strengths in ways in principle available to other cultures and other confessions.[30]

Going further still, Louis Weil has suggested that in light of the multicultural reality of the world today, it behooves Anglicans to balance faithfulness to tradition with openness to a very different future:

> We all wish to hold to continuity with the previous generations of the church, back to its origins in Jesus Christ. Yet continuity itself is not static; it is not merely an adherence to models from the past. The challenges of inculturation oblige us to find authentic continuity within change. The characteristics of our Anglican heritage that we most cherish will live into the future of the church not as fossils of the past but through their *incarnation* in the widely diverse cultures of our world.[31]

In this invitation to a deep inculturation of Christian faith, Weil puts the stress not on the specific details of liturgical or devotional practice but on the underlying patterns of ecclesial life, which elsewhere in the same article he identifies with the four marks of the Chicago-Lambeth Quadrilateral: the Holy Scriptures, the Apostles' and Nicene Creeds; Baptism and Eucharist; and the historic episcopate locally adapted to varying needs.[32] It may seem strange to think of a distinctive denominational ethos in terms of its multifaceted expression of common elements intended to represent an ecumenical consensus, but that is precisely how a church's ethos is supposed to work. The distinctiveness of a spiritual tradition is to be found not so much in what is done as in how it is done, by whom, and toward what end.

Hearing and Speaking in Ecumenical Dialogue

All of the words that we use to talk about spiritual traditions carry both positive and negative connotations. "Charism" reminds us that distinctive spiritualities are gifts of the Holy Spirit, but may fail to account for the hybridity and fluidity of traditions as they develop and change. "Patrimony" acknowledges the precious value of a tradition's inheritance, but the implication of detachable portability tends to objectify the specific text or artifact or practice by separating it from its context in the vibrant life of an ecclesial community. "Ethos" honors the ways in which any spirituality is embedded

---

30. Rowell, Stevenson, and Williams, *Love's Redeeming Work*, xxxiii.

31. Weil, *A Theology of Worship*, 79.

32. Ibid., 78.

in the hearts of a people both in its history and in its future prospects, but may tempt us to identify that spirituality too closely with a particular ethnic or cultural group. Whatever words we choose in ecumenical discussions, we will do well to note that our choices are not neutral. Every word contains a world of meaning; every word *creates* a meaningful world.

Since this essay has focused on the language of Anglican-Roman Catholic ecumenical relations, it seems fitting to close by recalling what the Anglican poet W. H. Auden had to say about the prospects for genuine dialogue between Protestants and Catholics. Having first remarked that both the Protestant minister and the Catholic priest ought to thank one another—and modern secular culture too—for the competition that compels them to present their respective traditions in the best possible light, Auden turned to consider the story of Pentecost in the book of Acts. Was the miracle of Pentecost not both a gift of tongues and a gift of ears? Whenever Christians come to mutual understanding, Auden observed, it is always a marvelous exchange of reciprocity involving humility as well as grace.

> The Curse of Babel is not the diversity of human tongues—diversity is essential to life—but the pride of each of us which makes us think that those who make different verbal noises from our own are incapable of human speech so that discourse with them is out of the question. . . . That we may learn first how to listen and then how to translate are the two gifts of which we stand most urgently in need and for which we should most fervently pray at this time.[33]

---

33. Auden, "Introduction," 38.

Bibliography

Auden, W. H. "Introduction." In *The Protestant Mystics*, edited by Anne Fremantle, 13–38. New York: Mentor, 1964.

Benedict XVI. "Anglicanorum Coetibus: Providing for Personal Ordinariates for Anglicans Entering into Full Communion with the Catholic Church," November 4, 2009. http://www.vatican.va/holy_father/benedict_xvi/apost_constitutions/documents/hf_ben-xvi_apc_20091104_anglicanorum-coetibus_en.html.

"Bishops' Conference Issues Guide to the Ordinariate." *CatholicHerald.co.uk*, January 11, 2011. http://www.catholicherald.co.uk/news/2011/01/11/bishops-conference-issues-guide-to-the-ordinariate/.

"Customary of Our Lady of Walsingham by Andrew Burnham." *Canterbury Press*, n.d. http://www.canterburypress.co.uk/books/9781848251229/Customary-of-Our-Lady-of-Walsingham#Description.

Davies, Oliver. *Celtic Christianity in Early Medieval Wales: The Origins of the Welsh Spiritual Tradition*. Cardiff, UK: University of Wales Press, 1996.

Edwards, Samuel L., David A. Ousley, and Michael D. LaRue. "What Is the Anglican Patrimony?" Church of St. Michael the Archangel, Philadelphia, June 22, 2011. http://www.anglicanphiladelphia.org/articles/Anglican%20Patrimony.pdf.

Guthrie, Harvey H. "Anglican Spirituality: An Ethos and Some Issues." In *Anglican Spirituality*, edited by William J. Wolf, 1–16. Wilton, CT: Morehouse-Barlow, 1982.

Keble, John. *Keble's Lectures on Poetry, 1832–1841*. Translated by Edward Kershaw Francis. 2 vols. Oxford: Clarendon, 1912.

Liddon, Henry Parry. *Life of Edward Bouverie Pusey*. 4 vols. 4th ed. London: Longmans, Green and Co., 1898.

Murphy, David. "Thesaurus of Quotations and Excerpts on Anglican Patrimony." *Ordinariate Expats*, August 8, 2011. http://ordinariateexpats.wordpress.com/anglican-patrimony-thesaurus/.

Newman, John Henry. "Letter to John Rickards Mozley," December 3, 1875. http://www.newmanreader.org/works/miscellaneous/jrmozley.html.

Paul VI. "Canonizzazione Di Quaranta Martiri dell'Inghilterra e Del Galles," October 25, 1970. http://www.vatican.va/holy_father/paul_vi/homilies/1970/documents/hf_p-vi_hom_19701025_it.html.

Peake, F. A. "The Anglican Ethos." In *The Future of Anglican Theology*, edited by M. Darrol Bryant, 27–41. Toronto Studies in Theology 17. New York: Mellen, 1984.

Pereiro, James. *"Ethos" and the Oxford Movement: At the Heart of Tractarianism*. Oxford: Oxford University Press, 2008.

Quinn, Frederick. *To Be a Pilgrim: The Anglican Ethos in History*. New York: Crossroad, 2001.

Rowell, Geoffrey, Kenneth Stevenson, and Rowan Williams, editors. *Love's Redeeming Work: The Anglican Quest for Holiness*. Oxford: Oxford University Press, 2001.

Schaff, Philip. *Christ and Christianity*. New York: Scribner's Sons, 1885.

Sheldrake, Philip. "Christian Spiritual Traditions: Reframing Boundaries, Theory and Method." In *Towards a Theory of Spirituality*, edited by Elisabeth Hense and Frans Maas, 29–42. Studies in Spirituality Supplement 22. Leuven: Peeters, 2011.

———. *Explorations in Spirituality: History, Theology, and Social Practice*. New York: Paulist, 2010.

———. "Types of Spirituality." In *Spirituality and History: Questions of Interpretation and Method*, 196–221. rev. ed. Maryknoll, NY: Orbis, 1995.

Stevenson, W. Taylor. "Lex Orandi—Lex Credendi." In *The Study of Anglicanism*, edited by Stephen Sykes, John E. Booty, and Jonathan Knight, 187–202. London: SPCK, 1998.

Thornton, Martin. *English Spirituality: An Outline of Ascetical Theology according to the English Pastoral Tradition*. Cambridge, MA: Cowley, 1986.

Vatican II. "Orientalium Ecclesiarium (Decree on the Catholic Churches of the Eastern Rite)," November 21, 1964. http://www.vatican.va/archive/hist_councils/ii_vatican_council/documents/vat-ii_decree_19641121_orientalium-ecclesiarum_en.html.

———. "Unitatis Redintegratio (Decree on Ecumenism)," November 21, 1964. http://www.vatican.va/archive/hist_councils/ii_vatican_council/documents/vat-ii_decree_19641121_unitatis-redintegratio_en.html.

Weil, Louis. *A Theology of Worship*. New Church's Teaching Series 12. Cambridge, MA: Cowley, 2001.

———. "Worship and Pastoral Care." In *Anglican Theology and Pastoral Care*, edited by James E. Griffiss, 115–31. Anglican Studies. Wilton, CT: Morehouse-Barlow, 1985.

Williams, Isaac. "Indications of a Superintending Providence in the Preservation of the Prayer Book and in the Changes Which It Has Undergone." In *Tracts for the Times*. Vol. 5, Tract 86. London: Rivington, 1840.

Yeago, David S. "Theological Renewal in Communion: What Anglicans and Lutherans Can Learn from One Another." In *Inhabiting Unity: Theological Perspectives on the Proposed Lutheran-Episcopal Concordat*, edited by Ephraim Radner and Russell R. Reno, 206–23. Grand Rapids: Eerdmans, 1995.

Baptismal Life Transforming the World

12

Committed to Earth's Waters for Life

Baptism in a Time of Global Water Crisis

Mary E. McGann, RSCJ

"The many hued, infinitely flexible matter known as water exists as one of humankind's most important sources of the sacred."[1] Water cradles humans in the amniotic sac and slakes the thirst of the whole Earth community "with its delightfully sensuous fluids."[2] Water's majesty and power can evoke praise in the heart of the psalmist and lament in the soul of a poet.[3] Water, "bubbling fresh from the imagination of the living God,"[4] is a sacred gift as well as a central symbol in all religious traditions.[5] Christian use of water in rites of initiation symbolizes rebirth in Christ and a public proclamation of faith. In the waters of Baptism, persons are welcomed into the Christian family and the beloved community of all life. For Hindus the waters of the Ganges are a sacred bridge to the divine that find their origin is the very heavens themselves.[6] Bathing in this sacred river cleanses away spiritual and

1. Donaldson, "Covenanting Nature," 100–101.

2. Ibid.

3. Psalm 93 sings of the "waters lifting up their voices" and declares that God is "greater than the roar of mighty waters, more glorious than the surgings of the sea" (Grail). In contrast, a Sri Lankan poet Wickrema Udawatta, writing after the destructive inundation of a tsunami in 2004, cries out to God that the sea, once the friend of his people, has turned against them. This text was performed at the Asian Concert, National Association of Pastoral Musicians, 2005.

4. MacDonald, "The Truth," 68.

5. Maryknoll Office of Global Concerns, "Water," 2.

6. Shiva, *Water Wars*, 131–33.

material impurities, while mourning one's dead at its banks brings peace after death and prosperity in life.[7] References to water abound in the Christian Scriptures, as they do in the sacred writings of all religions. Perhaps no other dimension of earthly life has such spiritual meaning as water.[8]

Yet water has become an endangered species. The past few decades have witnessed an unprecedented assault on the Earth's waters, described by one author as aquacide.[9] Analysts claim that dwindling fresh water supplies, inequitable access, and the control of water by large corporations pose the greatest threat of our time to the planet and its creatures.[10] Moreover, the degradation, privatization, and scarcity of Earth's waters threaten the very meaning and integrity of our sacred rites.[11]

One needs only to view a film such as *Flow: For the Love of Water*,[12] or to explore the statistics referenced in many of the sources for this essay,[13] to realize that life is threatened on a massive scale by human choices that are degrading Earth's waters:

- 1.2 billion people lack safe drinking water.
- Half the world's population is without adequate sanitation.
- Twelve million deaths a year are caused by water-borne diseases resulting from biological and toxic contamination.
- Twenty tons of trash wash into the seas of the world every minute.
- Fish stocks in rivers and seas are being destroyed by rampant pollution and sewage dumping, aggravating problems of world hunger and reducing biodiversity.
- Underground aquifers around the world are being drained at a rate far beyond their capacity to be replenished, endangering future generations that will depend on these supplies.
- Wetlands, vernal pools, and marshes that are the habitat of birds and wildlife are being destroyed by escalating development.

7. Ibid., 135.

8. Maryknoll Office of Global Concerns, "Water," 2.

9. Donaldson, "Covenanting Nature," 100.

10. Barlow, *Blue Covenant*, 1–2.

11. See Hart, *Sacramental Commons*, 90–91.

12. Salina, *Flow: For the Love of Water*.

13. Such as those in Arrojo Agudo, *Global Water Crisis*; Barlow, *Blue Covenant*; Gleick, *Bottled and Sold*; McCully, *Silenced Rivers*; Pearce, *When the Rivers Run Dry*; Rogers and Leal, *Running Out of Water*.

- Disruption of the planet's climate is contributing to severe droughts and widespread water shortages that spike global food prices and leave whole populations with inadequate drinking water.

The litany could go on. Indeed water is in crisis, and with it Earth's creatures, both human and non-human. As people around the globe awaken to this situation, local groups and governments, international bodies and NGOs, scientists and ecologists are raising alarm signals and moving aggressively to design new policies and instigate new practices.[14]

But what about communities of faith engaged in the practice of Baptism? What implications does this crisis have for Christians, for whom the sacramental waters signify a "change in human consciousness and conduct and a renewed relationship with the Spirit" of God alive in the universe?[15] In this essay I will explore how the practice of Baptism commits us in a compelling way to the waters of the planet and to solidarity with all who share them. I will do this by examining three related assertions: first, that Baptism pledges us to follow Jesus, who in his deep incarnation embraced the waters of the Earth in all their beauty and suffering, and in his resurrection claimed them as part of God's redemptive future; second, that the practice of Baptism forms us as the body of Christ—a theopolitical community with social and ecological responsibilities that flow from the gospel we embrace and the discipleship we undertake; and third, that Baptism brings with it an ethical imperative, which, at a time of global water crisis, calls us to cultivate four restorative virtues: social-equity, bioresponsibility, sustainability, and frugality.

Deep Incarnation

We begin with my first assertion: that Baptism pledges us to follow Jesus, who in his deep incarnation embraced the waters of the Earth in all their beauty and suffering, and in his resurrection claimed them as part of God's redemptive future. The term deep incarnation,[16] used by a growing number of theologians, signifies that in becoming flesh (John 1:14), Christ became incarnate in "the very tissue of biological existence."[17] In coming

---

14. Maryknoll Office of Global Concerns, "Water," 2.

15. Hart, *Sacramental Commons*, 90.

16. The term was coined by Danish theologian Niels Henrich Gregersen.

17. Gregersen, "The Cross of Christ in an Evolutionary World," 205. See also Gregersen, "Deep Incarnation," 175–77. Gregerson argues that in ancient Greek thinking, *sarx* /flesh refers not only to individual bodies but to how these bodies are part of a

into the world, the divine Logos embraced not only human existence in all its uniqueness—consciousness and awareness of God, as well as bodily frailty and vulnerability—but likewise entered the "whole interconnected world of fleshly life"[18] that emerged from the primal waters of creation. As Word incarnate, Christ united himself with the "biological world of living creatures and interrelated organisms . . . in the web of life,"[19] and with the "flux of material beings . . . composed of Earth, water and fire."[20] In Christ-become-flesh, "God became an earth creature, a sentient being,"[21] entering "evolving creation in a radically new way,"[22] embracing all forms of life in their suffering and limitation, and revealing God's redemptive presence to all creatures that face destruction, decay or defilement.

Deep incarnation thus signifies a radical, divine reach into the whole biophysical world,[23] the identification of Christ with the interconnected ecosystem of nature, and with the "particularity of each individual, vulnerable creature"[24]—sparrows and playing children, grasses and water courses. In his deep incarnation, Christ dwells with and within the Earth community as a "communion of subjects,"[25] interdependent in their life and destiny. In the words of Paul, Christ is the living bond in and between all that exists, whether material or spiritual: "in him all things hold together," and "through him God was pleased to reconcile to himself all things" (Col 1:18–20).

In light of these understandings, Jesus's Baptism in the Jordan becomes a compelling icon of his profound embrace of Earth's waters and of

---

whole flux of material beings, always in contact with each other (ibid., 176). Moreover, the concept of deep incarnation reflects the insights of evolutionary biology regarding the interconnectedness of all living things. Human beings are here understood as "interrelated with the other life-forms of our planet and interconnected with the atmosphere, the land, and the seas that sustain life." See Edwards, *Ecology at the Heart of Faith*, 60.

18. Edwards, *Ecology at the Heart of Faith*, 58. Edwards argues, with Gregerson, that flesh implies "the whole related world of organisms" and includes, in some way, "the whole universe to which flesh is related and on which it depends."

19. Ibid., 58, summarizing the work of Australian theologian Duncan Reid.

20. Gregersen, "Deep Incarnation," 177.

21. Darragh, *At Home in the Earth*, 124. As quoted in Edwards, *Ecology at the Heart of Faith*, 58.

22. Edwards, *Ecology at the Heart of Faith*, 59, summarizing Gregersen, "The Cross of Christ in an Evolutionary World."

23. Johnson, "An Earthy Christology."

24. Gregersen, "Deep Incarnation," 184.

25. See Berry, *The Sacred Universe* for treatment of the universe as a "communion of subjects."

all who share these fragile resources. The Gospels record that Jesus "immersed himself"[26] in the river Jordan, plunged himself into Earth's waters, source of life for all living creatures. Patristic authors, exploring the cosmic import of the Jordan event, claim that "in the Baptism of Jesus all the waters of the Earth were sanctified and renewed."[27] As Jesus stepped into the Jordan, claims Jacob of Serugh, all living "waters perceived that Christ had visited them—seas, deeps, rivers, springs, and pools all thronged together to receive a blessing from [his] footsteps."[28] Earth's waters were first made holy in the creation of the world, claims Tertullian, when they became "the resting place of the Spirit," receiving their holiness from the Spirit of God who was borne upon them at the beginning of time and who continues to abide with them: "a holy thing . . . carried upon a holy thing."[29]

In Jesus's Baptism, this fructifying Spirit hovers once again over Jesus and over the waters in which he is immersed, revealing not only their holy origins in first creation but also their future eschatological destiny. According to the *Teaching of St. Gregory*, the God who made the Earth to emerge from the primal waters of first creation, enabling "plants and reptiles, wild animals, beasts and birds" to spring from the earth "by the freshness of the waters,"[30] now in Jesus's Baptism "nurtures a second creation,"[31] "renewing and rejuvenating the universe once and for all."[32]

Killian McDonnell points out that this perception that a new creation begins in Jordan's waters is rooted in "antiquity's broader conviction: that the universe in all its materiality . . . is destined for transfiguration through the power of the Spirit manifested in the risen body of Christ."[33] In this vision, "humanity stands within the laboring universe as it wails and cries out for the Jordan event, reaching out in hope of a joint liberation" that would touch "visible and invisible creation."[34] According to Philoxenus, "as Jesus steps

---

26. Killian McDonnell notes that the Greek term used in the texts of Matthew, Luke, and Mark regarding Jesus's Baptism means to "undergo immersions" or "immerse oneself." See McDonnell, *The Baptism of Jesus in the Jordan*, 9.

27. McDonnell, *The Baptism of Jesus in the Jordan*, 55.

28. Jacob of Sarug, *Homiliae Selectae Mar-Jacobi Sarugensis*, I:188, Cited in McDonnell, *The Baptism of Jesus in the Jordan*, 61.

29. Tertullian, *Tertullian's Homily on Baptism*, 7; McDonnell, *The Baptism of Jesus in the Jordan*, 55.

30. Gregory the Illuminator, *The Teaching of Saint Gregory*, #412, 89.

31. Ibid., 169.

32. McDonnell, *The Baptism of Jesus in the Jordan*, 62.

33. Ibid., 243.

34. Ibid., 243–44.

down into the waters of the Jordan . . . he takes the first step toward this ulti-mate cosmic freedom and transformation,"[35] as "mystically, God [is revealed as] in all and all in God."[36] This belief is vividly portrayed by Gregory Na-zianzus when he describes Christ ascending from Jordan's waters "carrying the cosmos with him," [37] identifying the destiny of the created universe—its waters, soil, plants and all living beings—with his own resurrected life.

For communities which practice Baptism, this icon of Jesus's Baptism invites them to ponder their own engagement with Earth's waters—their living of Christ's deep incarnation as members of his body in time and history. Committed to the water in Baptism, are they not committed to Earth's waters for life? Joined with Christ in their baptismal immersion, are they not plunged more fully into the interconnected web of life that depends on water for its existence? As Christ went down to death in union with all suffering beings, embracing the frailty, struggle and pain of all creation, must those who are initiated into his death and resurrection not also struggle on behalf of Earth's waters, in all their beauty and diminish-ment, their promise and their defilement? Must they not live in solidarity and mutuality with the least of God's beloved creatures, whose very lives are threatened by a lack of clean water and basic sanitation?

Sacramental Commons

We turn now to my second assertion: in forming us as the body of Christ, Baptism invites us to a theopolitical vision of water as a sacramental com-mons for all creatures. First, a word about theopolitics. William Cavanagh has proposed that all political realities are products of the human imagina-tion and hold together only in so far as they are imagined.[38] Politics, he claims, is a "practice of the imagination" in that it constructs a convincing image of space and time, a sense of civil, national, and global territory, and of our identity within these constructs. To imagine a nation state, for example, requires that one be "convinced about the reality of borders" and about one's union with a "wider national community that stops abruptly at [these] borders" dividing "fellow-citizens from strangers." I submit that the practice of Baptism, as the incorporation of new members into the body

35. Ibid., 244.

36. Ibid., 67.

37. Ibid., 243.

38. Cavanaugh, *Theopolitical Imagination*, 1–7. Images in this paragraph taken from the same source.

of Christ, involves a similar engagement of our political imagination—one which Cavanagh describes as "theopolitical"—because its foundational understandings of space, time, and human relationship are rooted in the Christian story and the Christian gospel.

In contrast to the nation state as described by Cavanagh, with its borders and relationships, the divine-human *body-politic* that is the body of Christ, built up and imaged in the practice of Baptism, is rooted in a theological vision of co-abiding in love that includes the whole human-biotic family: a co-abiding in love that springs from the very life of the Triune God.[39] To be baptized into the body of Christ is to enter a radical inclusiveness in which there is no longer Jew or Greek, slave or free, male or female (Gal 3:28). Within this divine-human body-politic, this body of Christ, Christians are called to redraw their borders and realign their relationships; to recognize their responsibility for the most vulnerable in this world; and to grow in a creational-consciousness that is faithful to Jesus's deep incarnation.

In going down into the waters of Baptism, Christians are called not only to a conversion of heart, as Don Saliers points out, but to a conversion of their "social imagination"—and, I would add, of their ecological imagination—"to the rule and reign of God,"[40] enabling them to envision their interrelatedness with the peoples of this Earth and with all creation in light of God's justice: that is in solidarity, in right relationships, in compassion, and with a special care for the poorest and most vulnerable.[41]

In the practice of Baptism, communities embody this theopolitical vision of God's justice precisely around water—around waters that are meant to nourish life and fruitfulness, waters that are the common good of all creatures, intended by God for all. "No single species, nor any region of Earth, no economic class or political party can claim water as its own. . . . In the presence of water, all creatures and all creation stand in need, side-by-side, dependent and grateful."[42] Water is an essential part of the Earth commons,[43] and within the Earth commons, is a finite and a fragile gift. Indeed, "all the water now in circulation has been here since the Planet was first formed, no more, no less."[44] A theopolitics of water recognizes that as common good, this precious legacy must remain for the good of

---

39. Méndez Montoya, *Theology of Food*, 113–16. Both Montoya and Cavanagh explore theopolitics in relation to Eucharist.

40. Saliers, *Worship as Theology*, 175.

41. Deane-Drummond, "Deep Incarnation, Theo-drama and Eco-Justice," 7.

42. Maryknoll Office of Global Concerns, "Water," 2.

43. Hart, *Sacramental Commons*, xvii.

44. Maryknoll Office of Global Concerns, "Water," 1.

all in the Earth commons.[45] Whatever violates the right of all people and creatures to adequate, clean, and available water, especially through human greed or carelessness, is a concern of the body of Christ.

Moreover, in Baptism, communities enact their theopolitical vision of God's justice precisely around their local waters, drawn from the interconnected waterways of their local watersheds—streams, rivers, lakes, oceans—that create home and habitat for all God's creatures who co-abide there, and that are dependent on the care, as well as susceptible to the degradation, of those who use them. Within the larger Earth commons, local waters are part of a community's bioregional commons[46]—a constant sign of God's provident care and a call to live interdependently with all persons and creatures who share this interlocking ecosystem. A theopolitics of water commits us to responsibility for the health and just distribution of our local waters, and to the maintenance of the delicate ecological balance necessary for the well-being of future generations who will inhabit this place. Whatever violates the right of all who dwell in this bioregion to clean and adequate water, whatever destroys natural habitats or ecosystems, especially through human greed or carelessness, is a concern of the body of Christ.

Perhaps most profoundly, in the practice of Baptism communities embody their theopolitical vision of God's justice around sacramental waters. Baptism celebrates the sacredness of Earth's waters as natural sacrament:[47] as a locus of encounter with the Spirit of God that reveals the immanent divine presence in the natural world, drawing people into deeper relationship with God and with all living and non-living creation. As natural sacrament, Earth's waters—experienced as cascading waterfalls, crashing oceans, delicate mountain streams, or tranquil lakes—are a material-divine sign of

45. The Catholic bishops of Alberta, Canada address this expanded notion of the "common good" in their 1988 pastoral letter "Celebrate Life, Care for Creation": "Today [the] traditional understanding of the common good needs to be expanded to include a healthy natural environment. . . . We need to speak of a global common good, going beyond all provincial and national boundaries." See Roman Catholic Bishops of Alberta, Canada, "Celebrate Life: Care for Creation," 3.

46. Hart, *Sacramental Commons*, xvii.

47. Term and definition that follows from Hart, *Sacramental Commons*, xiv. Hart's use of the term natural sacrament implies the sacramental principle: that all life is potentially revelatory of the divine; that creation has taken on a special relation to God in the event of Jesus Christ; and that sacramentality is experienced when God's action in and through creation is met with human response. See: McBrien, *Catholicism*, 731; Ross, *Extravagant Affections*, 34–41; Osborne, *Christian Sacraments in a Postmodern World*, 74. Osborne contends that only if individual beings experience sacramentality in their encounter with creation/the world will their ecclesial sacramental action be meaningful (ibid., 80).

God's precious life poured out in abundance. Used lavishly in Baptism, this natural sacrament has the power to awaken our imagination to God's self-disclosure in creation, in redemption, in the life of this community, and in the hearts of those who go down into waters of this font. It's no wonder that the Scriptures are replete with images of water as life-giving spring and healing grace to which all Earth's peoples are invited: "Everyone who thirsts, come to the waters; and you who have no money, come!" (Isa 55:1). Graced with this vision, a theopolitics of water invites us to embrace water as a sacramental commons[48]—a spiritual legacy with intrinsic value and God-given integrity; imbued with spiritual and sacramental qualities that can summon "human participation in the . . . caring compassion of the Spirit of God";[49] a sacred "habitat and resource for countless sacred subjects";[50] and a shared resource that must be loved and protected for both the material and the spiritual good of all in the commons.[51]

Restorative Virtues

We turn now to my third assertion: that Baptism brings with it an ethical imperative,[52] which, in a time of global water crisis, calls us to cultivate four restorative virtues: social equity, bioresponsibility, sustainability, and frugality. These virtues, identified by James Nash as necessary for Christian response to the current water crisis,[53] are an ethical expression of our following of Jesus Christ who embraced Earth's waters in his deep incarnation, and a tangible witness to our theopolitical formation as the body of Christ, co-abiding in love and interdependence with all God's creation. While part of the character formation of each member of the body, I propose that these are critical social virtues, essential for the transformation that the community of the baptized is called to bring about in the world through the power of Jesus's Spirit.

---

48. Hart, *Sacramental Commons*, xviii, describes a sacramental commons as a place where the social meanings and ethical responsibilities we have toward water take on potent spiritual meaning.

49. Ibid., 90.

50. Nash, "Healing an Ailing Alliance," 121.

51. Hart, *Sacramental Commons*, viii.

52. Louis-Marie Chauvet contends that it is "the sacrament that gives ethics the power to become a 'spiritual sacrifice' [while] it is ethics that gives the sacrament a means of 'veri-fying' its fruitfulness." See *The Sacraments*, 65.

53. Nash, "Healing an Ailing Alliance," 120–21.

Social equity is an essential mode of justice within the human community. It insures that all who have a right to the common good receive their fair share. To hold that water is part of the Earth commons is to assert that water is not a private commodity but belongs to all.[54] Yet this equity is often violated. The rich and powerful, be they individuals, corporations or nations, "get the most benefits and bear the fewest burdens. They have greater access to water, they waste more, and they pollute more, but they usually pay less in proportion to their use and effects."[55] Social equity is a moral compass in decisions about the care and just distribution of water. It is concerned with both overconsumption and underconsumption, with abundance and scarcity, requiring those of us who overconsume and abuse water to reduce our use, and to work knowledgeably to insure that those denied adequate water have enough to live and flourish.

Vandana Shiva points out that we live in a world where two differing "water cultures" are in conflict with each other: "a culture that sees water as sacred and treats its provision as a duty for the preservation of life, [and] a culture of commodification [in which] ownership and trade [of water] are fundamental corporate rights."[56] The first of these cultures is based in a universal ethic of water as a human and ecological necessity, with sharing, receiving, and giving water as free gift considered intrinsic to human dignity and survival.[57] In contrast, the culture of commodification is based in a market rationality that views water as an economic asset, to be appropriated and exchanged, to be bottled and sold, while remaining in the control of a few multi-national corporations who derive all the economic profit from its use.[58] As governments around the world privatize their wa-

54. Ibid., 120. While the right of all to water seems self-evident, the first internationally binding declaration of this right came only in July 2010, when the General Assembly of the U.N. "recognized the right to safe and clean drinking water and sanitation as a human right that is essential for the full enjoyment of life and all human rights." This was followed in October 2010 by a landmark decision of the Human Rights Council in Geneva affirming that the right to water and sanitation is derived from the right to an adequate standard of living, which itself is a legally binding treaty obligation in existing human rights law.

55. Nash, "Healing an Ailing Alliance," 120.

56. Shiva, *Water Wars*, ix–xii. Images that follow taken from this source.

57. Shiva finds icons of this culture in the "water temples" and *piyanos* found in much of India, where water is available in earthenware pots as free gift to all who are thirsty, especially in times of drought.

58. Arrojo Agudo, *Global Water Crisis*, 15–16. See Barlow, *Blue Covenant*, 34, for summary of the profit-producing water services that are now in the hands of elite multi-national corporations, many of whom are Fortune 500 companies. In some parts of the world, a gallon of water already costs more than a gallon of oil. See Magnuson,

ter supplies,[59] authorizing corporations to manage and distribute water as a profitable source of business, the poor who cannot pay for their services are left with scarce resources that are often contaminated and most often at great distance from their homes.[60]

Only a major ethical response will counteract this injustice, since values of social equity and cohesion are simply beyond the sensitivities of market logic. Corporations have "no responsibility to guarantee human and social rights," including the right to clean water.[61] Communities whose baptismal practice has shaped their theopolitical vision of God's justice and nurtured their sense of water as sacramental commons for all are called to translate that vision into action. The challenge to embrace the virtue of social equity will only increase in the decades ahead, as the world's population increases and conflicts over the right to water intensify.[62] Gandhi once wrote, "The earth has enough for the needs of all, but not for the greed of a few."

Bioresponsibility, the second restorative virtue, extends the "covenant of justice to include all lifeforms." [63] It recognizes that all species are entitled to a fair share of Earth's water. It begins with valuing the countless creatures with whom we share this planet, acknowledging their intrinsic worth as God's handiwork, and making room for them to thrive as an integral part of the web of life. For these species, water is both nourishment and often habitat. Bioresponsibility calls us to examine our patterns of consumption that pollute and destroy aquatic habitats, and to work to restore spaces where wildlife and wildlands can thrive along with human communities.

Bioresponsibility will require a fundamental shift in attitudes toward water. For the past few centuries, water has been treated as an isolated

---

"Great Lakes, Troubled Waters," 902; also Solomon, "Water: The New Oil."

59. Water privatization, often funded by the World Bank, is on the rise in every part of the world. In most cases of privatization, water rates rise precipitously to exorbitant levels and controlling corporations renege on their contracts to improve water delivery to the poor and to invest in new water infrastructure. See Barlow, *Blue Covenant*, 102–41.

60. See ibid., 34–101. Barlow points out that women and indigenous people suffer disproportionately from the negative impact of corporate control of water, bearing the brunt of water inequity. Women now carry out 80 percent of water-related work throughout the world, and indigenous peoples are most vulnerable to water theft and appropriation.

61. Arrojo Agudo, *Global Water Crisis*, 16

62. Clashes over water rights have occurred in cities as diverse Detroit, MI, Cochabamba, Bolivia, and Kathmandu, Nepal. Analysts project that wars over water in the twenty-first century will parallel those over oil in the twentieth century.

63. Nash, "Healing an Ailing Alliance," 120. Images in this paragraph from this source.

resource, rather than as part of the ecosystem of which it is an integral part. As such, water is managed through a large-scale manipulation of the hydrologic cycle—massive dams, water management systems, irrigation canals, aqueducts, piping systems, treatment plants, and irrigation systems—all to move, control, process and provide water for an ever-expanding population.[64] Yet the cost of these interventions has been great: destruction of eco-systems; the drying up of rivers and lakes, killing of massive numbers of fish and destroying biodiversity; loss of flood plains that are essential to soil fertilization; desertification of large areas of Earth; and the draining of our underground aquifers at a rate well beyond their ability to be replenished.[65]

These patterns are untenable for the future and must give way to a new eco-system approach to water, one that restores and preserves the ecological integrity of lakes, rivers, and wetlands, while maintaining the health of whole aquatic habitats. This new water ethic partners with water's natural cycles, conserving and managing its flows, learning its wisdom, and recognizing that "nature is the ultimate provider of water rather than a wasteful withholder."[66]

This new ecological vision of water is beautifully expressed in "The Columbia River Watershed: Caring for Creation and the Common Good"—an international pastoral letter by the Catholic bishops of the Region."[67] The drafters of this document, after "listening sessions" with politicians, environmentalists, hydrologists, native peoples, and local residents, present a comprehensive vision for the 259,000 square mile ecosystem that comprises the Columbia River watershed. Spiritual, ecological, ethical, economic, and political perspectives are integrated into a call to the people of the region to take responsibility together for the future of this richly blessed ecosystem. Such vision is a model for communities whose theopolitical vision of God's justice moves them to embrace the virtue of bioresponsibility, acting locally on behalf of those creatures and habitats that are being destroyed or mistreated because of our ways of using and abusing water.

Sustainability, the third restorative virtue, extends the covenant of water-justice to future generations, be they human or other species. It is a commitment "to live within the regenerative capacities of [our planet]

64. See Gleick, *Bottled and Sold*, 171–75; Arrojo Agudo, *Global Water Crisis*, 12–13, 16–17; McCully, *Silenced Rivers*; Pearce, *When the Rivers Run Dry*, 306.

65. See Pearce, *When the Rivers Run Dry*, 67–106, 131–54, for a sampling of the effects of our management systems.

66. See Shiva, *Water Wars*, 119–30; Pearce, *When the Rivers Run Dry*, 283–312.

67. Brunett et al., "Columbia River Watershed."

indefinitely.[68] Sustainable use of the Earth's waters acknowledges that they are finite and fragile, and demands that we balance our current use with the needs of future generations. Pollution of our waterways, depletion of our underground aquifers, and leakage of pesticides and toxic chemicals into essential fresh water supplies—challenges to be faced in every country on the planet—violate the well-being of the Earth and seriously threaten future generations who will inhabit it.

One thing is clear at the beginning of the twenty-first century: we are living on borrowed time with regard to our water supplies. One million people are eating food from aquifers that are not being replaced, and economists project that by 2025, "water scarcity will be cutting global food production by 385 million tons a year."[69] Sustainable approaches that combine ancient conservation practices and cutting-edge new water technology need the serious investment of local communities and governments: using local water to meet local water needs; limiting new development to areas with adequate water supplies; irrigating crops by direct rainfall as alternative to massive irrigation systems that drain aquifers; turning paved cities into "porous cities";[70] harvesting rainwater where it falls; building "green roofs" that catch and hold water for local use; replacing concrete surfaces with porous pavement.[71] In all of these efforts, nature itself is a dynamic partner and bounteous provider: every day, more than eight hundred million acre-feet of water rains onto the Earth.[72]

Sustainability invites communities to remember that "We are only users and not owners of nature. We have no more rights over it than our children, our grandchildren, and the generations we will never meet."[73] In the words of an oft-quoted adage, "We do not inherit nature from our ancestors; we borrow it from our grandchildren." Communities of faith,

68. Nash, "Healing an Ailing Alliance," 120. Italics in original.

69. Pearce, *When the Rivers Run Dry*, 306.

70. Los Angeles, one of largest "paved cities" in the world and among the most dependent on water supplies piped from other parts of California, is implementing numerous strategies to become a "porous city" that can catch the rain, banish floods, and become self-sufficient in water. See "Low Impact Development Standards Manual."

71. St. Lucy's Parish in Syracuse, NY, replaced its parking lot with porous pavement as part of a city-wide initiative to prevent oil-contaminated storm water from draining into Lake Onondaga. In July, 2011, the new parking lot, and the rain-garden they created to surround it, were blessed at the conclusion of a Sunday liturgy at which five new members were baptized.

72. Pearce, *When the Rivers Run Dry*, 307. 800 million acre-feet of water is approximately 260 trillion gallons, or 240 cubic miles.

73. Arrojo Agudo, *Global Water Crisis*, 19.

embracing sustainability as a baptismal virtue, build bridges of hope to generations still unborn.

Frugality, the fourth restorative virtue, is described by Nash as "the most subversive of virtues," because it revolts against the sacred values of consumerist societies.[74] Frugality—living moderately and with less—is a prophetic stance toward all wasteful and greed-ful use of water. As Nash points out, it is "an earth-affirming" virtue "that delights in the less-consumptive joys of mind and flesh, especially the enhanced lives for human communities and other creatures that only constrained consumption can make possible on a finite planet."

"Frugality is an expression of love," and a necessary condition for the other three virtues we have just explored: social equity, bioresponsibility, and sustainability.[75] It is the daily attentiveness to issues of water as they affect us personally and communally, sending a beam of light through our consciousness, reminding us that there is enough for all, and that we are called to share. Frugality is a sophisticated and informed virtue, that recognizes the complex ways we use and "consume" water: thirty-seven gallons for each cup of coffee; forty gallons for a serving of toast; six hundred fifty gallons for a pound of cheese; one thousand, three hundred twenty gallons for a small steak.[76]

Frugality is integral to the "church's servanthood in the social order" which flows from Baptism.[77] It enlightens the heart and restores the soul of our baptismal nature: as receivers of all good gifts, sharers in the community of life, partners with God's desire for the world. Frugality is a way of living "cruciform," as Sally McFague proposes,[78] conformed to the dying and rising of Jesus into which we are submerged in Baptism. Frugality keeps the larger issues of water-justice—scarcity, disease, over-consumption—close at hand, training our vision, concretizing our dedication, and embodying our solidarity with the whole earth community who together receive water as a free gift of God, to be cherished and used with thanksgiving and praise.

---

74. Nash, "Healing an Ailing Alliance," 121. See also Nash, "Toward the Revival."

75. Nash, "Healing an Ailing Alliance," 121. See also McFague, *A New Climate for Theology*, 35. McFague claims that discipleship for well-off Christians means living a life of limitation, of "enoughness," and of sacrifice.

76. See Pearce, *When the Rivers Run Dry*, 4, and other sources cited in this essay for more details.

77. See Saliers, *Worship as Theology*, 180–85.

78. McFague, *A New Climate for Theology*, 35.

Bibliography

Arrojo Agudo, Pedro. *Global Water Crisis: Values and Rights at Stake.* Barcelona: Cristianisme i Justícia Booklets, 2010.

Barlow, Maude. *Blue Covenant: The Global Water Crisis and the Coming Battle for the Right to Water.* Toronto: McClelland and Stewart, 2007.

Berry, Thomas. *The Sacred Universe: Earth, Spirituality, and Religion in the Twenty-First Century.* Edited by Mary Evelyn Tucker. New York: Columbia University Press, 2009.

Brunett, Alex J., John G. Vlazny, Eugene J. Cooney, Michael P. Driscoll, Robert C. Morlino, Carlos A. Sevilla, William S. Skylstad, et al. "Columbia River Watershed: Caring for Creation and the Common Good." Washington State Catholic Conference, January 8, 2001. http://www.thewscc.org/images/stories/Resources/Statements/colrvr-e.pdf.

Cavanaugh, William T. *Theopolitical Imagination.* London: T. & T. Clark, 2002.

Chauvet, Louis-Marie. *The Sacraments: The Word of God at the Mercy of the Body.* Collegeville, MN: Liturgical, 2001.

Darragh, Neil. *At Home in the Earth: Seeking an Earth-Centred Spirituality.* Auckland, NZ: Accent, 2000.

Deane-Drummond, Celia E. "Deep Incarnation, Theo-drama and Eco-Justice." The Assunta Kirwan Lecture, Blackfriars, Oxford, May 2, 2009.

Donaldson, Laura. "Covenanting Nature: Aquacide and the Transformation of Knowledge." *Ecotheology* 8.1 (2003) 100–118.

Edwards, Denis. *Ecology at the Heart of Faith.* Maryknoll, NY: Orbis, 2008.

Gleick, Peter. *Bottled and Sold: The Story behind Our Obsession with Bottled Water.* Washington, DC: Island, 2010.

Gregersen, Niels Henrich. "The Cross of Christ in an Evolutionary World." *Dialog: A Journal of Theology* 3 (2001) 192–207.

———. "Deep Incarnation: Why Evolutionary Continuity Matters in Christology." *Toronto Journal of Theology* 26.3 (2010) 173–88.

Gregory the Illuminator. *The Teaching of Saint Gregory: An Early Armenian Catechism.* Edited by Robert W. Thomson. Cambridge: Harvard University Press, 1970.

Hart, John. *Sacramental Commons: Christian Ecological Ethics.* Lanham, MD: Rowman & Littlefield, 2006.

Jacob of Sarug. *Homiliae Selectae Mar-Jacobi Sarugensis.* Edited by Paul Bedjan and Sebastian P. Brock. Vol. I. 6 vols. Leipzig: Harrassowitc, 1905.

Johnson, Elizabeth A. "An Earthy Christology." *America Magazine,* April 13, 2009. http://www.americamagazine.org/content/article.cfm?article_id=11566.

MacDonald, George. "The Truth." In *Unspoken Sermons, Third Series,* 56–82. London: Longmans, Green, and Co., 1889.

Magnuson, Jon. "Great Lakes, Troubled Waters." *Christian Century* 116, September 22, 1999, 902–5.

Maryknoll Office of Global Concerns. "Water and the Community of Life." Catholic Foreign Mission Society of America, 2006. http://www.maryknollogc.org/ecology/Maryknoll%20Water%20document%20final1.pdf.

McBrien, Richard P. *Catholicism.* Minneapolis, MN: Winston, 1980.

McCully, Patrick. *Silenced Rivers: The Ecology and Politics of Large Dams.* London: Zed, 1996.

McDonnell, Kilian. *The Baptism of Jesus in the Jordan: The Trinitarian and Cosmic Order of Salvation*. Collegeville, MN: Liturgical, 1996.

McFague, Sallie. *A New Climate for Theology: God, the World, and Global Warming*. Minneapolis, MN: Fortress, 2008.

Méndez Montoya, Angel F. *Theology of Food: Eating and the Eucharist*. Malden, MA: Wiley-Blackwell, 2009.

Nash, James A. "Healing an Ailing Alliance: Ethics and Science Face the Ambiguities of Water." *The Journal of Faith and Science Exchange* (2001) 111–24.

———. "Toward the Revival and Reform of the Subversive Virtue: Frugality." *The Annual of the Society of Christian Ethics* (1995) 137–60.

Osborne, Kenan B. *Christian Sacraments in a Postmodern World: A Theology for the Third Millennium*. New York: Paulist, 1999.

Pearce, Fred. *When the Rivers Run Dry: Water, the Defining Crisis of the Twenty-First Century*. Boston: Beacon, 2006.

Rogers, Peter P., and Susan Leal. *Running Out of Water: The Looming Crisis and Solutions to Conserve our most Precious Resource*. New York: Palgrave Macmillan, 2010.

Roman Catholic Bishops of Alberta, Canada. "Celebrate Life: Care for Creation," October 4, 1998. http://www.inee.mu.edu/documents/24CelebrateLifeCareforCreation-Alberta_000.pdf.

Ross, Susan A. *Extravagant Affections: A Feminist Sacramental Theology*. New York: Continuum, 1998.

Saliers, Don E. *Worship as Theology: Foretaste of Glory Divine*. Nashville, TN: Abingdon, 1994.

Salina, Irena. *Flow: For the Love of Water* Documentary. Oscilloscope, 2008. http://flowthefilm.com.

Shiva, Vandana. *Water Wars: Privatization, Pollution, and Profit*. Cambridge, MA: South End, 2002.

Solomon, Steven. "Water: The New Oil." In *Water: The Epic Struggle for Wealth, Power, and Civilization*, 367–83. New York: Harper, 2010.

Tertullian. *Tertullian's Homily on Baptism*. Translated by Ernest Evans. London: SPCK, 1964.

"Low Impact Development Standards Manual." County of Los Angeles, CA, January 2009. http://dpw.lacounty.gov/wmd/LA_County_LID_Manual.pdf.

13

Practical Ecclesiology

Reflections on Anglican Eucharistic Faith and Practice

J. Neil Alexander

Long before I came to know Louis Weil and to count him as a colleague and friend, I was fortunate to know many priests of The Episcopal Church who counted it a high privilege to have studied the great tradition under his tutelage. Getting to know Professor Weil through the eyes of his students has been a unique vantage point that I cherish because it is consonant with the scholar, teacher, priest, and friend I have come to know. I remember well one of Professor Weil's former pupils summarizing all that he had learned in several years of study in one sentence: "According to Louis, the liturgy is practical ecclesiology." I have no reason to believe that one can even begin to capture a long and distinguished vocation in so brief a sound bite, however clever, but how wonderful that a working priest and eucharistic presider would remember from his teacher such a strong anchor from which to secure a sacramental and priestly ministry. Oh, that all who teach were so lucky!

This essay will consider some aspects of practical ecclesiology refracted through the lens of Anglican eucharistic faith and practice, historical and contemporary. Its goal is not to challenge or even re-cast any particular received position, but rather, to reconsider for the present life of the church the juxtaposition of ecclesiology, eucharistic theology and practice, and the role of presbyters in the eucharistic assembly as a stimulus to continued reflection. The purpose here is not to prove a new theory but to reflect on our inheritance and ask if within it there is a refreshing way forward.

Students of ecclesiology recognize fairly quickly that what the church teaches about itself is comprised of dynamic and constantly shifting collections of cognate theologies. This rich complex of theologies becomes static and immovable only when the desire is to freeze a particular moment in time and so protect that moment from the inevitability of continued theological development and the relentlessness of the Holy Spirit's urgings. A wonderful image for this is to picture a mobile that is hung over the crib of a child for his or her entertainment and stimulation: as the child grows and becomes more familiar with the mobile, one of the things the child learns is that one cannot pull on a singular dangle without setting all of the others in motion. There are no autonomous, freestanding dangles. Ecclesiology works exactly the same way. Although it is possible to suggest that almost any dimension of the church's theology might have some impact on the movement of an ecclesiological mobile, there are particular aspects directly related to the life of the assembly at prayer that are fully interrelated and integrated and whose dangles on the mobile are inevitably put into motion when any other dangle begins to move.

Consider, for example, the inseparable relationship between theologies of holy orders and theologies of the Eucharist, both of which shape ecclesiology. With due allowances for details, if one imagines a eucharistic assembly in the late second century, the picture is of a Sunday gathering of the baptized with perhaps a visible cadre of unbaptized seekers lingering around the periphery. The Sunday rite unfolds with intentionality but not rigidity. Because there are no books or bulletins, the faithful have only a sense of the broad ritual shape of what is about to transpire, but the rite is still possessed of a kind of elasticity that allows some measure of flexibility according to the day and the place. The assembly is presided over by someone who has pastoral responsibility for their common life, in many cases a bishop, but perhaps a presbyter. A sort of restrained freedom of movement guides the deacons, cantors, assorted acolytes and other assistants as they go about their duties in service to the assembly's work. The bishop or presbyter who presides, and others who assist, are experienced less as being in control of the assembly's actions, as they are thought of as pastoral and sacramental *animateurs* of a eucharistic celebration that belongs to the whole assembly and not to its leaders alone. To the extent there are liturgical books at all, they are provisional, still developing, and are to a large degree role specific: a book of prayers for the presider, a book of the Gospels for the deacon, and perhaps a book of psalms and simple chants for the cantor.[1]

---

1. An excellent survey of the history and development of liturgical books may be

As the assembly goes about its work of praise, proclamation, intercession, and Eucharist, the presence of Christ around, among, and within them is palpable. Sharing song, sharing word, sharing prayer, and sharing the eucharistic gifts made holy by thanksgiving, combine to welcome the Holy Spirit of the Risen One into their midst in ways that are unpredictable and uninhibiting. On any particular day, no particular aspect of the assembly's celebration stands out as more important than another; Christ is present as they gather, as they celebrate their Sunday rites, and as they return to their workaday worlds.

This picture is admittedly imaginary and represents a fairly romantic composite of what a Sunday eucharistic assembly in the late second century may have looked like. It does not describe any particular local rite, but each part of this imaginary rite is visible in the extant liturgical texts or descriptions of such rites from the period. It is invented only in the sense of its composite nature.

What does this rite suggest to us about an embodied, practical ecclesiology? Consider first the shape of the assembly, gathered in a single room where very little if anything separates the liturgical ministers from the assembly as a whole. The bishop (or presbyter) is clearly a recognized leader of the community, with visible charisms that are described as apostolic, catechetical, and pastoral, and thereby presides at the assembly's public witness. Although the mantle of leadership is clearly shouldered by ordained leaders, strong images of hierarchy are barely visible when the assembly is celebrating.

As the assembly goes about its ritual work, those who are able are attentive and engaged, participating actively in the assembly's actions. Only those who are aged or infirm appear to be playing a passive role. The whole of the assembly is celebrating its public witness to the death and resurrection of Jesus. They are not mere spectators to the ritual machinations of the leadership. When the Scriptures are read, they hear them with a kind of active listening that suggests a powerful sense of immediacy. The presider's preaching is not received as though it is a detached word coming from outside the assembly. The preaching is the assembly's word, the assembly's proclamation, the assembly's story of Jesus.

When their gifts for the poor are gathered at the table a new dimension of community and life together begins to come into focus. A strong sense of common life, common toil, and common prayer begins to emerge.

---

found in Palazzo, *A History of Liturgical Books from the Beginning to the Thirteenth Century.*

From among these offerings the deacon finds a loaf of bread and a vessel of wine of sufficient size for the assembly's celebration. The presider prays a lengthy prayer of thanksgiving, breaks the bread, and shares it with all the baptized so that everyone experiences a holy communion with the Risen One and with each other. There is a strong sense of interconnectedness in the moment that is best described as the presence of the Christ animated by a sort of awe-like wonder that is a gift of the Holy Spirit.

This roughly sketched composite is but a single interpretation of what a Sunday assembly at the end of the second century might have looked and felt like.[2] Its details are recognizable even if the whole is imagined. It helps us see how the assembly's self-understanding, its ecclesiology, its theology of holy orders, and its theology of the Eucharist are inseparably intertwined. The assembly's identity is active and corporate, not passive and individualistic. The presider, deacon, and assisting ministers stand among, not over against the assembly. Their service to the assembly is best described not as a privileged one, but rather a pastoral one. The authority to preside is less the result of some externally applied rite conferring a socially complex set of rights and privileges, but an authority recognized by the assembly itself as a natural outgrowth of pastoral relationships. A strong sense of the presence of Christ is experienced in the whole of the assembly's action—praise, proclamation, intercession, and Eucharist— and is not yet localized to specific actions within the rite, particularly with respect to the eucharistic gifts of bread and wine.

If this composite is not an unreasonable snapshot of the interrelationship between ecclesiology, holy orders, and Eucharist at the end of the second century, then it is easy to see the mobile model relentlessly moving as liturgical and theological development takes place in the succeeding centuries. By the time we reach the full bloom of the missal at the beginning of the thirteenth century, we have a very different picture of the Sunday assembly, of the theological and practical understanding of those who serve the assembly, and of the theology and practice of the Holy Eucharist. The main outlines of this are well known, but it is important to note a few of the broad strokes of this development so the larger point being made here is clear.

In the intervening centuries a number of changes have taken place. By the high Middle Ages, the assembly gathered in buildings that were purpose-built and that had evolved over time to reflect developing theologies

2. See also Shepherd, *At All Times and in All Places*, 7–34, and Foley, *From Age to Age*, 1–78.

of holy orders and the Eucharist. One-room eucharistic halls of the late second century, centered on word and sacrament, became multiple room temples that separated much of the ritual action from the people and often physically elevated the clergy above the laity. The fluid movement of liturgical ministers, each with their own liturgical book, guiding the assembly through its rite had given way in most places to a singular minister employing a singular book enacting the rite from a singular position and assisted in most cases by a singular acolyte or server. The participation of the faithful in the ritual action was characterized by a reverent passivity, and private devotions occupy the attention of the faithful while the rite is carried out on their behalf by a largely detached priesthood.[3]

Between these two vignettes, roughly a millennium apart, the ecclesiological mobile has been in relentless motion. Consider just a few of the major shifts. There is a dramatic change in the shape and understanding of the assembly. First we see the baptized engaged with their clergy in celebrating the Eucharist, while later we see the baptized present but largely perfunctory to the ritual action, the clergy no longer presiding but now celebrating on behalf of the assembly. This recast shape of the assembly was caused by at least two other interacting factors, e.g., changes in the theology of the priesthood and changes in eucharistic theology.

It is impossible to determine a direct causal effect from one to the other and in the mobile model of development that concern is probably irrelevant; even the slightest shift in one compels a responsive shift in the other. What we do know, however, is this: in the thousand years or so between our two examples, the role of presider in the assembly, increasingly the domain of presbyters, changes rather dramatically. The physical placement of the presider shifts from *within* the assembly to *over* the assembly with attendant changes in architecture, vesture, vessels, books, and liturgical assistants that emphasize the change.

Further developments in the theology of holy orders will place increasing emphasis on the presbyterate as the locus of priesthood, increasingly conferred externally, and alone possessed with the capacity to confect the Eucharist, now detached to a great extent from the prayers and participation of the assembly. Such changes naturally have impact upon the understanding of the Eucharist, and a predictable result was that the eucharistic gifts become the near exclusive domain of the priesthood and the core of the action appears less and less like a meal made holy by prayer. Alongside these

3. See Shepherd, *At All Times and in All Places*, 35–47, and Foley, *From Age to Age*, 185–240.

developments, theologies of the Eucharist emerge that are focused almost entirely on providing a satisfying explanation of the presence of Christ in the eucharistic action at the altar, particularly with respect to how that presence is localized in the eucharistic species of bread and wine. Recognizing the presence of Christ in the assembly of the baptized, palpably present in the whole of its praise, proclamation, prayer, and sacramental sharing, gives way to ever stronger emphasis on the objective presence of Christ in the sacramental species, enacted solely by the actions of the priest alone.

These two vignettes, admittedly theoretical reconstructions, help us to capture several themes. First, they make clear the first premise of this essay, that however you filter the data, the action or non-action of a eucharistic assembly, the theology of the Eucharist that is embodied and exhibited in the assembly's action, and the theology of holy orders, particularly that of priesthood, are so inextricably intertwined that one simply cannot speak of one without speaking of the others simultaneously. This is the ecclesiological mobile in full swing. Second, these stories are a cautionary tale of sorts that remind us that one never tampers with the dangles on the ecclesiological mobile without launching inevitable change far greater than one might anticipate, change that will be replete with unintended consequences.

Let us now consider another example of the movement of the ecclesiological mobile as background upon which some present-day reflections will be made. The sixteenth century reform of liturgy and worship among Anglicans shares a common heritage with the Latin rite and struggles, more or less, with many of the same issues as the other churches of the Reformation. We inherited the buildings, ritual patterns, and theological positions of late medieval Roman Catholicism while at the same time partaking in the spirit of the sixteenth century reforms with respect to the centrality of Scripture, the desire for a less passive mode of participation by the laity in the rites, and less philosophically driven understandings of the mode of the presence of Christ in the eucharistic species. Laying the medieval catholic inheritance alongside the spirit of reform puts the ecclesiological mobile in a state of relentless movement.

A great example of the multiple forces at work in the mobile may be seen in Archbishop Cranmer's creation of the first Anglican ordinal in 1550.[4] There one can see a number of forces at work. The ordinal ostensibly maintains the three historic orders of ministry arranged hierarchically,

---

4. The most complete treatment of the Anglican Ordinal is to be found in Bradshaw, *Anglican Ordinal*. Another useful resource is *Franklin, Anglican Orders*. And more recently, Holeton, *Anglican Orders and Ordinations*.

deacon, priest, and bishop, visible in the tradition from the second century, with glimpses already to be seen in the New Testament. In Cranmer's ordinal, the ordination proper is conferred by a liturgical formula pronounced by the bishop to accompany the laying on hands, the ordination prayer taking place separately. This ritual pattern is first visible in the tradition in the middle of the ninth century that did not reach its full flower until the end of the thirteenth century.[5] This ritual pattern suggests that the bishop is dispensing what the bishop alone possesses, an understanding that gives rise over time to further theologies of cumulative orders. This picture is in rather dramatic contrast to pre-medieval pictures of ordination where the gifts and graces for the ordained are less the possessions of the bishop to be dispensed, but charisms for ministry received by means of a fresh outpouring of the Holy Spirit, sought by the church in prayer, and presided over by their bishop and chief pastor.

The complexity of this may be seen in the terminology that Cranmer uses for the ordination rites, which is surely a result of his conversations with the chameleon-like Martin Bucer, the Lutheran, turned Reformed, turned Anglican theologian of the middle of the sixteenth century.[6] The first rite is for the *making* of deacons, the second for the *ordination* of priests, and the third for the *consecration* of bishops. Cranmer evidently wants to maintain the three historic orders of ministry, but for several centuries by his time, the medieval church had elevated the priesthood to a place of such prominence that the other orders had come to be understood merely as stepping stones to priesthood. By the high Middle Ages the priesthood was the pinnacle of the three sacred ministries, along with the orders of diaconate and subdiaconate, the episcopate being recognized only as a dignity within the ministry of the priesthood. The primacy of the priesthood among the orders of ministry developed alongside increasingly severe theologies of eucharistic presence and theologies of ministry

5. By the middle of the tenth century, the unity of prayer and the laying on of hands was beginning to dissemble as the importance of the *traditio instrumentorium* increased. See Vogel and Elze, *Le Pontifical Romano-Germanique Du Dixième Siècle I*, 28–36. This process continues through to the thirteenth-century pontifical of William Durandus that sets the stage for medieval developments leading up to the Reformation. See Andrieu, *Le Pontifical De Guillaume Durand*.

6. Martin Bucer, *De ordinatione legitimae ministrorum ecclesiae revocanda*. The text survives in *Scripta Anglicana* (Basel, 1577), 238f. A convenient English translation of the relevant portion may be found in Whitaker, *Martin Bucer and the Book of Common Prayer*. There has been some debate around the relationship between Cranmer's *Ordinal of 1550* and Bucer's *De ordinatione legitimae*. While some have argued that Bucer's work is more likely a description and defense of the *Ordinal 1550*, the standard view subscribed to here is that Bucer's work was a principal source for Cranmer.

that separated the consecrating priest still further from the prayerful work of the assembly. This is reflected in Cranmer's choice of titles: the priesthood is *ordained*, the lesser order (in this scheme) are *made deacons*, and the bishops receive *consecration*, thereby giving us one ordained office and two variations upon it rather than three distinct ordained ministries. Because all three rites contain ritual actions that are associated with ordination, one might suggest all we are seeing is three distinct names for three types of ordination. That solution, however, fails to pay due attention to both the medieval inheritance and the historical context, and ignores the complex motion of the ecclesiological mobile.

Cranmer can be excused for seeing the world this way. As noted above, Martin Bucer was by now in England and was consulting with the archbishop on these matters. As one who had been heavily influenced by the reform in two of the major cities on the Continent, Wittenberg (Lutheran) and Strassburg (Reformed), Bucer was familiar with the arguments for a one-order ministry and was a vigorous proponent of it. All of the Continental Reformers had inherited an ordained ministry that was focused upon the centrality of priesthood to such a degree that reducing three or more orders to one ministry of word and sacrament was not as radical a change as has often been posited. It can be read as merely taking the medieval inheritance to its logical conclusion: if the primacy of priesthood had for some centuries eclipsed the importance of other orders, it was not a major leap to see it as the sole order of word and sacrament ministry. So Cranmer works out a solution that maintains the three historic orders of ministry—deacons, priests, and bishops—but he does that in such a way as to maintain the primacy of the priesthood among them, the ordained order, seeing the diaconate and episcopate as diminutions or enrichments of the principal order of priesthood and not full, separate, and equal orders. Here it would be tempting to continue this discussion and observe the movements of the ecclesiological mobile as Cranmer's ordinal gives way to that of the 1662 prayer book, and on to the twentieth century and the reforms of the Church of South India and, ultimately, those of the American Book of Common Prayer, 1979. An essay of this length, however, does not provide the space for such an investigation and following that development would take us far afield from the principal point being made here.

Against this background, several reflections about eucharistic faith and practice in the Anglican tradition might be considered as we look to the future to see what may be in motion on the ecclesiological mobile. If one takes the whole of the foregoing and reflects upon its various aspects, several reflections emerge that are worthy of our consideration in the present time. Because of space constraints, I will offer here only three such reflections, but I think they point to potential outcomes of the continuing motion of the ecclesiological mobile.

The motion of the mobile invites us to reconsider the centrality of the assembly for liturgical practice, with respect to our theology of orders, and consequently as the principal embodiment of our ecclesiology. One of the gifts of the 1979 prayer book is the stronger sense, at least compared to earlier prayer books, of the gathered assembly. The centrality of holy Baptism as the sole sacrament of belonging and the singular sign of full fellowship in the church is underscored throughout the rites. The perceptible shift from the strongly vertical rites of earlier prayer books, sometimes caricatured as multiple liturgies going on at the same time and place, has given way to a more horizontal sense of the baptized before God making public witness to the resurrection and offering its prayer and praise as a community of faith, not as an enclave of individuals.

This shift in the centrality of the assembly has been accompanied by a fair amount of architectural adjustment to the new reality. Although many of our buildings were constructed for liturgies of another age, and while some congregations continue to build edifices to shelter their worship that are romantically inclined toward the devotion of another era, there is also evidence that the present rites are reshaping the consciousness of many parishes with the result that new or completely re-modeled facilities that accentuate the centrality of the assembly are on the increase. A clear movement from the three-room eucharistic hall—nave, choir, sanctuary—to a one-room space that emphasizes the interaction of the assembly—the baptized, the liturgical leaders and clergy, the musicians, etc.—seems to be underway in many places. In the Diocese of Atlanta, for example, in recent years no less than a dozen parishes have built new or dramatically remodeled worship space emphasizing the assembly. In some places dealing with the constraints of previous construction has meant compromises in the outcome, but there is no doubt that the intention was to move in a direction that facilitates the centrality of the assembly, shapes a less passive congregation, and provides space for more interactive participation in the rites.

The shift toward greater centrality of the assembly puts in motion a reconsideration of the place of the clergy in the assembly and the attendant theology of holy orders. If the assembly is reshaped by its rites and the buildings in which they are enacted, giving up its former role as largely passive spectators, then it is inevitable that the role of clergy in the assembly will change. For over a millennium, even in those churches that would claim to blur the theological distinctions between laity and clergy, the clergy have been central to the performance of the church's rites. One might go a step further, perhaps, and suggest that in some protestant, non-liturgical contexts, the almost cult-like centrality of the clergy has risen to a level that would make a high-ranking priest of the middle ages blush with embarrassment. The entertainment model rampant in much of the church continues to shape the faithful into postures of passivity.

This is a more complicated question than at first meets the eye. In recent decades the church has sought to declericalize the liturgy by the almost universal addition of multiple lay readers, lay eucharistic ministers of various sorts, and a seemingly endless growth in the number of acolytes, servers, and vergers to assist with increasingly simpler rites (irony intended). The motivation behind these changes is worthy to be sure, but I am inclined to believe that in many cases what we are observing is not the declericalization of the liturgy, but the clericalization of the laity at worship. I am also inclined to believe that, in terms of natural ritual development, this is almost surely a stage that we must go through and, hopefully, survive.

The point here, however, is not to predict how all this is going to turn out, but only to suggest that as the assembly is restored to centrality in the ritualization of our public life, that fact alone will change the role of the clergy within the assembly, as opposed to over against it, and will, over time, demand that the ecclesiologists provide fresh interpretations of the nature and mission of the church. This is also not the beginning of an apologia for a severely diminished or clergy-less church. Far from it. Ordained clergy in distinct orders are essential to the life and well-being of the church. The shift suggested here will actually raise the stakes considerably and demand clergy whose formation resonates more deeply with the best of the tradition and will require a sort of adaptability and creativity as *animateurs* of intelligent public liturgy that those of us of earlier generations could sometimes escape by hiding behind the altar.

Another consequence of the motion of the ecclesiological mobile will be shifts in eucharistic theology. As we noted above, in the early centuries of the church where the assembly and the clergy were in a more interactive, dynamic relationship, the presence of Christ was thought to pervade the whole of the eucharistic action and was less focused upon some sort of priestly action upon the bread and wine. I am not suggesting that the re-emergence of the centrality of the assembly will simply re-create premedieval eucharistic theology. The strength of devotion and piety in the intervening millennium and a half is too strong to believe that will happen quickly, if ever. What is inevitable is that reclaiming the centrality of the assembly and re-positioning the sacred ministers as servants of the assembly rather than as ministers functioning over against the assembly on its behalf will, over time, significantly nuance, if not change, the next generation of eucharistic theology.

Related to this is another aspect of the assembly's life worthy of mention. The tradition that shaped Jesus was embodied in meals made holy by prayer, both domestic and communal. And it was a meal made holy by prayer that Jesus shared with his disciples that the church continues to claim as the eschatological banquet of the resurrection. Our early documentation of eucharistic celebration seems clearly to have maintained a strong sense of a communal meal that over time gradually gave way to an increasingly stylized ritual meal that after some centuries can be seen to resemble a communal meal only to those with the most vivid imaginations. Again, this is the ecclesiological mobile in full motion as the shape of the assembly, the building that houses it, the clergy who serve it, and the underpinning theologies of all of it are relentlessly shifting. A powerful consequence of the mobile's movement in our own time would be a strong recovery of the Eucharist as a communal meal made holy by prayer wherein the presence of Christ is recognized in the whole of the assembly's action and not isolated to a few discreet moments focused upon the priest and accompanied by bells.

"Liturgy is practical ecclesiology." I don't know whether Louis Weil actually said that or if it is simply the executive summary of a former pupil's good learning. Either way I find it to be an immensely helpful tag line that is a helpful reminder of the inextricability of the various dangles on the ecclesiological mobile. The church at worship is without question our clearest and most profound window into ecclesiology. Looking through that window does not show us everything, but it does reveal those dimensions of our common life that most clearly define us. We see not an enclave of like-minded souls, but a diverse community publicly gathered as the living expression of the faith it professes. The assembly is possessed of innumerable gifts and charisms for the benefit of its common life, some lay, others ordained. The main things the assembly does are to pray, to proclaim God's Word, and to celebrate the sacraments of the resurrection. All of the theological reflection in the world cannot replace the doing of these things, together, week upon week, for a lifetime. The ecclesiological mobile has been in unstoppable, relentless motion since resurrection morning. There's no reason to think it's going to settle down now!

Bibliography

Andrieu, Michel. *Le Pontifical De Guillaume Durand*. Studi e Testi: Le Pontifical Romain Au Moyen-Âge 88. Rome: Biblioteca apostolica vaticana, 1938.

Bradshaw, Paul F. *The Anglican Ordinal: Its History and Development from the Reformation to the Present Day*. Alcuin Club Collections 53. London: SPCK, 1971.

Foley, Edward. *From Age to Age: How Christians Have Celebrated the Eucharist*. Collegeville, MN: Liturgical, 2008.

Franklin, R. W., editor. *Anglican Orders: Essays on the Centenary of Apostolicae Curae, 1896–1996*. Harrisburg, PA: Morehouse, 1996. (Also available in *Anglican Theological Review* 76 (1996) 1–149.)

Holeton, David, editor. *Anglican Orders and Ordinations: Essays and Reports from the Interim Conference at Jarvenpää, Finland, of the International Anglican Liturgical Consultation, 4–9 August 1997*. Joint Liturgical Studies 39. Cambridge: Grove, 1997.

Palazzo, Eric. *A History of Liturgical Books from the Beginning to the Thirteenth Century*. Translated by Madeleine Beaumont. Collegeville, MN: Liturgical, 1998.

Shepherd, Massey H. *At All Times and in All Places*. 3rd ed. New York: Seabury, 1965.

Vogel, Cyrille, and Reinhard Elze, editors. *Le Pontifical Romano-Germanique Du Dixième Siècle I*. Studi e Testi, 266. Rome: Biblioteca apostolica vaitcana, 1963.

Whitaker, E. C. *Martin Bucer and the Book of Common Prayer*. Alcuin Club Collections 55. Great Wakering, UK: Alcuin Club, 1974.

14

Baptized into the Catholic Future

Ralph McMichael

Do all of the baptized share a common future? Should they then share a common present? Can this common present have an ecclesial expression or constitution? These questions raise the perennial topic of the relationship between Baptism and membership in a, or the, church. Through the recent decades of liturgical scholarship and the renewal of the rites of initiation, we have grown in our appreciation of Baptism as an ecclesial event; Baptism is a corporate act and should be enacted accordingly. How would we begin to engage the mutuality between Baptism and ecclesiology, and what might be the consequences of this mutuality for ecumenism? In this essay, I will explore this question from the perspective of the trinitarian relationship between past, present, and future as this relationship is embodied as the body of Christ.[1] God's future for us is a catholic reality to which we are called as church, and into which we are baptized. I wish to engage the temporal and accountable consequences for ecclesiology and for ecumenism that issue from the act of baptizing persons in the name of the Father, and of the Son, and of the Holy Spirit.

Whatever theological understanding or ecclesial significance we ascribe to Baptism, it should be a trinitarian construction. When we move on quickly from the rhetorical act of Baptism to something we have wanted to say, or to some church strategy we have wanted to justify, Baptism can become simply a cipher for meanings constructed elsewhere. For example, Baptism can become merely an entry into the egalitarian and

---

1. For a detailed analysis and critique of ecumenical agreements from the perspective of Trinitarian theology and the future, see Jenson, "Part Three: The Basis."

democratic church/society in which all the baptized have rights and voice, and in the name of this "Baptism" we revolt against pernicious hierarchies. Conversely, Baptism can be the singular salvific act of forgiving sins, rendering the Christian a saved individual who then chooses to gather with other saved individuals, while referring to this gathering as their church. However, if we are to go beyond our efforts to turn Baptism into an instrument of our own making, a sacramental means toward our chosen and desired end, then we must appreciate and engage the trinitarian reality and significance of Baptism. This trinitarian understanding of Baptism allows for a trinitarian ecclesiology, and hence, a trinitarian re-shaping of ecumenism.[2] To achieve this understanding, we must talk about God before we talk about ourselves, and we have to lay aside our ecclesial agendas and personal theological preferences, and we will confess the Trinity before telling our story: We will contemplate the revelation of God in Jesus before expressing our experience of the divine.

Baptism and the Paschal Mystery

A traditional approach to the theological significance of Baptism is to understand it within the paschal mystery of Jesus. This location maintains Baptism within the economy of salvation, and it preserves the connection between Baptism and soteriology. One of the primary textual warrants for this is taken from Romans 6:

> Do you not know that all of us who have been baptized into Christ Jesus were baptized into his death? Therefore we have been buried with him by Baptism into death, so that, just as Christ was raised from the dead by the glory of the Father, so we too might walk in newness of life. For if we have been united with him in a death like his, we will certainly be united in a resurrection like his. (Rom 6:3–5)

Baptism into Jesus Christ places us within the reality enacted by his death and resurrection. What happened to Jesus will happen to us because we have been located where this happens.

What is a death like his? The historical trajectory of the life of Jesus could be characterized as moving from gathering to dispersal, from companionship to abandonment. Starting with the calling of the twelve, to the gathering of other disciples, including all the crowds that formed to hear

2. A good overview of the renewal of trinitarian theology for ecclesiology is provided by Thompson, *Modern Trinitarian Perspectives.*

Jesus teach and to be touched, culminating with those who lined the road into Jerusalem to cheer, the life of Jesus is a story of gatherings and followers. And yet, this dynamic of association could not be sustained. There were others plotting the demise of Jesus, finding ways to ensure they would retain authority over the people when it comes to God, and co-operating with the authority of the state if need be. They perceived the crowds following Jesus, attending to his teaching, as straying from the accepted ways of acting and understanding. When authoritative push came to shove, the cheering throng became the deriding herd, while some stragglers slipped into the shadows of silence and fear. The conclusion of Jesus's historical life was marked by abandonment. Those around him on the road to death were not listening for his teaching; they were enforcing the rhetoric of the status quo. Jesus was left alone with his Father; and then seemingly, he was left alone to die.

The life and ministry of Jesus was one of discernment and fidelity; he sought to do the will of his Father, while being guided by the Holy Spirit. What he had to say and do was given to him from beyond his historical and relational context. He did not seek his vocation in the past or in the present. What he was given to say and do allowed him to interpret the past and to effect the present. Jesus became the occasion for interpreting the Scriptures so that they were truly about him; they signified his arrival. How people related to Jesus became a decision about how they would relate to God. The past and present that those who gathered after the death of Jesus knew was bent toward him. So the one who was abandoned by the guardians and interpreters of past and present becomes the one whose presence bestows the true meaning of past and present to those who now gather in and for this presence.

However, the outward appearance of the course of Jesus's life, his history, tells the story of defeat. His vulnerability to other historical agents and dynamics led to his historical death. He did not "combat" these agents and forces on their own terms; he did inhabit the past and present as others did. The irony is that while he did not navigate history by charting a course with the co-ordinates of past and present, he did share its common end. Jesus's death does not signify the "inevitability of history," of the recurring passage from past to present, rather his death signifies "newness of life."

What is a resurrection like his? The resurrection is not an act of self-expression, self-affirmation, or self-determination; it is the realization of an existence by another distinct agency. The Father raises Jesus; henceforth, Jesus is present as the risen one. He becomes the epiphany of one for whom life happens beyond the grave and not before it. He acts as one on whom another has acted and through whom God's future arrives. The one who seemingly was abandoned by the Father and the Spirit is now the presence of their gathering, and this becomes our future when we are baptized into him. The resurrection of Jesus by the Father in the power of the Holy Spirit liberates him from the contingencies and vulnerabilities of history, but history is not left behind. History is re-constituted from that place where the future makes the difference between life and death. The place of reconstitution is the baptismal font, and the life that is raised from its waters is the body of Christ.

Baptism into the Body of Christ

We are baptized into the body of Christ, and thus our identity belongs to a body whose profile is not an outline of our individual visage. As a members of the body of Christ, we are incorporated into a way of living which has been chosen for us. Henceforth, we are formed to choose what has been chosen: a faithful member of this body lives into new life. In temporal terms, members of this body are formed to live their future now. We are baptized into a tri-temporal life that is the body of Christ. We share a past, present, and future with all members of this body even though we may not share other identifying factors arising from particular and contrasting corporate entities. Those who have received the gift of the Holy Spirit in Baptism now breathe the future of God. This future has a history; it has a past and present. However, the past and present are no longer there or here for their own sake; they too belong to the future. Faithful regard for the past (tradition), along with fidelity in the present, places us where resurrection happens, and this resurrection is always an event enacted on us from a distinct other.

The ecumenical question becomes: "are we willing to hear this body speak these words: 'Unbind them and let them go'?" Are we willing to cast off the vestments of immobility and walk out of our cathedrals of security and self-reference? The church is the body of Christ,[3] and the existence of this identity is not rooted in a self-referent or self-contained entity. The church does not possess the character of this body, rather, the church is the body of Christ because this body identifies with it; this body shares its life completely, including its future. In this way, identity is not construed from origins or from the persistence of sameness through time. Identity is rooted in a distinct other, another agent and another time than one's own. The church is always facing the vocation to become the body of Christ, while

3. For a concise exposition of the ramifications of an ecclesiology of church as the body of Christ, see Tillard, *Flesh of the Church, Flesh of Christ.*

living as this body. The church's past and present places it where resurrection happens. All localized churches are but provisional manifestations of the one body of Christ. The risen body of Christ is free to show up and inhabit many places and gatherings, even those taking place behind locked doors.

The Vocation of Becoming

Since the church has the baptismal vocation to become the body of Christ, a vocation that reaches beyond the boundaries of any one church or denomination requires us to live vocationally. In ecumenical interchanges, we have faced each other, but have we faced Christ together? We have sorted out some of our disagreements of the past, and we have gotten along better in the present, and now we must explore the implications of a common future.

Baptism, ecclesiology, and ecumenism are appropriately understood within a trinitarian reality, focused on the vocation to be and become the body of Christ; and as such, the future is the determinative dimension of the tri-temporal life into which we are baptized. This argument is advanced by pneumatology, by an emphasis on the Holy Spirit as the one who frees us from the bondage of separation for the bonds of communion.[4]

From nature and history we can project future possibilities, but the resurrection of Jesus cannot be located within either projection. This resurrection does not negate nature or history; it manifests what can become of nature and history when the Holy Spirit becomes the primary agent of reality, when the future breaks into the tombs where nature and history are bound (both as destiny and as limitation). A future realized by the Holy Spirit is distinct from other possible futures. Baptism places us into a pneumatologically realized future as the body of Christ before the Father in heaven. All ecclesiological and ecumenical strategies and speculations will be unfulfilled if they are not grounded in the trinitarian future, God's catholic vision for the church and for the world.[5]

The Catholic Future

We are baptized into the trinitarian life, into the life of divine communion. This is a tri-temporal life where the future represents wholeness.

---

4. A comprehensive guide to the Holy Spirit in the life of the Christian and the Church is Congar, *I Believe in the Holy Spirit*, especially especially vol. 2, 5–38.

5. For a view of catholicity as the transcendence of differences in the world, see Zizioulas, *Being as Communion*, particularly chapter 4, "Eucharist and Catholicity."

"Catholic" is that which pertains to the whole, and we supplement wholeness with universality. This concept of catholicity can function as an ecclesiological mirror held up by the so-called Vincentian canon: that which is believed everywhere, always, and by all. Coupling wholeness with universality can give the impression that if something is everywhere, then we have the whole thing. It is in the future that we will become our whole baptismal self.

> So if you have been raised with Christ, seek the things that are above, where Christ is, seated at the right hand of God. Set your minds on things that are above, not on things that are on earth, for you have died, and your life is hidden with Christ in God. When Christ who is your life is revealed, then you also will be revealed with him in glory. (Col 3:1–4)

In light of the preceding argument, we could paraphrase this text to say "seek the things that are ahead, and not the things that are behind." The wholeness of who we are within the body of Christ, and the church as this body, will be revealed. In an ultimate sense, our future as the body of Christ has been decided. So the proper baptismal, ecclesial, and ecumenical question is not what will the future be like. Rather, the question is how do we live this future now; how do we embody the wholeness of Christ's life of communion from and to the Father, realized and revealed by the Holy Spirit. How do we manifest the catholicity of God?

A pneumatologically conceived present is determined ultimately by the future, and this future is the primary temporal dimension of catholicity. Baptism is nothing less than a yielding to the agency of God, and as such, there is no body of Christ, baptismal or eucharistic, without epiclesis (whether textually articulated or not). Catholicity resides with the wholeness of God's life and agency and not with the church. Catholicity is the future. But this is not a future delayed so much as it is desired. Catholicity arrives not as reward but through repentance. We are always tempted to mistake a part for the whole, to exalt one temporal dimension placing the other two in its shadow. Those of us who have been baptized into the catholic future are not to practice the demarcation of past from present and present from future. We are not to make idols of the past, the present, or of the future. The theological reality is that the past and present are sacraments of the future. The wholeness of the body of Christ is not achieved but revealed.

Disciplines of Baptismal Ecumenism

Catholicity is no longer the process of spatial expansion through time from a singular origin. Catholicity does not spread; it arrives. Recognition of wholeness is not by the identification of prior causes and of common historical genealogies but by the significations of a common future. As a tri-temporal reality, the recognition of catholicity is not confined to the future: Catholicity can and does arrive from the past, and from the present, as well as from the future. In order to practice this recognition, to faithfully inhabit the catholic future, we do well to nurture three theological disciplines: contemplation, invocation, and imagination.

Contemplation is the discipline of waiting for another's presence without conditions or distractions. It is the offer of our presence to what is as it is. Thus, our engagement with the past as the possible arrival of the catholic future is characterized by contemplation. We place ourselves before the tradition as a whole allowing ourselves to be surprised and changed. We do not scour the past for answers to contemporary questions. We permit the past to pose its questions to us, provoking us to grapple with a wholeness that includes accepting what may seem at first an alien perspective. Contemplating the catholic past can lead us into a surprising future, a realization that wholeness cannot be gained at the expense of the past. In this way, the catholic tradition does not serve as an inviolable trajectory but as the formation of expectation. Contemplation does not exclude scholarly study. Rather, contemplation is nurtured by such study when we are not driven to conclusions of our liking but to ever-focused attentiveness on what might be revealed about the nature of baptismal and trinitarian wholeness for the church and for the world. Contemplation of the past places us within a present characterized by invocation.

The ecclesial movement of the present to the future is marked by invocation. That is, a church accountable to the wholeness of God's tri-temporal reality of communion will not be satisfied by the present; it will not be enough. The present is not preserved for ecclesial advantage. One cannot guard catholicity from the future. Instead, the present is the time for invoking the Holy Spirit, for the realization of the body of Christ beyond the possibilities of the church's nature or history. The catholic future arrives following the sacrificial departure of the church's claims of self-sufficiency and of power. Baptism does not happen without invocation, and neither should any other ecclesial event. What would a pneumatologically constituted ecumenism look like? It would have the profile of a "death and resurrection like his." The Holy Spirit realizes the life of the body of Christ where there is no claim of human agency: the womb of Mary of Nazareth and the tomb of Joseph of Arimathea. We become the body of Christ through invocation, when we receive the arrival of the catholic future.

Contemplation of the past along with the presence of invocation provides for the imagination of the catholic future. Imagination is not fantasy. While fantasy is untethered from any expectation of a possible reality, imagination is populated by images bestowed by Scripture, tradition, and the church's contemporary life. When we imagine the catholic future, we participate in God's catholic image of all of the baptized inhabiting their common future as the pnuematologically realized body of Christ.[6] This imagination can free us from overly defining and determining what common life we are willing to permit. Imagination of the catholic future can move us from ecumenical negotiation to ecclesial transformation. For the catholic future in which we have been baptized in not far away; it is hewn from the past and invoked from the present. It is where we now "live and move and have our being." Imagining the catholic future sounds like this:

> For this reason I bow my knees before the Father, from whom every family in heaven and on earth takes its name. I pray that, according to the riches of his glory, he may grant that you may be strengthened in your inner being with power through his Spirit, and that Christ may dwell in your hearts through faith, as you are being rooted and grounded in love. I pray that you may have the power to comprehend, with all the saints, what is the breadth and length and height and depth, and to know the love of Christ that surpasses knowledge, so that you may be filled with all the fullness of God. Now to him who by the power at work within us is able to accomplish abundantly far more than all we can ask or imagine, to him be glory in the church and in Christ Jesus to all generations, forever and ever. Amen. (Eph 3:14–21)

---

6. See again Zizioulas, *Being as Communion*, chapter 3, "Christ, the Spirit, and the Church."

Bibliography

Congar, Yves. *I Believe in the Holy Spirit*. New York: Crossroad, 1997.

Jenson, Robert W. "Part Three: The Basis." In *Unbaptized God: The Basic Flaw in Ecumenical Theology*. Minneapolis, MN: Fortress, 1992.

Thompson, John. *Modern Trinitarian Perspectives*. New York: Oxford University Press, 1994.

Tillard, J.-M.-R. *Flesh of the Church, Flesh of Christ: at the Source of the Ecclesiology of Communion*. Translated by Madeleine Beaumont. Collegeville, MN: Liturgical, 2001.

Zizioulas, John D. *Being as Communion: Studies in Personhood and the Church*. Crestwood, NY: St. Vladimir's Seminary Press, 1985.

15

Toward a Baptismal Spirituality

Frank T. Griswold

I AM DELIGHTED TO have been asked to contribute to this collection of essays in honor of my very good friend, Louis Weil. We first met, appropriately enough, after a celebration of the Eucharist at the monastery of the Society of St. John the Evangelist in Cambridge, Massachusetts. At the time, Louis was a graduate student at Harvard and I was an undergraduate. Our friendship continued at the General Seminary in New York, and has been sustained over the years through the many turnings of our lives and ministries. It has been further enhanced by a shared sense that liturgy is integral to the life of the church and to its ability to know itself and its mission.

Foundational to any understanding of the place of liturgy in the life of the church is the awareness that liturgy does not stand on its own: it is Christ whose presiding presence enlivens and authenticates every liturgical action. Accordingly, the original impetus of the Liturgical Movement of the last century was an urgent concern that, through the rites of the church, men and women would be able to encounter the risen Christ and be caught up into his life and ongoing work of removing the obstacles to the reconciliation that had been achieved through his death and resurrection. Among Louis's many gifts are his pastoral sensibility and his deep respect for the people of God. Therefore, at the core of much that Louis and I have pondered and discussed over the years is the issue of how well God's people are served by the liturgy. That is, do the ritual patterns of the church, with their multiple languages of sign and symbol and text—particularly texts drawn from Scripture—speak to and engage hearts and minds? If not, how might their reordering in response to history and pastoral urgency renew the liturgy, allowing it proclaim and enact the mystery of our life in Christ with greater transparency, authenticity and force?

In his teaching, preaching and pastoral practice, Louis has sought to set before the church a deeper appreciation of the paschal mystery into which we are plunged in Baptism—properly celebrated with an extravagant deployment of water and not a sanctified dribble—and sealed by the Holy Spirit with a generous outpouring of chrism, symbolizing the unimagined abundance of the Spirit of Christ. And it is "the Spirit of [God's] Son" (Gal 4:6) in our hearts that makes it possible for our spirit authentically to utter as our own Jesus's intimate address to God: "Abba, Father. "

The 1979 Book of Common Prayer, which Louis was deeply involved in bringing before the church, seeks to ground the consciousness of the worshiping community in the mystery of Baptism. Mystery here is to be understood as a reality so full and deep that it passes our ability to comprehend it in its fullness. Baptism is both a discrete event in a person's life and a life-long process of "growing up in every way into him who is the head, into Christ" (Eph 4:15) and acknowledging with St. John that "what we will be has not yet been revealed" (1 John 3:2).

William Law, the eighteenth century priest and mystic, speaks of "the process of Christ."[1] This evocative phrase suggests an ongoing dynamic of being stretched and transformed, taken apart and restructured according to God's mad love, to use a phrase from the Eastern church. This outpouring of God's love, which exceeds all that we might ask or imagine, is able to embrace and reconcile the various dimensions of our personhood, even when we are unable to do so. This includes even the thorns that burden us, causing us shame and self-alienation.

St. Augustine of Hippo in a mystagogical homily (Sermon 272) encourages the newly baptized to "become who you are." Augustine foresees a life-long process of growth and discovery as we come to maturity, "to the measure of the full stature of Christ" (Eph 4:13), not as we would like to construct ourselves, but according to the imagination and loving desire of God. Baptism is the identification of our selfhood with the selfhood of Christ, not by way of obliteration but by way of maturation. Our life "hidden with Christ in God" (Col 3:3) becomes the means by which we grow into the fullness and uniqueness of who we are called to be. This growing

---

1. I was introduced to this phrase in Law, *Selections*, 18. Law's greatest use is in *The Spirit of Love*, second dialog (for example at Law, *Serious Call*, 445), but also in *A Short Confutation of Dr. Warburton's Defence*, and in *Of Justification by Faith and Works*.

up into Christ is ordered by a repeating pattern of dying and rising, losing and finding. In the water of Baptism "we are buried with Christ in his death. By it we share in his resurrection" (Book of Common Prayer 1979, 306). Thus, we are called to live the paschal mystery of Christ and willingly embrace the dynamic of death and resurrection as it reveals itself throughout our process of moving through the different seasons of our lives.

Baptism is also a corporate reality. To be baptized into Christ is to be incorporated into a community, into Christ's risen body, the church. The Book of Common Prayer 1979, 298, declares that "Holy Baptism is appropriately administered within the Eucharist as the chief service on a Sunday or other feast." The promise of support and the welcome of the newly baptized by the members of the worshiping community underscore the reality that our growth toward maturity in Christ involves life with others. As St. Paul makes clear in his description of the church as the body of Christ, the wholeness of the body depends on multiple limbs and organs, in relation to each other, yet each with its own unique function and differentiation contributing to the life of the whole. All the disparate and distinct limbs and members bound together make up the embodied presence of the Risen Christ in the world.

Classical baptismal liturgies include a series of renunciations and affirmations. The renunciations involve turning away from evil, that is all that draws us away from collaborating with the motions of the Holy Spirit who guides and leads us toward maturity. In this way Christ is "formed" in us, and we are "conformed to the image of [God's] Son" (Rom 8:29). The affirmations oblige us to turn toward Christ and to acknowledge with St. Paul that "it is no longer I who live, but it is Christ who lives in me" (Gal 2:20). This Christ-life is animated by God's love poured into the depths of our being—our hearts—by the Holy Spirit. And this love is nothing less than God's own trinitarian life shared with us in order that the risen Christ may embody his healing and reconciling, his compassion and truth, in the incarnate reality of our lives. The baptismal affirmation of this trinitarian life at work in us is reflected in the Apostles' Creed.

The 1979 Book of Common Prayer sets forth a baptismal covenant that includes, first of all, the Apostles' Creed. It then calls for a willingness to be shaped and formed by ongoing encounter with Christ in his body and its members, in word, sacrament and common prayer. The force and power of evil is also acknowledged along with the call to resist it. Our falling into sin is presupposed, along with the need for ongoing *metanoia*: a return to the Lord when we have fallen away. The baptismal covenant concludes with three questions that seek to articulate the life of apostolic witness and service that flow from our prior avowals and, above all, from our baptismal union with Christ:

> "Will you proclaim by word and example the Good News of God in Christ?"

> "Will you seek and serve Christ in all persons, loving your neighbor as yourself?"

> "Will you strive for justice and peace among all people, and respect the dignity of every human being?"

The reply to each of the questions is, "I will, with God's help."

While these questions are altogether appropriate as an articulation and outworking of our life in Christ, for many they have displaced the earlier portions of the covenant and become its primary focus. To be sure we assent to each question ". . . with God's help." Unfortunately, the way in which these questions are frequently divorced from the preceding five, and any acknowledgement of God's help in carrying them out, suggests that they have taken on a life of their own. They risk being seen as an agenda without the clear understanding that the living of them presupposes a relationship with Christ and a willingness to be formed by the paschal mystery as it overtakes us within the concrete realities and demands of our daily lives.

During my years serving as the Presiding Bishop of The Episcopal Church in the United States, I was exposed to the length and breadth of theological opinion and practice that exists, at times uneasily, within the Church. What became increasingly clear as I listened to various voices, engaged in conversations with different groups, and participated in a variety of meetings and church councils, was that there are two dominant vocabularies in use among us: one is the language of "holiness" and the other that of "justice." On many occasions, it became apparent that if a person speaking the language of holiness encountered another whose preferred speech was justice, an atmosphere of discomfort and mistrust could easily engulf them both. The result was that neither of them was able to understand or appreciate the perspective or urgent concern of the other. In addition, declarations such as "It's a matter of holiness," or "It's a justice issue," could be used to draw a line in the sand and end all conversation. The baptismal covenant was frequently drawn in as well. The first four questions belonged to the "holiness" camp and the last three to the "justice" camp. The fifth question regarding continuing in the apostles' teaching and fellowship belonged in differing degrees to both groups, with various "conservative" or "liberal" articulations.

What became increasingly clear was that we need to become bilingual and be able to speak the language of both holiness and justice, and that The baptismal covenant must be taken as a *whole*. Furthermore, we must ask, "whose holiness?" and "whose justice?" Are they simply our own notions projected onto God? "Be transformed by the renewing of your minds," Paul tells us, "so that you may discern what is the will of God, what is good and acceptable and perfect" (Rom 12:2). To what extent, we are obliged to ask, are our notions of holiness and justice shaped by the Spirit of truth who renews our minds and conforms them to the mind of Christ, and to what extent are they our unrefined biases reinforced by listening only to the voices of those who are likeminded? This raises the question of our relationship to the One into whom we have been baptized: our relationship to the One who, in addition to being model for faithful discipleship, is also its source.

We frequently make mention of "baptismal ecclesiology," but say little about "baptismal spirituality." It would seem that we focus more on what Baptism means for us as part of the life of the church and are inattentive to an awareness of the mystery and power of Baptism to shape and form us at the core of our being. What does being baptized reveal in terms of our *identity* in order that we may be faithful to the call to witness and service? Our neglect of the true depth of Baptism can cause us to look upon Christ as being essentially external to us as a source of inspiration, and an exemplar of righteousness, rather than being encountered as the intimate ground of our personhood through Baptism, and the sealing of the Holy Spirit.

In the Letter to the Romans, St. Paul speaks about our being baptized "into" Christ. This leads quite naturally to his understanding of the baptized as actual members—body parts—of the risen Christ who is the head of the body, and thereby its regulating and ordering force. "Do you not know," Paul tells us, "that all of us who were baptized into Christ Jesus were baptized into his death? Therefore we have been buried with him by Baptism into death, so that, just as Christ was raised from the dead by the glory of the Father, so we too might walk in newness of life" (Rom 6:3–4).

Being buried into Christ's death effects a profound union between Christ and the person baptized: "you have died, and your life is hidden with Christ in God" (Col 3:3). This dying, however, is the narrow door through which we pass to "newness of life." Or again, "If anyone is in Christ, there is a new creation: everything old has passed away: see, everything has become new!" (2 Cor 5:17). Such is the dynamic nature of the paschal mystery into which we are plunged through Baptism, and by which we are shaped and molded and conformed to the image of Christ. As it unfolds, our life in Christ involves many dyings and risings, many relinquishments and losses that open the way—not without pain—to new growth and discovery.

St. John of the Cross observes, "When [the soul] shall be perfectly dispossessed, it will remain with the perfect possession of God,"[2] and T. S. Eliot echoes the paradox in "East Coker."[3] This paradox lies at the heart of the paschal mystery, and it makes sense only to those who, in union with Christ, dare to embrace it in all its stark reality. And yet, at the end, what is revealed is not death and diminishment, but life—not life as we formerly knew it, but as revealed by the One who is our life.

For many of us, all memories of our Baptism are buried in the distant and forgotten days of our infancy, but for Jesus it was a profound and life changing moment at his own Baptism. The Gospel accounts of Jesus's Baptism tell us that it was a profound experience of his being loved. "And just as he was coming up out of the water, he saw the heavens torn apart and the Spirit descending like a dove on him. And a voice came from heaven, "You are my Son, the Beloved; with you I am well pleased" (Mark 1:10–11).

As Jesus emerges from the waters of the Jordan, he experiences a deep and all-embracing oneness with God, and an overwhelming sense of being God's Beloved. At that moment of intense self-awareness, Jesus was not presented with a task to be done or an agenda to be attended to. Quite simply, he knew himself to be God's Beloved. From that moment on, his baptismal awareness is expressed in his words and actions with passionate urgency. And the love which passes between Jesus and the Father in the Holy Spirit becomes the animating force of his life.

Jesus's Baptism was a profoundly personal experience of being encountered by love. And love, by its very nature, must give itself away. Jesus's Baptism opened his heart to the world around him, and impelled him to move about teaching and preaching. God's reign is embodied in the person of Jesus, who does the work of the Father in seeking to draw all to himself. Ultimately, it is this passionate desire to bring all things together and to break down all walls of division that drives him to the cross. All that followed from his Baptism, right up to the cross, was a response to his deep sense of being loved.

2. John of the Cross, *Ascent of Mount Carmel*, pt. 3.7.2.

3. "East Coker," lines 140–41, from Eliot, "Four Quartets," 127.

And what have our Baptisms done to us? In our Baptism God says to us, through sign and symbol and the community of faith gathered around the font or standing at the water's edge, "*You* are my Son, my Daughter, the Beloved; in you I take pleasure and delight simply because you are." Baptism, before it is a ritual of incorporation or covenant of discipleship, is an act of love: God loving us for no reason whatsoever, loving us simply and passionately because we *are*.

Through Baptism God's love becomes embodied in us. Baptism, therefore, is God's act before it is our own. Through Baptism we are bound together with others and declared limbs—beloved body parts—of the risen Lord who lives his life of reconciling love in and through us. God draws us to himself and takes us out of our presumed separateness into a new web of relationships that unites us with others beyond all thoughts of personal affinity. Questions of whether we like someone or not, whether we agree or not, are no longer relevant. Something far more fundamental has happened: God has knit us together in a body not of our own making, and Christ is the head and consciousness of this body.

The mystery of our Baptism is that in Christ we have all been made irrevocably one—beyond all imagining or desire. And, difficult as it may seem at times, our lives are ordered in Christ such that we are instruments of one another's salvation. "Life and death are in the hands of my brother [or sister]," the Desert Tradition informs us. It is important to remember this when strains occur within the body and one limb begins to question whether another body part properly belongs. As Rowan Williams reminds us, through Baptism "we are caught up in solidarities we have not chosen."[4] The very angularities and unsettling points of view of another may be exactly the way in which the risen Christ is seeking to liberate us from an opinion or perception that is partially true or entirely false, and to deepen and expand our experience of his truth, a truth that is always unfolding: "I still have many things to say to you, but you cannot bear them now. When the Spirit of truth comes, he will guide you into all the truth. . . . [He] will take what is mine and declare it to you." (John 16:12–15)

The Spirit continues to draw truth from Christ who declares "*I am the truth*" (John 14:6). Truth, therefore, is essentially personal, and growing into the truth involves a living relationship with Christ. It is the work of the Spirit in Baptism to establish a bond of communion between Christ and the limbs of his risen body that renders us permeable to the truth, "as truth is in Jesus" (Eph 4:21).

---

4. Williams, "Sacraments of the New Society," 93.

One of the most moving experiences for a member of the clergy is to preside at a Baptism, particularly that of an adult. To anoint a person emerging fresh from the font and to declare, "You are sealed by the Holy Spirit in Baptism and marked as Christ's own forever," touches some very deep place within me, which can move me to the point of tears. Though I am addressing the person who has been baptized, I realize that I am calling to mind what happened to me many years ago when I too was sealed by the Holy Spirit and marked as Christ's own forever.

Of the many certificates and citations presented to me over the years, the one I have displayed most prominently was given to me by a group of catechists from the Catechesis of the Good Shepherd. It reads *Frank Tracy Griswold, A Child of God, Marked as Christ's own forever, January 1, 1938.* Over the years, and in a wide range of circumstances involving many deaths and resurrections, that certificate, bearing the image of Jesus the Good Shepherd, has reminded me again and again of my fundamental relationship to Christ, who invites us to follow him through the waters of Baptism into the depths of his own fidelity which took him to the cross and through it into the open space of the resurrection. For him, and for us in union with him, the paschal mystery is revealed in the various demands and choices that confront us day by day.

How might we, as members of Christ's body, recover a fuller and deeper sense of what it means to be baptized? One way is through prayer, and to that end, I offer the following prayer:

> Gracious God, through the waters of Baptism and the working of the Holy Spirit, you have made us one with Christ in his death and resurrection. We have become limbs and members of Christ's risen body, the church. You have sealed and marked us by the Holy Spirit as Christ's forever and called us to share in his eternal priesthood. Sustain and strengthen us with your Spirit day by day. Give us inquiring and discerning hearts, the courage to will and to persevere, a spirit to know and to love you, and the gift of joy and wonder in all your works. In the face of difficulty and distress help us to remember that our lives are not our own but the life that Christ lives in us, and that your power working in us can do infinitely more than we can ask or imagine. To you be glory in the church, and in Christ Jesus, now and forever. Amen.[5]

5. Griswold, *Praying our Days*, 59.

Bibliography

Eliot, T. S. "Four Quartets." In *The Complete Poems and Plays, 1909–1950*. San Diego: Harcourt Brace Jovanovich, 1971.

Griswold, Frank T. *Praying our Days: A Guide and Companion*. Harrisburg, PA: Morehouse, 2009.

John of the Cross. *Ascent of Mount Carmel*. Translated by E. Allison Peers. 3d rev. ed. Garden City, NY: Image, 1958.

Law, William. *A Serious Call to a Devout and Holy Life: The Spirit of Love*. Edited by P. G. Stanwood. New York: Paulist, 1978.

———. *Selections on the Interior Life*. Edited by Mary Chase Morrison. Wallingford, PA: Pendle Hill, 1962.

Williams, Rowan. "Sacraments of the New Society." In *Christ: The Sacramental Word*, edited by David Brown and Ann Loades, 89–102. London: SPCK, 1996.

16

Louis Weil

An Appreciation

WALTER KNOWLES

As LIZETTE LARSON-MILLER AND I discussed producing a volume to honor Louis Weil's fifty years of teaching, Fr. Weil weighed in with a firm request that this collection was "to be a contribution to the conversation about Baptism and the life of the church,—and not to be about him." This is classic Fr. Weil; he is a scholar in service to the church, neither a career climber in ecclesiastical politics nor a pedagogical cloner attempting to produce copies of himself. Indeed, that self-effacing teacher and conversationalist created a challenge for the editors; both of us were mentored by Fr. Weil to be liturgists, not only deeply indebted to his thought but also quite different from him, and we were tasked in working with Louis to find contributors for this volume.

It is a long-standing tradition that the *Doktorkinder* of a scholar gather to produce a present to their *Vater* on these commemorative occasions. However, most of the students whose dissertations Professor Weil directed have chosen to apply their scholarship in direct service to the church rather than through the academy, and those who are active academics are exploring issues that do not fit easily into the topic area that Fr. Weil gave us. As a result, this collection comes from colleagues and those whom he mentored in various ways, including a couple of his academic "children."

Thus it is that, as the last doctoral protégé of Dr. Weil's full-time academic career, I yield to his first student from Nashotah House days to receive a doctorate in liturgical studies, David Holeton. Professor Holeton presented Professor Weil to the 2012 Annual Meeting of the North American Academy of Liturgy (which Dr. Weil helped to found in 1969 as a newly minted STD from the Institut Catholique in Paris) with these words:

> C'est un grand honneur et un plaisir d'être invité à présenter Louis Weil, un des membres fondateurs de cette académie et récipiendair cette année de son Prix *Berakah*.
>
> I have known Louis Weil for a little over forty years. One might think that would make introducing him relatively easy; in fact it has made it rather difficult. I know too much! I will mention just a few aspects of his rich life.
>
> I was beginning my second year of seminary studies [at Nashotah House in Wisconsin] when Louis arrived as the youngest member of the faculty. I had more or less given up on liturgy after our required introduction to the history of the liturgy taught by someone whom I later came to respect as a very great liturgical scholar. During the course, our heads and notebooks had been filled with liturgical facts that seemed completely irrelevant to anything that would face us in our immediate future as liturgical leaders in parishes—notably an overly generous amount of time devoted to Chrodegang of Metz. More useful, perhaps, was the very detailed and recurring account of how to negotiate with Hortense, the dragon-like keeper of MS Paris, Bibliothèque Nationale lat. 12048—the Gellone—for we all knew that every parish came with at least one dragon! We all remembered Hortense; few of us remembered Chrodegang.
>
> Louis's arrival transformed the teaching of liturgy at the seminary and, as a consequence, the lives of many students—including mine. It quickly became clear that it was possible (no, necessary) to be both *wissenschaftlich* and pastoral. Lectures were captivating—filled, as they were, with allusions to great works of literature, music, and remarkable personal anecdotes which both made the point at hand and enlivened our minds. If the liturgy was to embrace all of this, we wanted more.
>
> Étudiant à l'Institut Catholique de Paris pendant et juste après le Concile Vatican II, Louis a été amené en contact immédiat avec ceux qui, par leurs travaux, contribuaient alors à la réforme liturgique du Concile. Des grands personnages comme Pierre-Marie Gy, Pierre Jounel, Aimé-Georges Martimort, Louis Bouyer, et Yves Congar entre autres, insistaient alors, dans leur enseignement, sur l'importance d'une connaissance profonde des sources liturgiques pour le renouvellement de la vie liturgique de l'église.

As a teacher, the spirit of *aggiornamento* and *ressource-ment* imbued Louis's lectures. We were to know the sources and the evolution of the liturgy (as well as its periods of devolution) not as an end in itself but for the renewal of the life of the church in which we lived. Teaching in a church where cold water is *not* regularly poured on those who still burn with a passion for liturgical renewal, that passion has never died in Louis and it imbues his teaching to this day.

Alors que nous célébrons ces jours-ci le cinquantiéme anniversaire de l'ordination de Louis au presbytérat, on ne peut que se réjouir d'un ministère ordonnee consacré à la pastorale dans des paroisses aussi éloignées que Porto Rico et Paris. Il a dirigé des programmes liturgiques dans presque tous les diocèses de l'Église épiscopale ainsi qu'en Amérique latine, aux Philippines, à Hong Kong, et au Royaume Uni.

For many of us, it would not be possible to honour Louis without also remembering his mother, LaRue, for whom he was the primary care giver for many years. A formidable woman whose opinions were held passionately and which often seemed chosen explicitly to provoke Louis's liberal views on politics and life, she was given time that would otherwise have been devoted to the world of scholarship. For many of us, these years of care are held in great respect and admiration.

And Louis today? Two years ago, at the age of 74, Louis retired . . . allegedly. But every time I communicate with him, he is just off to or back from leading another diocesan program. He continues to undertake writing commissions which will be fulfilled only if he lives to be a hundred.

New in his life is a return to his early studies both in piano performance and musicology. In his new home, his grand piano has been restored to its rightful place as musical instrument rather than as the book shelf as which it served for decades, and Louis now plays for a few hours a day. I hope that you will join me in the wish that he may play forever.[1]

The Berakah Award is the North American Academy of Liturgy's recognition of the value of the work and life of one of its members. In receiving the Berakah, Louis Weil joins his predecessor at the Church Divinity School of the Pacific in Berkeley, CA, Fr. Massey Shepherd (the third Berakah laureat), effectively bracketing the renewal of the American *Book of Common Prayer* between the first and the most recent Anglican recipients of

---

1. David R. Holeton, "Introduction of *Berekah* Recipient," *Proceedings of the North American Academy of Liturgy* (2012) 23–24.

the award. Dr. Weil is in rarefied company; the only other Episcopalian recipient has been Dr. Thomas Talley, who taught at General Theological Seminary in New York, and who is also an important figure in the renewal of worship in the Episcopal Church.[2]

Dr. Don Saliers's Berakah citation for Dr. Weil reads:

> Texas born, Harvard, General & Paris trained
> with Caribbean seasoning: priest, musician and scholar,
> exemplary teacher from Paris to San Juan,
> from Nashotah to Berkeley, with South America between,
> you lavishly open the heart of Anglican traditions,
> teaching "liturgy for living" with elegance and love.
>
> Relishing the Feast, you know the taste and fragrance of Christ
> in many cultures, sounding the deep waters of Baptism.
> The world has been your classroom,
> the ecumenical Church your care,
> the surprise of God your idiom,
> the gracious cadence of prayer your music,
> wit and good theology for worshiping assemblies, your style.
>
> Intrepid Traveler,
> Sagacious Servant,
> Loving Critic,
> Faithful Friend.
>
> For your life and work, the Academy gives thanks and praise.[3]

Indeed, Fr. Weil, we, the contributors to this volume, praise God in God's holy sanctuary, around font and altar, in song and structure, in both history and our own time, for your ministry as teacher, scholar, and friend, and as a priest who is truly "Drenched in Grace," and offer you thanks!

---

2. A priest of the Church of England, Dr. Paul Bradshaw, has also received the Berakah Award, bringing the total of Anglicans to four.

3. Don E. Saliers, "2012 Berakah Award," *Proceedings of the North American Academy of Liturgy* (2012) 25.

Selected Lectures
and Writings of Louis Weil

Selected lectures

Lecturer at Conferences in the Diocese of Olympia:

- "The Great Paschal Days," Tacoma, WA, January 1991.

- "Kids in Church," Medina, WA, January 1993.

Lecturer at the College of Preachers, Washington, DC:

- "In Every Time and Place: Liturgy, Anglicanism and Culture," March 1992.

- "The Sermon within the Liturgy," March 1993.

- "Children, Preaching, and the Nature of Worship," March 1994.

- "Children and Worship: Preaching, Sacrament and Space," May 1995.

- "Liturgy at the Crossroads," April 1996.

- "Future Imperatives for Anglican Liturgy," April 1999.

- "The Magic of Ritual," March 2000.

"Changing the Focus in Worship." The Theodore Parker Ferris Lecture (2000) at Emmanuel Church, Baltimore, MD. November 18, 2000.

"Living Out Our Baptism: Children, Liturgy and Christian Community." A conference sponsored by the Diocese of Ely, at the New Divinity Faculty, The University of Cambridge, March 21, 2002.

"Anglican Liturgical Pluralism: An Oxymoron?" A lecture presented at the Epiphany West Conference "Anglicanism(s) Identity and Diversity in a Global Communion," Church Divinity School of the Pacific, Berkeley, CA, January 29, 2003.

"The Bible in the Liturgy." A lecture presented at the Epiphany West Conference "Truth and Dialogue: Friends or Enemies?" Church Divinity School of the Pacific, January 26, 2005.

"The Good Friday Veneration in the Light of the Johannine Passion." A Case Study jointly presented with The Rev. Dr. Ryan Lesh at the Societas Liturgica Congress, Palermo, Sicily, August 18, 2007.

"Setting a Table in the City: The Eucharist and the Hunger of the World." A talk presented at St. John's Church, Los Angeles, CA, September 16, 2007.

"Looking at the Liturgy: (1) As it was . . . (2) is now . . . (3) and shall be." The Paddock Lectures, presented at the General Theological Seminary, New York, October 2–3, 2007.

"The Integrity of the Eucharist: The Role of Music and Preaching in the Eucharistic Celebration." A program presented in the Diocese of Utah at St. Mark's Cathedral, Salt Lake City, UT, November 3, 2007.

"When Signs Signify." An address presented at the Inclusive Church National Conference *Drenched in Grace,* Hayes Conference Centre, Swanwick, Derbyshire, UK, November 21–23, 2007.

"The Shape of Liturgical Formation: [1] Vertical/Horizontal; [2] Horizontal/Vertical." The Bayard Jones Lectures, presented at St. Luke's School of Theology, Sewanee, TN, February 25–26, 2008.

"Baptism as the Model for a Sacramental Aesthetic." Lecture presented at the Epiphany West Conference "Baptismal Water: Thicker than Blood," at the Church Divinity School of the Pacific, 30 January 30, 2009.

Books

1977   *Christian Initiation: A Theological and Pastoral Commentary on the Proposed Rites.* Alexandria, VA: Associated Parishes, 1977.

1979   with Charles P. Price. *Liturgy for Living.* Church's Teaching Series, 5. New York: Seabury, 1979. (Revised edition: Harrisburg, PA. Morehouse, 2000.)

1983   *Sacraments & Liturgy: The Outward Signs.* Oxford: Blackwell, 1983.

1986   *Gathered to Pray: Understanding Liturgical Prayer.* Cambridge, MA: Cowley, 1986.

1992   with J. Robert Wright and Richard Norris. *The Ministry of Bishops.* New York: Trinity Institute, 1992.

2001   *A Theology of Worship.* Cambridge, MA: Cowley, 2001.

2013   *Liturgical Sense: the Logic of Rite.* New York: Church, 2013.

Publications

1968   "The Imperatives of Renewal." *Bulletin of The General Theological Seminary,* 1968.

1969   "The Liturgy: Law or Liberty." *Canterbury Papers,* 1969.

"La Liturgia Anglicana y su adaptacion en Hispanoamerica." *Dialogo Ecumenico* 4.16 (1969) 483–94. Translated as: "The Problem of Adaptation in Anglican Worship." *Worship* 44 (1970) 143–53.

1971 "Pre-Liturgical Priorities." *Nashotah Review* 11.3 (1971) 97–103.

1972 "Documentation and Reflection: Confirmation Today." *Anglican Theological Review* 54 (1972) 107–19.

1974 "The Christian as Player before God." *Nashotah Review* 14.1 (1974) 5–19.

"Christian Initiation: A Theological and Pastoral Commentary on the Proposed Rites." *Nashotah Review* 14.3 (1974) 202–23. Republished in *The Saint Luke's Journal of Theology* 18.2 (1975) 95–112.

1975 "Penance in Episcopalian Liturgical Reform." *Liturgy* 20.2 (1975) 53–54.

"Priesthood in the New Testament" In *To Be a Priest,* edited by Robert Terwilliger and Urban Holmes, 63–69. New York: Seabury, 1975.

"A Response to Bishop Neill." *Anglican Theological Review* 57 (1975) 336–38.

1977 "Confirmation: Some Notes on Its Meaning." *Anglican Theological Review* 59 (1977) 220–24.

"Algunas Relaciones Entre la Renovacion Liturgica de los Catolicos y de los Anglicanos." *Liturgia* (1977) 29–35.

"Christian Initiation in the Anglican Communion: A Response." *Studia Liturgica,* 12 (1977) 126–28.

1978 "The Liturgy on Great Occasions: Notes on Large-Scale Celebrations." *Living Worship* 14.2 (1978). Translated as "Einige Bemerkungen zu Liturgischen Grossveranstaltungen" *Liturgisches Jahrbuch* 28.1 (1978) 57–64. Expanded as "The Liturgy on Great Occasions: Notes on Large-Scale Celebrations—with a Focus on Holy Week." *The Cathedral—A Reader,* 37–41. Washington, DC: U.S. Catholic Conference, 1979.

with Louis Coddaire. "The Use of the Psalter in Worship." *Worship,* 52 (1978) 342–48.

"The New Lutheran Book of Worship: Ministers Edition." *Worship* 52 (1978) 400–403.

"The Pastoral Implementation of Liturgical Principle." In *Prayer Book Renewal,* edited by H. Barry Evans, 17–34. New York: Seabury, 1978.

1979 "Articulations of Authenticity." *Hymn 598* (Nashotah House) 1.1 (1979).

"La Teologia Anglicana de la Presencia Real y el Documento de Windsor." *Liturgia* (1979) 61–65.

1980 "Benedictine Insight for the Divine Office Today." In *Journey to God: Anglican Essays on the Benedictine Way,* 83–98. West Malling, UK: St. Mary's Abbey, 1980.

"Liturgy in a Disintegrating World." *Worship* 54 (1980) 291–302.

"Shaping the Environment of Initiation." In *The Environment for Worship,* 53–59. Washington, DC: The Bishops' Committee on the Liturgy, National Conference of Catholic Bishops and the Center for Pastoral Liturgy of the Catholic University of America, 1980.

1981   "Liturgical Creativity." In *Parish: A Place for Worship*, edited by Mark Searle, 81–96. Collegeville, MN: Liturgical, 1981.

1982   "Anglican Understanding of the Local Church." *Anglican Theological Review* 64 (1982) 193–200.

"Continuing Education of the Assembly." In *Building and Renovation Kit for Places of Catholic Worship*, edited by Bill Brown, sec. 1, 18–19. Chicago: Liturgy Training, 1982.

1983   "The Role of the Bishop in the Liturgy." *Open: The Journal of Associated Parishes for Liturgy and Mission* 27 (April 1983) 1–7.

"Children and Worship." In *The Sacred Play of Children*, edited by Diane Apostolos-Cappadona, 55–59. New York: Seabury, 1983.

"Tractarians and Baptism." *The Seminarian* (Nashotah House), Easter 1983.

"The Oxford Movement: A Restrospective Consideration of its Sacramental and Liturgical Teaching on the 150th Anniversary." *Studia Liturgica*, 15 (1982/1983) 118–23.

"The Practice of Infant Communion." *Liturgy* 4.1 (1983) 69–73.

"El Ministerio, Formas del Futuro." *Conciencia* 8.4 (1983) 7–11.

1984   "The Meaning of Ordination." *The Seminarian* (Nashotah House), Michaelmas 1984.

"The Collect as a Theological Statement." *Studies and Commentaries* (1984) 37–40.

"The Structure of Christian Community." In *Theology in Anglicanism*, edited by Arthur A. Vogel, 115–41. Wilton, CT: Morehouse-Barlow, 1984.

1985   "The History of Christian Litanies." *Liturgy* 5.2 (1985) 33–37.

"Worship and Pastoral Care." In *Anglican Theology and Pastoral Care*, edited by James E. Griffiss, 115–31. Wilton, CT: Morehouse-Barlow, 1985.

"American Perspectives: Confirmation." In *Nurturing Children in Communion*, edited by Colin Buchanan, 19–22. Bramcote, UK: Grove, 1985. (Revised as "American Perspectives: ii) Confirmation." In *Children at the Table*, edited by Ruth A. Meyers, 71–78. New York: Church Hymnal, 1995.)

1986   "The Arts: Language of the Spirit." In *Called to Prayer*, edited by Lawrence J. Johnson, 69–81. Collegeville, MN: Liturgical, 1986.

"The Tractarian Liturgical Inheritance Re-assessed." In *Tradition Renewed*, edited by Geoffrey Rowell, 110–19. London: Darton, Longman and Todd, 1986.

1987   "The Theologian and Ecumensim." In *The Trial of Faith: Theology and the Church Today*, edited by Peter Eaton, 163–72. Worthing, UK: Churchman, 1987.

"Disputed Aspects of Infant Communion." *Studia Liturgica*, 17 (1987) 256–63. (Revised as "Disputed Aspects of Infant Communion." In *Children at the Table*, edited by Ruth A. Meyers, 188–93. New York: Church Hymnal, 1995.)

"The Musical Implications of the Book of Common Prayer." *Occasional Papers*, 6 November 1984. (Republished in *The Occasional Papers of the Standing Liturgical Commission*, I, 51–56. New York: Church Hymnal, 1987.)

1988   "The Spirituality of Holy Week." *Reflections from the DeKoven Center*, Lent 1988. Republished as "The Spirituality of Holy Week." *Tuesday Morning: Resource for Ministry and Liturgical Preaching*. 3.2 (2001) 5–6.

"The Sanctification of Time: What Does It Mean?" *Open: The Journal of Associated Parishes for Consistency* 32 (June 1988) 1–5.

"The Gospel in Anglicanism." In *The Study of Anglicanism*, edited by Stephen Sykes and John Booty, 49–76. London: SPCK, 1988. (Revised edition, edited by Stephen Sykes, John Booty, and Jonathan Knight, 55–83. London: SPCK, 1998.)

1989   "Prayer Book Studies #26, Revised and Expanded." *Anglican Theological Review* 71 (1989) 88–94.

1990   "A Response to *Food for the Journey*. Study on Eucharistic Sharing (1985)." *ARC Soundings: A U.S. Response to ARCIC I*, edited by Ernest R. Falardeau, 47–49. Lanham, MD: National Association of Diocesan Ecumenical Officers, 1990.

"Facilitating Growth in Faith Through Liturgical Worship." In *Handbook of Faith*, edited by James Michael Lee, 203–20. Birmingham, AL: Religious Education, 1990.

"The Church Does Not Make a Marriage." *Anglican Theological Review* 72 (1990) 172–74.

"Prayer, Liturgical." In *The New Dictionary of Sacramental Worship*, edited by Peter E. Fink, 949–59. Collegeville, MN: Liturgical, 1990.

"Proclamation of Faith in the Eucharist." In *Time and Community*, edited by J. Neil Alexander, 279–90. Washington, DC: Pastoral, 1990.

1991   "Worship: What is Central?" *The Evangelical Outlook* 28.2 (1991) 1–3.

"Spirituality and Children." *Crossings* (Fall 1991) 1, 4–5.

"A Larger Vision of Apostolicity: The End of an Anglo-Catholic Illusion." In *Fountain of Life*, edited by Gerard Austin, 183–97. Washington, DC: Pastoral, 1991.

1993   "Baptism and Mission." In *Growing in Newness of Life*, edited by David R. Holeton, 74–79. Toronto: Anglican Book Centre, 1993.

"Reclaiming the Larger Trinitarian Framework of Baptism." *Creation and Liturgy*, edited by Ralph N. McMichael, 129–43. Washington, DC: Pastoral, 1993.

1994   "Preaching through the Church Year: Advent." In *Breaking the Word*, edited by Carl Daw, 39–48. New York: Church Hymnal, 1994.

"The Contribution of the *Anglican Theological Review* in Recent Liturgical Perspective." *Anglican Theological Review* 76 (1994) 184–96.

1995   "Episcopal Services," I:133–6; "Bede, The Venerable," II:331; "Bernard of Cluny," II:336–7; "Hall, William John," II:449–50; "John of Damascus," II:489;

"Joseph the Hymnographer," II:492; "Keeble, John," II:493; "Neale, John Mason," II:540–41; "Theodulph of Orleans," II:633; "Tisserand, Jean," II:636; "New every morning is the love," III:22–25; "O God, creation's secret force," III:30–31; "O God of truth, O Lord of might," III:37–40; "O Trinity of blessed light," III:57–58; "Of the Father's love begotten," II:155–9; "Alleluia, song of gladness," III:253–55; "All glory, laud and honor," III:309–14; "Come, ye faithful, raise the strain," III:400–401; "The Lamb's high banquet called to share," III:405–7; "Alleluia, alleluia, alleluia! O sons and daughters," III:407–11; "The day of resurrection," III:423–25; "Let us now our voices raise," III:471; "Blessed feasts of blessed martyrs," III:471–74; "Gabriel's message does away," III:522–23; "The great forerunner of the morn," III:523–27; "Draw nigh and take the Body of the Lord," III:616–18; "Christ is made the sure foundation," III:971–73; "Light's abode, celestial salem," III:1141–43; "O what their joy and their glory must be," III:1144–45; "Jerusalem the golden," III:1145–47; "Blest are the pure in heart," III:1201–3; "O very God of very God," III:1243. In *The Hymnal 1982* Companion. Edited by Raymond F. Glover. New York: Church Hymnal, 1995.

"The Place of the Liturgy in Michael Ramsey's Theology." In *Michael Ramsey as Theologian*, edited by Robin Gill and Lorna Kendall, 141–58. London: Darton, Longman and Todd, 1995.

1996   "Should the Episcopal Church Permit Direct Ordination?" In *The Orders of Ministry: Reflections on Direct Ordination, 1996*, edited by Edwin F. Hallenbeck, 53–65. Providence, RI: North American Association for the Diaconate, 1996.

"Aspects of the Issue of *Per Saltum* Ordination: An Anglican Perspective." In *Rule of Prayer, Rule of Faith*, edited by Nathan Mitchell and John F. Baldovin, 200–217. Collegeville, MN: Liturgical, 1996.

1997   "The Practice of Ordination: Distinguishing Secondary Elements from Primary." In *Anglican Orders and Ordinations: Essays and Reports from the Interim Conference at Jarvenpaa, Finland, of the International Anglican Liturgical Consultation, 4–9 August 1997*, Edited by David R. Holeton, 46–49. Cambridge: Grove, 1997.

1998   "The Dublin Lecture: Issues concerning the Anglican Eucharist in the Twenty-first Century." In *Our Thanks and Praise: The Eucharist in Anglicanism Today*, edited by David R. Holeton, 15–31. Toronto: Anglican Book Centre, 1998. (Also published as "Scope and Focus in Eucharistic Celebration." In *A Prayer Book for the Twenty-first Century*, edited by Ruth A. Meyers, 34–55. New York: Church Hymnal, 1996.)

"Children in the Liturgy." *God's Friends* 9.1 (1998) 3–5.

"The Liturgical Sense of Advent." *Journal of the Association of Anglican Musicians* 7.8 (1998) 1, 4.

"The Split Personality of Lent." *Journal of the Association of Anglican Musicians* 7.10 (1998) 1, 4.

1999   "The Feast of Feasts." *Journal of the Association of Anglican Musicians*, 8.1 (1999) 1, 4.

"Those Sundays after Epiphany." *Journal of the Association of Anglican Musicians* 8.9 (1999) 1, 4.

"A Perspective on the Relation of the Prayer Book to Anglican Unity." In *With Ever Joyful Hearts,* edited by J. Neil Alexander, 321–32. New York: Church, 1999.

"Teaching Liturgy: A Subversive Activity." In *A New Conversation,* edited by Robert B. Slocum, 278–87. New York: Church, 1999.

2000   "Those Sundays after Epiphany: A Second Look." *Journal of the Association of Anglican Musicians* 9.9 (2000) 1, 4.

"Children and the Liturgy—A Perspective." Foreword to Caroline Fairless, *Children at Worship: Congregations in Bloom,* viii–xiii. New York: Church, 2000.

"Essential Reading." *Anglican Theological Review* 82.4 (2000) 865–67.

2001   "The Holy Spirit: Source of Unity in the Liturgy." *Anglican Theological Review* 83.3 (2001) 409–15. (Republished in *Engaging the Spirit,* edited by Robert B. Slocum, 39–45. New York: Church, 2001.)

2002   "'*Kennst du das Land?*': Comments on the Implications of a 'Lied' of Goethe as a Source of Insight for the Ordinary of the Mass." In *Postmodern Worship & The Arts,* edited by Doug Adams and Michael E. Moynahan, 59–66. San Jose, CA: Resource, 2002.

"The Handmaid of the Lord." *Ave* (St. Mary the Virgin, New York) 71.3 (2002) 6–7.

"A Sabbatical at St. Matthew's." *Oasis—The Magazine of St. Matthew's, Westminster* (London, UK), Summer 2002, 11–14.

"Book of Common Prayer." In *New Catholic Encyclopedia,* 2nd ed., 2:524–25. Washington, DC: Catholic University Press of America 2002.

2003   "Reflections on a Visit to Rome." *CDSP Crossings,* Summer 2003, 9.

"Not Requiem but Celebration." *Ave* (St. Mary the Virgin, New York) 72.4 (2003) 15–16.

2004   "The Papacy: An Obstacle or a Sign for Christian Unity." *International Journal for the Study of the Christian Church* 4.1 (2004) 6–20.

2005   "Rome and Canterbury—Steps toward Reconciliation through the Sharing of Gifts." *Centro Pro Unione Bulletin* 67 (2005) 16–20.

"Eucharist." In *Christianity: The Complete Guide,* edited by John Bowden, 395–400. London: Continuum, 2005.

2006   "Sacramental Aspects of Reconciliation: Impaired Communion and Eschatological Hope." In *I Have Called You Friends: Reflections on Reconciliation,* edited by Barbara Braver, 99–113. Cambridge, MA: Cowley, 2006.

"Baptismal Ecclesiology: Uncovering a Paradigm," In *Equipping the Saints: Ordination in Anglicanism Today,* edited by Ronald L. Dowling and David R. Holeton, 18–34. Blackrock, IE: Columba, 2006.

"The Solemn Reproaches of the Cross." Archives and History, Church of St. Mary the Virgin, New York, March 2006. http://www.stmvirgin.org/archives/article19433c2290727.htm.

2007   "When Signs Signify." *Open: The Journal of Associated Parishes for Liturgy and Mission* (Spring 2008) 5–9.

2008   "'Remembering the Future': Reflections on Liturgy and Ecclesiology." In *Anglican Liturgical Integrity,* edited by Christopher Irvine, 31–45. Joint Liturgical Studies 65. Norwich, UK: Canterbury, 2008.

"The Shape of Liturgical Formation: Vertical/Horizontal, Horizontal/Vertical." *Sewanee Theological Review* 52 (2008) 33–47.

2009   "Ritual Considerations in Same-Sex Marriage," In *Christian Holiness and Human Sexuality,* edited by Gary R. Hall and Ruth A. Meyers, 21–24. Chicago: The Chicago Consultation, 2009.

"Updating a Text on Marriage," In *Writings on Marriage: Journal of the Bishop's Task Force on Marriage,* edited by Gregory Jones, 25–28. Raleigh, NC: The Episcopal Diocese of North Carolina, 2009.

2010   "Baptism as the Model for a Sacramental Aesthetic." *Anglican Theological Review* 92 (2010) 259–70.

2012   "Berakah Response: Invitation into a Larger Room." *Proceedings of the North American Academy of Liturgy,* Montreal, Quebec, 2012, 27–32.

Made in the USA
Las Vegas, NV
30 May 2023

72712060R00140